History and Heresy

History and Heresy

How Historical Forces Can Create Doctrinal Conflicts

Joseph F. Kelly

A Michael Glazier Book

LITURGICAL PRESS
Collegeville, Minnesota

www.litpress.org

A Michael Glazier Book published by Liturgical Press

Cover design by David Manahan, OSB. Illustration of Saint Augustine, *The City of God*, France, 14th century, courtesy of Thinkstock.

1	2	3	4	5	6	7	8	9

Library of Congress Cataloging-in-Publication Data

Kelly, Joseph F. (Joseph Francis), 1945–
    History and heresy : how historical forces can create doctrinal conflicts / Joseph F. Kelly.
       p.   cm.
    "A Michael Glazier book."
    Includes bibliographical references (p.   ) and index.
    ISBN 978-0-8146-5695-2 — ISBN 978-0-8146-5999-1 (e-book)
    1. Christian heresies—History.   2. History—Religious aspects—Christianity. I. Title.
BT1315.3.K45   2012
273—dc23   2012018231

To Valerie Flechtner and Brenda Wirkus

Contents

Preface

In 2010 Hans Christoffersen of Liturgical Press asked me about writing a book on heresy. It seemed like a good idea, but I did not want to do one that would basically list heresies *seriatim* with brief accounts and explanations. Very good encyclopedias of Christianity do that. Instead I wanted to work a theme familiar to church historians if not to the general religious public, and that was the impact of historical forces on heresy.

Many Christians believe that because doctrines claim to define divine or spiritual—that is, nonhistorical—realities, the doctrines themselves have somehow escaped from or risen above history. That is simply not so. Every doctrine came into being at a certain time in a certain place under certain circumstances. Christians believe in a deity who is beyond time, but formulas about that deity have a definite historical framework. Furthermore, as the historical framework changes, so does the "timeless" doctrine. The Christians of the apostolic era were Jews who venerated a deity understood from their own tradition. By the fourth and fifth centuries, when most Christians were intellectually Greco-Roman, the doctrine of God had taken on very Platonic overtones and ones that the first-century Christians would have had trouble recognizing. By the twelfth century Aristotle was replacing Plato as the theologians' philosopher of choice, and by the thirteenth century the doctrine of God had become very Aristotelian among the scholastic theologians of the European universities. By the twentieth century theologians were questioning or even abandoning much of the Aristotelian understanding.

There is no issue of right or wrong in this process. Before the twelfth century European Christian theologians knew little of Aristotle. When his works became well-known, the theologians carefully appropriated them for their work. And even in the High Middle Ages there were theologians who did not use Aristotle's works. Today theologians live in an era that forces them to keep up with scientific discoveries that alter our view of the physical world and even of human bodies, a great burden for scholars not always well trained in the sciences.

But just as doctrinal formulations were and are products of history, so too are heresies, as this book hopes to demonstrate, and they must be understood historically as well as theologically.

This book will also try to demonstrate that many heresies were not purely doctrinal issues and not necessarily attempts to corrode the true faith. Sometimes conflicts about doctrine resulted from purely or mostly historical forces. For example, as chapters 5 and 6 will show, the dominance gained by science over nineteenth-century Western intellectual life guaranteed that biblical exegesis would have to change. To be sure, many Christian scholars, independent of the scientists, had initiated some new methods of study, but even if they had not, science on its own would have challenged the traditional understanding of Scripture.

Antiquarianism is the study of the past for its own sake. History is the study of the past for some insight about and relevance to the present. True heresy represents a clear and present danger to Christian teaching, should never be taken lightly, and demands a response from church leaders and theologians. Yet those leaders and theologians should examine the historical situation and forces that may have caused a supposed or potential heresy to arise. The "heretic" may not be challenging a doctrine so much as saying that it should be reformulated to meet the needs of modern Christians. As so many of us know, the biblical account of creation, a raging problem even in public schools, offers a classic case.

This book ranges widely, from the first to the twenty-first century. For help with this large, historical range, I turned to some specialists. For chapters 1, 2, and 7, on the New Testament and Montanism, my John Carroll University colleague and friend Dr. Sheila McGinn provided valuable help. Even in the rare cases where I did not take her advice, her comments still sharpened my understanding of the issues.

For the chapter on the Monophysites, my old friend Dr. Frederick Norris, now emeritus from Emmanuel School of Theology, graciously provided advice, even though my request for help came when he was struggling with an illness, now happily behind him.

Dr. Paul Murphy, another JCU colleague and friend, directs the Institute of Catholic Studies at John Carroll University. He knows a great deal about institutional Roman Catholicism, and, in spite of a very busy schedule, he made that knowledge available to me for the chapter on Roman Catholic modernism.

Dr. John Spencer, chairperson of the Department of Theology and Religious Studies at JCU, a friend and colleague for thirty-five years, used his knowledge of the Bible and of modern Protestant exegesis to help with the chapter on Protestant fundamentalism.

Most of this book was prepared during a sabbatical leave for the spring 2011 semester. My thanks to Dr. Spencer, chairperson of the department, for supporting my request, and to the JCU University Committee on Research and Service and its chairperson, Associate Academic Vice President Dr. Lauren Bowen, for recommending me for the sabbatical to Dr. Beth Martin, Acting Dean of the College of Arts and Sciences, and Dr. John Day, Academic Vice-President, who both approved the committee's recommendation. My thanks also to Rev. Robert Niehoff, SJ, president of JCU, who saw to the funding of the sabbatical.

My sincere thanks also to my graduate assistant Shannon Edwards, who read this text several times and provided valuable help.

As always, the person to whom I owe the most thanks is Ellen Marie Kelly, my loving wife of more than four decades, who saw to it that I had time to work on this book, who graciously understood when my writing took away from our time together, and who was always there when I needed her.

This book is dedicated to two old friends, Valerie Flechtner and Brenda Wirkus, two JCU colleagues who know how much their friendship has meant to me over the years.

Defining Heresy and Authority

"Heresy" conjures up a number of images in the modern mind, most of them negative and often associated with inquisitions or worse. That religious people committed vicious acts against those they deemed heretics remains a stain on the history of every religion, but this does not mean that there is no such thing as heresy or that religious people should not oppose it. For moderns, living in a world that accepts diversity and values freedom of thought and of speech, the issue is often not so much opposition to heresy but rather the form this opposition takes. Yet even moderns must concede that a religious people cannot stand by silently or idly while someone maligns their received teachings.

For this text, we will define heresy as the conscious deviation from a publicly proclaimed teaching of a religious group or church. This is a working definition, but it includes the basics: the church has stated and explained its position publicly and clearly so that the heretic, one of the believers, knows that her or his view differs from that of the church and in what way it does so. It also means that the heretic wishes to disagree with that position so that no one would equate her or his view with that of the church. For example, a church teaches the real presence of Christ in the Eucharist, and the "heretic" denies the real presence. This could just be a minor disagreement, but should the heretic's position become sufficiently threatening, the church then rightly responds to it. Not to do so would imply indifference at best or a tacit acquiescence at worst. The modern approach for a church would be to criticize the heretic's teachings and then explain its contrary position. Modern Christians would not condone the use of force or intimidation, so common in the past.

This sounds straightforward enough, but that has rarely been the case. Heresy implies orthodoxy, and often in Christian history orthodoxy on some points simply did not exist, either because of a fluid situation or because the church had not yet found a way to define its teaching.

1

Heterodoxy means disagreement from a commonly accepted teaching. It differs from heresy because "commonly accepted" does not mean officially defined. Let us consider a classic example.

The earliest Christians, those alive shortly after Christ's death, believed that their message should go only to Jews. In the Acts of the Apostles 2:46, a theologized account of the first Christians, the evangelist Luke says that the disciples (a term that means both women and men) actually met in the Jerusalem temple. Inevitably, their public preaching reached the ears of some Gentiles in Jerusalem. A few Gentiles might have expressed interest, but the acceptance of Gentiles into Christianity depended not upon the earliest disciples but upon one man, a Jew from Asia Minor (modern Turkey) named Saul, better known as Paul. Convinced that the risen Christ wanted his message to go to all people, Paul began evangelizing in the eastern Mediterranean Roman provinces to both Jews and Gentiles. He enjoyed considerable success but also encountered very powerful opposition against his mission to the Gentiles. In his Epistle to the Galatians, Paul tells us that his views gained apparent acceptance from the members of the Jerusalem community, including the twelve apostles and James, a relative of Jesus and head of that community. Yet when Paul was in Antioch with some Gentile converts, some Jerusalem Christians, representing James, refused to share table fellowship with the Gentiles. Peter, leader of the Twelve, likewise refused to eat with them and earned a severe public rebuke from Paul (Gal 2:11-14).

The evidence is clear. Paul was in the minority. He disagreed with the majority's focus on staying within a Jewish environment and was snubbed by both James and Peter. This provides a good example of heterodoxy. The first Christians had no formal method of pronouncing doctrines. Luke says that they stayed faithful to the teachings of the apostles (a group that included more than the Twelve and could have included women) and that "the community of believers was of one heart and one mind" (Acts 4:32). Paul did not share that "one mind" and worked to change it. Many Christians resented him and worked against him, sometimes even in communities that he had established. He asked the Galatians who had bewitched them (Gal 3:1), and he lamented that in Corinth, a church he founded and cared for very much, rival factions actually competed for primacy (1 Cor 1:11-13).

By later standards, Paul would have been a heretic. But in his day the community had not yet created enduring methods or standards by which to judge him. Paul may have been on the outs with the majority, but he was no heretic. And, of course, Christians eventually concluded that Paul was right, that the faith should go to all who had an interest in it. By the middle of the second century Paul's unwanted Gentiles had formed an enduring majority of the faithful.

But what made Paul right? Most obviously, the acceptance of his views by most other Christians, including the leaders of the communities. But why did they accept him?

Even allowing for Luke's heavy theologizing, the Acts of the Apostles clearly shows a people who followed the teachings of the Twelve and others who knew the earthly Jesus. But Paul did not know him; he knew only the risen Christ, not as modern believers know him through the Scriptures and in the community, but via visions. Could Paul authenticate those visions? No. People simply had to believe him, which most did. (One could say that Paul did miracles, as reported in Acts, and that these validated his vision, but those who opposed him also did miracles, likewise reported in Acts, and the churches discarded their views.) For some reason the first Christians chose to believe Paul.

But what about other people who had visions then and have visions now? Why do Christians not believe them? We will examine that in the next chapter.

Yet Paul's rise to prominence raises several fundamental problems that will occupy much of this book, and the most important is, what criteria can churches use to determine the authenticity of a particular teaching? Some modern churches, mostly conservative Protestant ones, rely on Scripture alone, although, as all Christians know, Scripture still has to be interpreted; indeed, some Protestant churches recognize a tradition of interpretation. Others, such as the Anglican and Episcopal churches, rely upon Scripture and also tradition but not in so overweening a way that tradition becomes binding. The Roman Catholic and Orthodox churches also rely upon tradition, which plays a far more determinative role for them. Tradition presents these churches with the same problem of interpretation that conservative Protestants must address.

First, just because "we have always done this," should we always do it? Consider the acceptance of slavery. In his letter to Philemon, a slave owner, Paul urged him to treat a runaway slave as he would treat Paul himself, but the apostle never asked Philemon to free the slave. Why not? Because Paul did not think slaves needed their freedom (1 Cor 7:21), a view shared by the anonymous author of the Epistle to the Ephesians who told slaves simply to be obedient to their masters (6:5) or the pseudonymous author of the Epistle to Titus who urged the leaders of the church to which he was writing to tell slaves to be submissive to their masters

(2:9). These views prevailed in the early church; many prominent early Christian theologians justified or defended slavery. Unsurprisingly, none of them was a slave. The only early Christian writer who had actually been a slave was Patrick, the sixth-century bishop of Ireland, who as a teenager had been kidnapped from Britain by Irish pirates and enslaved for six years. Patrick wrote about how vicious slavery was, and, unlike those who accepted and justified it, he saw no good in it.

What can be said of slavery can also be said of anti-Semitism. It is as old as the Gospel of John (cf. John 8:44), and it did nothing but get worse from the first century onward, diminishing only when the Holocaust showed Christians the horrifying consequences of anti-Semitism. Clearly, the endurance of a practice does not bestow Christian qualities upon it. Anti-Semitism and slavery have always been sinful, demeaning people by their ethnicity, race, or religion and justifying unfair, even criminal, treatment of them. Christians should treasure traditions and take them seriously but never equate hoary old age with God's truth.

Second, there are many instances of doctrines having changed. Let us consider the most obvious, an issue to which we will return again. Augustine of Hippo (354–430) created a new way to explain the Christian problem with evil; he called it Original Sin. He based his powerful and influential theology of evil upon the actual existence of Adam and Eve, who committed an actual sin, the consequences of which were passed onto all of their descendants, that is, the entire human race. We know now that Adam and Eve were not historical figures but fictional players in an ancient Semitic creation myth. Most Christians now treat the Genesis account symbolically or metaphorically, and although they still speak of Original Sin, they understand it not as an actual sin committed by our primeval parents but as an expression of our estrangement from God. (In saying this, we are speaking of Jewish, Roman Catholic, Orthodox, and mainline Protestant biblical exegetes and not of right-wing Protestants, as we shall see in chapter 6.)

Teachings have changed. But this raises yet another question or even a few questions. Under what circumstances should churches change traditional teaching? If they change one traditional teaching, is any teaching safe? More directly, is any tradition valid if it is even open to change? Occasionally, churches have had no choice but to change their teaching. Biblical cosmology envisioned a three-decker universe: heaven above, earth in the middle, hell below. This attitude explains many things about early Christian beliefs and practices, such as why angels have wings (because they had to fly back and forth between heaven and earth). But when the Scientific Revolution of the sixteenth and seventeenth centuries overthrew that cosmology, teachings that depended upon it had no choice but to change. Heaven could not be "above" since there was no "above" in the new, scientific cosmology, just endless, almost empty space with the occasional star or planet here and there. This also changed how churches visualized the ascension of Jesus. He could no longer ascend physically into heaven since it was no longer "up." Now we understand that Luke, the only New Testament writer who speaks of the ascension (Luke 28:51; Acts 1:9-10), meant that Jesus returned to his Father, not that he physically went up into the air.

Most changes in teaching occur internally, when church thinkers or leaders peer more closely into a particular doctrine. Here the classic case is the Trinity. The earliest words of the New Testament, the opening paragraph of Paul's First Epistle to the Thessalonians (ca. 49), speak of the Father, Son, and Holy Spirit, but the word "Trinity" appears nowhere in the New Testament. By the early second century many Christians had come to believe that all three were divine, which promptly raised the specter of polytheism, that is, multiple deities. Christians strongly denied this, but then theologians had to relate the threeness with monotheism. They proposed a number of theories, especially in the third century when the word "Trinity" (*Trinitas* in Latin) first appeared. In 325 at an ecumenical council in the town of Nicea in Asia Minor (modern Turkey), the assembled bishops under the leadership of the emperor Constantine declared that the Father and Son were "consubstantial"; that is, they were independent persons but shared the same divine substance. Nicea implied the same about the Holy Spirit, but it required a second ecumenical council, one at Constantinople in 381, to affirm the consubstantiality of all three persons of the Trinity.

When Nicea took this step, many conservative bishops objected on the logical and compelling ground that the word "consubstantial" (*homooúsios* in Greek) does not appear in Scripture. The great hero of Nicene orthodoxy, Athanasius of Alexandria (ca. 293–373), replied that the term represented the essence of Scripture; that is, although not in Scripture, the term had a biblical base, flowed from biblical teachings, and was thus consonant with Scripture. Not everyone accepted that assertion, and the Council of Nicea took decades to win widespread acceptance, but it triumphed in the end. (We will return to Nicea in chapter 3.)

To most readers this will sound like orthodoxy. It is a familiar teaching, promulgated by an ecumenical council, accepted by most Christians and familiar to all Christians. True, but that was not obvious in the fourth century. Besides, the Council of Nicea opened up two other difficult areas for discussion: mystery and development of doctrine.

Today the word "mystery" means a problem, usually a criminal one, that the great television detective will solve by means of little grey cells. But the Greek word *mystérion* meant something quite different. A mystery is something that can never be solved. To cite the classic case, in no way will humans be able to understand the nature of God, certainly not in this life. So if we cannot understand God, how can we talk about him all the time? (Notice that I referred to God as the traditional "he," thus transforming an incomprehensible being into a somewhat comprehensible male.) We can do this in two ways. First, we have God's Scriptures, and all of our beliefs about him, such as his goodness, his care for us, derive from that. Such an approach depends completely upon our faith that God spoke through those Scriptures, which is why all churches speak of the Christian "faith." That makes many people uncomfortable; they would prefer knowledge and proof to faith. So would many believers, but the Scriptures are books of faith, period. Note that Genesis begins simply with "In the beginning . . . God created the heavens and the earth." There is no attempt to prove God's existence, which both writer and reader simply took for granted. Nor does the Hebrew Bible attempt to prove that God called Moses or spoke through the prophets; the Bible simply says that these events were so. The New Testament takes the same approach. Mark, the earliest gospel (ca. 70), opens with "The beginning of the gospel of Jesus Christ the Son of God." No proof, just a proclamation of Jesus' divine paternity. So much of what we say about God derives from our faith in the revelation given by Scripture, but the essential nature of God remains a mystery.

Mystery leads to the discipline of "theology," literally "knowledge of God." The classic definition of this term was given by Anselm of Canterbury (ca. 1033–1109), who said it was *fides quaerens intellectum*, "faith seeking understanding," although the practice goes back to the New Testament.

Consider the three elements. "Faith" means that we believe—for example, that the Son of God became incarnate. "Understanding" means that we have to have some intellectual notion of what we believe—for example, that the Son of God took on humanity without compromising his divinity. But the operative word here is "seeking." We start from what we believe and we come to an understanding, but we recognize that our understanding, no matter how logical or sensible, does not correspond completely to the reality. We accept the mystery. We accept that we cannot truly understand how Jesus can simultaneously be human and divine, but we work out some formula that "does its best," so to speak, yet is always imperfect. No theologian has ever had the temerity or the ego to hold that her or his formulation exactly explains the spiritual reality.

The skeptic can dismiss all of this; Anselm does not care. Theologians are persons of faith seeking to explain their beliefs in a rational way. The bishops at Nicea did not "prove" that the Father, Son, and Holy Spirit are consubstantial, but they did theology; starting with their belief in one God and in three divine persons, they came up with the best formula, inevitably inadequate in relation to the divine being, by which to express their beliefs. So Christians can speak intelligently of the *ineffable* (beyond understanding) deity but only to those who share their faith or who recognize that they are speaking from a faith base.

The doctrine of the Trinity changed in the early church, as did that of Original Sin in the modern one, but theologians speak not of "change" but of "development." Why?

Because the church cannot teach one thing on Monday and the exact opposite on Tuesday. Theologians must look at some doctrinal formulation and wonder if some new approach or understanding might better address it because of some new knowledge (Original Sin and evolution) or challenge (does belief in three divine persons mean polytheism?). The theologians look at the current or traditional teaching and try to find a way to be loyal to its basics while simultaneously adapting the teaching to the new situation, as when Athanasius argued that the word *homooúsios* did not contradict Scripture but rather represented the essence of Scripture, and when modern theologians demonstrated that the doctrine of Original Sin need not rest on the historicity of the Garden of Eden.

Development may be necessary and inevitable, but does any church have a formal approach to development of doctrine? Not really. In the nineteenth century, John Henry Newman (1801–90), an Anglican at the time, wrote a book that delineated stages of development, although he focused mostly on the early church. When he became a Roman Catholic priest and later a cardinal, his book gained more influence but never became an official document. Most of its popularity came after 1950 when Newman's greatness was finally being recognized.

Practically speaking, development is recognized when a crisis has arisen with a particular teaching, and church leaders conclude that something must be modified. But an institution charged with guarding divine revelation cannot just change something, so its leaders must look carefully at alternatives to see if any of them can be reconciled with current teaching. The trinitarian situation exemplifies this—some formula was necessary to state that Christians believed in one deity but also in the divinity of the persons of the Trinity. Development of doctrine is simply a fact of life in the church, although one often recognized *post factum*.

So doctrines can and have changed, and doing so does not compromise Christian beliefs. Yet doctrines change only when they win approval of those entitled to approve them. Who are those persons? Answering that question brings us to the issue of authority.

Authority often gets confused with power, but they differ considerably. Power is the ability to coerce, the way a thug with the weapon can coerce someone to give up her or his valuables. Authority can include power, but it always includes the notion of legitimacy. A police officer can pull a driver over for violating a traffic regulation. The officer has the power of coercion because the driver knows that not pulling over could result in a very heavy fine or even loss of license. But the police offer is an agent of a legitimately elected government that has the authority to punish someone for violating a law.

Much authority does not involve coercion. People such as Mahatma Gandhi, Martin Luther King Jr., Mother Teresa, and Elie Wiesel exercise moral authority. Experts have authority because of their superior knowledge of things, from space exploration to fixing a car. Parental authority persists long after children have become adults. True authority in churches falls into this noncoercive category.

Where is church authority to be found? The answer to the question changes from church to church. For conservative Protestants, truth lies in the Scriptures, which overwhelm the judgment of any person or group of persons, yet every Protestant church has people with a specialized knowledge of Scripture who can assure the community that a particular teaching is consonant with the Bible. To use the most obvious example, when it became clear that the Bible contains many passages that could not be taken literally, nineteenth-century German scholars, mostly Lutherans, demonstrated that many biblical texts were not *meant* to be taken literally, and so fidelity to the Bible demanded that Protestants not hold on to interpretations shown to be erroneous. On the other end of the scale is Roman Catholicism, in which one man (and it is always a man) can make the final statement on any issue—including the decrees of ecumenical councils, which have no validity without papal approval. In fact, the popes do not go about daily proclaiming documents and interpreting scriptural verses, but they do stand as the final authority on any doctrinal issue, although modern theologians and biblical exegetes constantly hold papal teaching up to scholarly analysis and evaluation.

Between these extremes lies any number of authorities, always the Scriptures but also the voices of local congregations, of synods, and of ecumenical councils, as well as personal experiences (prophets and visionaries). Today these systems work rather well, largely because literate congregants know what is taught and why. This does not mean that all congregants are satisfied; some inevitably leave for another church or possibly no church.

But no matter how well modern approaches to authority may function, they, like all else in the churches, are products of history. Unlike theory, history tends to be messy, but history will demonstrate how the first Christians arrived at *orthodoxy*, or "right teaching," and set the pattern for later generations of Christians.

Since Christian churches claim their teachings ultimately derive from those of Jesus, that would be a good place for us to start, but such an approach runs into an insurmountable obstacle—the original teachings of Jesus do not survive.

How can that be? We all know what he said—"Blessed are the poor in spirit"; "Love one another"—but what we know are not Jesus' exact words but only a limited number of them preserved in Greek (not Jesus' original language) by some of his disciples, not one of whom experienced him during his life on earth, which ended no later than AD 36 when Pontius Pilate was recalled to Rome.

Jesus came from Nazareth of Galilee, the northern and rather backward part of the Roman province of Judea. Nazareth was so small and insignificant that it is not even mentioned in the Old Testament, and one of Jesus' disciples could actually make a joke to him about its obscurity (John 1:46).

No one in Galilee called him "Jesus"; rather, he was known as Yeshua bar-Joseph, "Yeshua, the son of Joseph." (*Christós* is an honorary term meaning "the Anointed One" or "Messiah," and it is not, as I was once asked by a student, Jesus' last name.) He preached to people in a language called Aramaic, a Semitic dialect widely spoken through the eastern Mediterranean region. None of his sermons, parables, or prayers survives in the original. The gospels preserve only occasional Aramaic words from Jesus' dealings with the people, such as *talithá cúmi* ("Little girl, stand up") and *éphphatá* ("Be opened"), both from Mark's gospel (5:41; 7:34) and both in the context of miracle stories, not words intended to teach an audience. In sum, we simply do not have Jesus' teaching in its original language.

Did Jesus record any of it? He could read (Luke 4:17) and write (John 8:6), but he left no written record. (In the fourth century, a Palestinian bishop named Eusebius of Caesarea published a letter supposedly written by Jesus to a king of Edessa named Abgar, but it is spurious.) At first this seems very problematic, but many great figures of the ancient world did not save their teachings in writing. We know of Socrates because of Plato and of the Buddha through many now anonymous disciples. The Prophet Muhammad did not write his revelations; the *Holy Qur'an* preserves the sayings of the Prophet during his twenty-year ministry as remembered by his faithful followers.

Why did the disciples who knew the earthly Jesus not record his words?

Before getting to that question, we should note that several New Testament books purport or were widely thought to have been written by those who knew Jesus. These would include the gospels of Matthew and John, along with the three epistles and the book of Revelation also attributed to John, two epistles by Peter, one by Jude, and one by James, either the Lord's disciple or his relative. Nineteenth-century biblical scholarship (to which we will return in chapters 5 and 6) changed all that, at least for educated believers. Led by German Protestants and now accepted by Catholics, Orthodox, and mainline Protestants, exegetes determined that the New Testament bristles with complexities, especially regarding authorship. Members of the twelve apostles did not write any of the books attributed to them, nor, for that matter, did Paul write several of the epistles hitherto confidently claimed for him (2 Thessalonians, Ephesians, Colossians, 1–2 Timothy, Titus).

So why did the first disciples not write? Many would have been illiterate, but Matthew, a tax collector (Matt 10:3), certainly could read and write; the same would have been true for the wealthy and aristocratic women who followed Jesus (Luke 8:1-3). The answer probably lies in the early Christians' imminent expectation of the Parousia or Second Coming.

Most early Christians expected to be alive at the end of the world. The apostle Paul had to further explain this teaching among his converts in Thessalonica who wondered why some of their number had died before Jesus returned, apparently concluding from Paul's preaching that they would all still be alive. The apostle vigorously defended an imminent Parousia: "For the Lord himself, with a word of command, with the voice of an archangel and with the trumpet of God, will come down from heaven, and the dead in Christ will rise first. Then we who are alive, who are left, will be caught up with them in the clouds to meet the Lord in the air" (1 Thess 4:16-17). Paul repeats this belief in 1 Corinthians 15:50-54, again asserting that at least some of the letter's recipients will be alive at the end. Since in both letters he used the word "we" for those to be caught up, he apparently expected to be alive himself.

Whatever the reason, and the Parousia seems logical, the disciples, both men and women, who knew the earthly Jesus and who, mostly Galileans, could speak Aramaic and thus recall his original words, did not write anything. Nor did they plan the wide-scale evangelization fostered by Paul and others. After all, they understood Jesus to have been the most unique person in history, so how could they possibly continue his work? Furthermore, as mostly Galileans of the lower classes, they may have wondered how they could actually carry it out. Forming a permanent community was not the most obvious choice these disciples could have made. Many may have decided to hold fast in their faith until Jesus soon returned.

Regrettably, what we know of the postresurrection early disciples lies in the pages of the Acts of the Apostles, a book written by the author of the Gospel of Luke, who was not one of those first disciples. He belonged to a universalizing group of Christians who agreed with the views of the apostle Paul that the message should go to all people and not just to the Jews as originally envisioned by the disciples. Three-fourths of Acts deals with Paul's spreading the message to Gentiles, so we must acknowledge that Luke's account of the early disciples in Acts 1–7 reflects his overall universalist concern. Allowing for that, we can see what he says about them.

As noted above, only Luke recounts the ascension. In the gospel Jesus tells the disciples that they must preach "his name to *all the nations*" because "You are *witnesses* of these things" (24:47-48; emphasis added). Here Luke claims that in pursuing the Gentile mission, Paul followed the intent of Jesus. Significantly, however, Paul himself was not a witness of those things (we will return to this later). To aid the disciples, Jesus will send upon them "what my Father promised" (Luke 24:49).

In Acts 2:1-4 the disciples were gathered for the Jewish feast of Pentecost when they had a mystical experience of the Holy Spirit, who appeared to them as tongues of fire, recalling the burning bush of Exodus (3:1-30) and the burning coal with which an angel touched the lips of Isaiah so that he might speak God's truth (Isa 6:5-7). Filled with the Spirit, the disciples could now preach to all peoples, symbolized by Luke via their ability to speak numerous languages (Acts 2:5-11). Luke does several things here. First, Jesus has sent the Spirit in fulfillment of his promise in the gospel (24:49). Second, Luke again justifies the Gentile mission. Third, he makes it clear that the disciples' continuation of Jesus' work and mission is something desired by Jesus and aided by the Spirit.

Jesus remains the unique presence of God in the world, but his disciples legitimately follow his example.

The presentation is too pat and is contradicted by the disciples' initial practice of preaching only to Jews, but Luke, writing in the 80s when Christians knew Jesus' original words of teaching were irretrievably lost, contends that the disciples had the right to continue their master's teaching and to do so in a variety of languages. Indeed, in his gospel he preserved, in Greek translation, some of Jesus' most famous teachings and parables (the Good Samaritan, the Pharisee and the publican). For the first generations of Christians, not having Jesus' authentic, original, Aramaic teachings was not a problem.

But there was more. Those who did preserve his words were commissioned by Jesus and aided by the Holy Spirit, who, Luke makes clear, continued to guide the Christian community, which from this point we will call the church. The Spirit inspired the deacon Stephen (Acts 7:55), spoke to Peter (10:19), spoke in an unexplained way to the church in Antioch (15:2), guided the deliberations of the Christian leaders assembled for the Council of Jerusalem (15:28), and continuously guided and aided Paul. Luke demonstrates and insists that only those having the Spirit can truly proclaim the Christian message.

But who would they be, what qualifications would they have, and how would the church recognize them? Several options existed.

The most obvious option belonged to those disciples who had known the earthly Jesus. What could be more compelling than someone saying, "When the Lord spoke about the prophecy of Isaiah being fulfilled by himself" (as in, for example, Luke 4:16-27), who could respond in a contrary way? It is not difficult to imagine even this conversation: "Look, Paul, you're a good man, but I knew Jesus personally, and . . ." But even among this cohort, some emerged with more weighty authority, especially the Twelve, a dozen male disciples specially chosen by Jesus for more knowledge and duties than the disciples as a whole. Therefore, we are not surprised when Luke recounts that Peter, leader of the Twelve, first addressed the Jerusalem crowd (Acts 2:14-41), and the Twelve became the community's leaders. They would delineate the primitive Christian understanding of Jesus.

What we know about Jesus is what the New Testament books, especially the gospels, tell us. One often hears of other sources that provide information about Jesus, but that is just not the case. Within a century of Jesus' death, only one Jewish writer, Flavius Josephus (ca. 37 to ca. 100), and three Roman writers, Tacitus (ca. 56 to ca. 118), Pliny the Younger (ca. 60 to ca. 115), and Suetonius (ca. 70 to ca. 130), mentioned him. They provided no information about him that was not already available in the New Testament, saying only that the religious group called Christians claimed him as their founder and that he was executed by Pontius Pilate.

The simple fact is that Jesus is known historically because his earliest disciples preserved information about him, and later Christians who did not know him personally wrote some of that material down. The disciples and writers did far more, such as theologizing about Jesus, establishing ways of venerating him, and passing his message along to Jews and pagans, but any information about his life and public career depends upon them. We cannot know if they misunderstood him or made factual errors or saw him primarily through their own lenses. If we wish to be Christians, we must begin with what the earliest church has given us.

Understandably, this upsets a lot of people because it means that faith in Jesus means faith in the early community, the church. Some Christians occasionally set the Scriptures against the church, but that makes no sense. The church came to be before the written Scriptures, and the church produced and approved the Scriptures. Some readers may think I am propounding a Roman Catholic view, but this is simply historical fact. Let me also add that accepting that the earliest church produced our understanding of Jesus does not impose any particular form of church organization or structure upon any believer. Modern biblical scholarship takes a very ecumenical approach, trying to determine what the Scriptures said but not insisting that a certain ecclesiastical stance must result from that. My real concern here is how standards of orthodoxy arose in the early church and how the Twelve and others in authority formed the standards of the earliest orthodoxy.

But other sources of authority existed besides the Twelve and other early disciples. Acts and two early historians, one Christian (Eusebius of Caesarea, fourth century) and one Jewish (Flavius Josephus, first century) mention James, brother (or at least a cousin) of Jesus and leader of the powerful community at Jerusalem where the Twelve first preached. He had respect from the local Jewish community. He could preside at the first council ever held by Christians and could pronounce and determine its final decision and wording (Acts 15:1-20). He could also send delegates to Antioch, a community in Gentile territory (Gal 2:12). Even Paul felt obliged to visit the Jerusalem community after his journeys (Acts 21:15-17).

From where did James derive this authority? The New Testament does not say, but in an era when royal and noble families routinely ruled for centuries and blood determined who would be the next ruler, and when the Gospel of Matthew (1:5-6, 17) could mention with pride Jesus' descent from King David, James's relationship to Jesus probably played a great role in his becoming head of the Jerusalem church. But when James died in 62, executed by his Jewish enemies, any hint of authority based on a bloodline simply disappeared. Yet the evangelist Mark, author of the first gospel, writing less than a decade after James's death, took no chances. He records this saying of Jesus: "'Who are my mother and [my] brothers?' And looking at those seated around in a circle, he said, 'Here are my mother and my brothers. [For] whoever does the will of God is my brother and sister and mother'" (3:33-35). This sentence strongly diminishes the value of blood relationships, and Jesus naturally does not include "father" among the relatives, since only one person can be his father.

For the record, the church historian Eusebius preserves a story that the emperor Domitian (81–95), fearful the Christians might be rebellious, had two of Jesus' relatives (apparently descendants of his relatives) brought to Rome to be examined. Domitian dismissed them unharmed after they had shown him their calloused hands, proof that they were poor farmers and, in the emperor's eyes, not community leaders.

Another form of authority, well-known from Jewish history, also existed, and that was prophecy. Jews and Christians believed that the Spirit of God (the Holy Spirit for the Christians) inspired the prophets so that they spoke with God's authority. This could easily make them rivals to rulers, and several Old Testament prophets did not shrink from telling the kings to change their behavior. But did early Christianity have prophets? Absolutely.

Luke says that prophets from Jerusalem came to the Antiochene community, "and one of them named Agabus stood up and predicted *by the Spirit* that there would be a severe famine all over the world, and it happened under Claudius" (Acts 11:27-28; emphasis added). The same Spirit that came upon the disciples at Pentecost and validated their mission also inspired later prophets.

Antioch soon had its own prophets (Acts 13:1), as did the port city of Caesarea, where the deacon Philip (6:4) had four daughters who prophesied (21:9). Agabus reappeared at Caesarea and prophesied to Paul that he would be arrested; the prophet told Paul, "Thus says the Holy Spirit . . ." (21:10-14). Noteworthy is that to make his point Agabus bound his own hands and feet with Paul's belt, a physically demonstrative act similar to ones performed by the Old Testament prophets, such as Isaiah, who at God's command walked about naked and barefoot (Isa 20:2), or Ezekiel, who drew a picture of Jerusalem on a clay tablet (Ezek 4:1). Paul spoke several times about prophets in the community (1 Cor 12:28-29; 14:29-33), and he considered prophecy one of several spiritual gifts (Rom 12:6; 1 Cor 12:10; 1 Thess 5:20).

Prophecy thus provided a separate locus of authority, different from the commissioned disciples and from those in turn commissioned by them. But, as the Old Testament kings learned to their continued distress, prophets were major pains. Like the wind, the Spirit blows where it wills (John 3:8). No one knew what a prophet might say or how troublesome the saying might be. No one wanted to contradict the Holy Spirit, but how could one tell if a prophet's saying came from the Spirit or was just the prophet's own idea? Basically, how could one know if the prophet were authentic?

Paul himself had a sense of this problem. He did not want his missionary work being undone, and he attempted to control the prophets. "So, [my] brothers, strive eagerly to prophesy, . . . but everything must be done properly and in order" (1 Cor 14:39-40). "[W]hoever prophesies builds up the church" (1 Cor 14:4). The apostle recognized that spiritual gifts could cause problems, although he worried more about glossolalia, or "speaking in tongues," a spiritual gift that enabled believers to speak in several languages and/or languages not necessarily understood by anyone. Of course, "building up the church" and "properly and in order" are broad—even vague—phrases, but Paul recognized the problem of false prophecy.

He was not alone. Mark said that false prophets would be one sign of the end (13:22), and a decade or so later Matthew (24:24) agreed with him. When warning some Asia Minor churches about their behavior, John the Seer pointed out a particular villain, a woman church leader in Thyatira "who calls herself a prophetess" (Rev 2:20) but is actually a manifestation of Jezebel, the pagan wife of the Israelite king Ahab (1 Kgs 16–21), a murderess of prophets and the archetypal evil woman of ancient Judaism. Significantly, "Jezebel" held her own against the Seer: "I gave her time to repent, but she refuses to repent of her harlotry" (Rev 2:21), and the Seer is reduced to making savage threats against her and "her children," that is, the community members who follow her. Clearly, prophecy could create serious problems in the early communities.

But "Jezebel" raises another issue. Prophecy could empower women since, as prophetesses, they spoke with the voice of the Spirit, and no man, no matter how prominent, could ignore that. Luke tells us that

Philip's four daughters prophesied—although he does not quote anything they said—and instead of avoiding them like the plague, Paul stayed in their home (Acts 21:8-9), a validation of their calling. This is the same Paul who wrote 1 Corinthians that says "women should keep silent in churches, for they are not allowed to speak, but should be subordinate" (14:34). Many biblical exegetes think Paul did not write those words and that they are a later interpolation. Regardless of authorship, this verse and the willingness of early Christians to accept it as Pauline illustrate a significant point: many early Christian men wanted to keep women in their customary subordinate status, but prophecy empowered women and thus made them a threat to men, as John the Seer learned. Let us further note that in his infancy narrative, Luke, who told of Philip's daughters, also mentioned a Jewish woman prophet named Anna (2:36-38).

Along these same lines, prophecy could also empower the poor, another group abused by ancient society. Isaiah came from an aristocratic Jerusalem family, while Amos was a shepherd, one of the poorest occupations in the ancient world.

Those accepted as prophets represented a challenge to those with institutional authority, both royal (2 Sam 12:1-12; 1 Kgs 22) and priestly (Isa 28:7; Jer 2:8). Yet in the earliest communities, no record survives outside of "Jezebel" of a prophet presenting any direct problem to the ruling groups in the communities.

The apostle Paul quite deliberately changed another aspect of authority in the early church. As Luke has Peter say in Acts 2:32, "we are all witnesses" to what they were preaching about Jesus; that is, they knew the earthly Christ. This gave them a very unique authority. If one of them were to say, "I recall when Jesus told the parable of . . . ," what could anyone reply? But, like all modern believers, Paul did not know the earthly Jesus, only the resurrected one, whom, Luke tells us, he encountered in very dramatic fashion when his vision of Jesus literally knocked him to the ground (Acts 9:1-9). Since Paul had persecuted Christians, many believers understandably had reservations about the authenticity of his conversion as well as of the apparition, but he slowly won them over, including members of the Twelve and the Jerusalem community. This was *the* decisive step for church history because if authority rested solely with those who knew the earthly Jesus, the movement would have to end with the Parousia or the deaths of the first generation.

The earliest disciples' acceptance of Paul's experience of the risen Christ changed the nature of authority, eliminating any need to have encountered the earthly Jesus. Paul sensed this quickly. In Galatians

2:1-14 he stood up to emissaries from James and rebuked Peter to his face (biblical episodes that have never made it into Christian art). But Paul was right. Teaching authority would not be limited only to the first generation.

Paul epitomized the first Christian generation; Luke epitomized the second. Paul went to his death in Rome in the early 60s still believing in an imminent Parousia. Luke realized that the church would be on earth for an indeterminate time. For many first-generation Christians, the "church" was group of believers worshiping together until the Parousia arrived. Luke realized that the church, under the guidance of the Holy Spirit, was actually a genuine continuation of Christ's work on earth, a view he enshrined, as we have seen, in the last chapter of his gospel and in the opening chapters of Acts. Earlier generations of Christians used to call the Acts of the Apostles "the gospel of the Holy Spirit," and they were right. To emphasize the continuity between the mission of Jesus and that of the Spirit-inspired, post-resurrection community, Luke deliberately has passages in Acts recall passages in his gospel. Like Jesus (Luke 17:26), Peter miraculously enables a crippled man to walk (Acts 3:1-10). Only in Luke's gospel does Jesus ask his father to forgive those who brought about his death (Luke 23:34), and the Christian protomartyr Stephen does likewise (Acts 7:60).

Luke's approach challenged widely accepted views, but time was on his side, literally. As the years and then decades went by and Jesus did not return, belief in an imminent Parousia inevitably began to fade. Trying to preserve this belief sometime between 120 and 130, an unknown Christian writing pseudonymously as Peter used the specious argument that Jesus is indeed coming soon, but "with the Lord one day is like a thousand years and a thousand years like one day" (2 Pet 3:8). But the church at large came to accept Luke's view.

Changing the Christian view of time naturally had endless consequences, the most obvious being in ministry. Here is Paul writing to the Corinthians in the mid-50s: "Some people God has designated in the church to be, first, apostles [coincidentally, Paul's own calling!]; second, prophets; third, teachers; then, mighty deeds; then, gifts of healing, assistance, administration, and varieties of tongues. . . . Strive eagerly for the greatest spiritual gifts" (1 Cor 12:28, 31). Note the predominance of spiritual gifts.

But by the time Luke was writing Acts, many practical problems had emerged. The church had gotten larger, still a minor religion in the Roman Empire, but growing nonetheless. Thanks to Paul and other, now anonymous missionaries, it had spread from Judea into Syria, Asia Minor,

Greece, Macedonia, and Italy. Many scholars believe with good reason that the faith also went to Alexandria. Acts shows Paul evangelizing in communities that had at least some Jewish residents. Alexandria had a large Jewish community, possibly one-fourth of the city's population, and it seems credible that if missionaries were going to Jews living small towns in Asia Minor, they would also have gone to the largest Diasporan (that is, outside Palestine) Jewish communities. Acts 18:24-25 mentions that Apollos, "a native of Alexandria" who had been "instructed in the way of the Lord," arrived in Ephesus on the west coast of Asia Minor. Since Apollos had obviously been travelling, we cannot be sure if he was instructed in Alexandria itself, but there were definitely Christians in Alexandria by the early second century.

The spread of the faith had not occurred without controversy and trouble. For example, Paul's successful preaching in Ephesus led to a riot by the pagans (Acts 19:23-40). More ominously, the emperor Nero (54–68) blamed the Roman Christians for the Great Fire of 64 and persecuted them. Circa 95 the emperor Domitian persecuted the Roman Christians at the same time John the Seer spoke of persecutions in western Asia Minor.

A growing, geographically extensive church occasionally threatened by persecutions was not one to be governed by people speaking in tongues. The charismatic ministries, so beloved of Paul, gave way to less exciting but more reliable, quotidian ministries. Now the church had *diákonoi*, or those who served the community in various ways; *presbýteroi*, or "elders" or respected people with experience in the community, an office that would evolve into something more official; and *epískopoi*, meaning "those who preside" or "overseers." By the second century *epískopos* had come to mean "bishop," the dominant office of early Christianity and, of course, in many churches today. To these men fell the task of leading the church through a most difficult period of its history, and part of their task, especially for the bishops, was guaranteeing orthodox teaching.

The first century also saw the origins of the other great force of orthodoxy, and that was the New Testament, which, combined with the Old Testament, would comprise the Christian Scriptures, inspired by the Holy Spirit.

Christians always had scriptures, the Old Testament, but even in Jesus' time the canon or official list of books had not been settled. (A rabbinic conference would do that toward the end of the first century.) Yet all Jews accepted a basic collection. Jesus could refer to the "law of Moses and . . . the prophets and psalms" (Luke 24:44), and his disciples knew what he was talking about.

The earliest known book of what would become the New Testament is Paul's First Epistle to the Thessalonians, which scholars date around the year 50. Presumably, educated Christians had done some writing between Jesus' death and then, but nothing survives. Many scholars believe that, once again, the anticipation of an imminent Parousia played a role. Who needed official church literature with the end so near? Even Paul did not disagree with that. His "inspired writings" were mostly letters to churches he had founded and were written to deal with specific problems. But the writing had begun, and it continued into the 80s with Paul's works, three gospels (all but John), and letters written by people claiming to be Paul.

Many scholars believe that one of these pseudonymous letters, that to the Ephesians, written in the 80s, may be an introduction to several Pauline letters, suggesting an incipient canon. But this is far from proven.

But another pseudonymous letter, the Second Epistle of Peter, written between 120 and 130 somewhere in the eastern Mediterranean, has more definite information. By that decade, a fourth gospel, several more non-Pauline epistles, and even an apocalyptic book had been composed. We also know of Christian literature that did not make it into the canon, such as the letter of a Roman writer named Clement to the Corinthian church, dated circa 95. This growing body of writings may have forced the issue of a canon. What we do know is that 2 Peter 3:15-16 speaks of "our beloved brother Paul" and "all his letters," showing that "Peter" knew of a collection of them. Equally if not more important, "Peter" compares them with "other scriptures," here using the Greek word *graphé*, the term used by Christians to refer to the Old Testament.

We wish we knew more. What moved "Peter" to say that when he did? Did he originate the idea of Christian *graphé*, or had it been around for a while? Which epistles did he include in "all" of Paul's writings? These questions may be unanswerable, but the central point is unmistakable. By the early second century, Christians had begun to accept that some of their own writings were inspired.

The earliest lines of development are not completely clear, but throughout the second century more and more writers refer to "sacred books" and compile "canon lists," that is, lists of books they considered inspired. Around 200 the scholar Clement of Alexandria could refer to a list of books as the "New Testament." Throughout the third century, scholars refined the list, and in 367 another Alexandrian, the bishop Athanasius, listed as the New Testament the twenty-seven books that all Christians now accept.

The canonization process was actually very complicated, but the central point here is that the early Christians produced their own set of inspired literature, which became a force of its own, although, of course, joined to the Old Testament to comprise a complete Bible. No Christian could ignore the New Testament, and church leaders, acknowledging its inspiration, had to align their own teaching with it. Scripture looked like a solid mountain, unassailable by mere humans, and a counterweight to episcopal authority. Indeed, many modern Christians will set the Bible against the church. But, inevitably, it was not that simple.

The biblical books are texts, finished products that cannot be changed. (This refers to the original texts; translations obviously can vary.) But the lives of persons and communities do change, and the text must be interpreted for particular situations. To use a secular parallel, governments pass laws in the form of texts, but judges interpret the laws in particular situations. The ancient Jews routinely interpreted their texts. For example, the desert community that produced the Dead Sea Scrolls believed that many biblical texts applied directly to that community, which would have been nonsense to the scholars at the temple in Jerusalem. A Diasporan Jew, Philo of Alexandria (d. ca. AD 50), interpreted parts of the Bible allegorically; that is, he thought that when the literal meaning of the text did not make sense, it must be pointing to a higher, spiritual truth. Scholars have long maintained that many of Jesus' debates with the Pharisees were not about the Mosaic Law but about the Pharisaic interpretation of it. Christians regularly interpreted parts of the Old Testament as foreshadowing if not outright predicting parts of the life and career of Jesus, such as his birth, yet we know how the temple priests responded when they learned that a group called the Christians believed that the prophecies about the Messiah, the *Christós*, were fulfilled by a Galilean carpenter turned itinerant preacher who was executed as a criminal.

Although some parts of the Bible can be read in a straightforward way, most passages demand interpretation. 1 Chronicles 1–9 is a huge genealogy, much of which just lists names with no information or content about the persons involved. The reader believes that this is inspired, but what is she or he to do about it? To this can be added many other genealogies as well as material in the book of Leviticus about the ancient Israelite cultic priesthood.

More problematically, narrative parts of the Bible sometimes conflict. In Matthew 8:18-22 Jesus talks about discipleship, using the image "Foxes have holes and birds of the sky have nests . . ." *before* he calms the storm at sea (8:23-27). In Luke Jesus utters those words (9:57-60) *after* he calms the storm at sea (8:22-25). Clearly, both gospels cannot be right about the sequence of events. To this example can be added two versions of the

Beatitudes (Matt 5:3-12; Luke 6:20-23) and two versions of the Lord's Prayer (Matt 6:19-23; Luke 11:2-4). The faithful reader needs help to understand how this can be.

Even more problematic, the Bible sometimes contradicts itself. Here is one of the most famous sayings in the Bible, found first in the book of Isaiah (2:4) and then reiterated in the book of Micah (4:3): in the messianic age "They shall beat their swords into ploughshares / and their spears into pruning hooks." But the prophet Joel (4:10) had a somewhat different take on this issue: "Beat your ploughshares into swords, / and your pruning hooks into spears." But if both verses are inspired, how can they be contradictory?

Scripture may be inspired by God, but it needs interpreters, and one crucial aspect of church authority is, who has the right to interpret the Scriptures? This matters to believers because for most of them the dominant interpretation becomes the "meaning" of the text. To use a familiar example, can any contemporary Roman Catholic read "you are Peter, and upon this rock I will build my church" (Matt 16:18) without envisioning the dome of Saint Peter's Basilica?

By the third century many bishops claimed that they alone had the right to interpret Scripture, although it took centuries for that view to become dominant, especially in the medieval West, where most biblical exegetes were monks. But the bishops, led by the bishops of Rome, prevailed by the end of the Middle Ages, only to find the Protestant Reformers accusing them of misinterpreting the Scriptures to justify their theology and authority. Today academic scholars insist that their professional qualifications give them the prevailing right to interpret the Bible, only to be challenged by fundamentalists who are refreshingly unimpressed by professors. But whoever makes the claim, the result is the same: the right to interpret the Bible is the right to speak for the Bible.

* * *

As the church entered the second century, the major elements for determining orthodoxy, ecclesiastical authority, and Sacred Scripture—the Old Testament and the nascent New Testament—were in place. It did not take long for these authorities to be tested as the church encountered what can safely be called the first heresy, Docetism.

Following Paul's lead, missionaries went into Gentile territory, including Alexandria in Egypt and other areas where, thanks to the conquests of Alexander the Great in the fourth century BCE, Greek culture and language had spread. Educated Greeks viewed God as a pure spirit who could not come into actual contact with the physical world and certainly could not get involved in history as blatantly as the deity of the Old Testament. For example, Deuteronomy 20:4 actually says, "For it is the LORD, your God, *who goes with you to fight for you* against your enemies and give you victory" (emphasis added). To ancient Greeks and Romans, God on the field of battle sounded more like the pagan *Iliad* than a biblical passage. Direct divine involvement in the material world also posed a serious philosophical problem. When Christians taught that Jesus, the Son of God, the divine Word of John's gospel, took on a physical body, some Greek-educated converts found that offensive, believing that flesh would demean the divine. These Gentiles began to advocate their own ideas or, rather, their own interpretation of Jesus.

They used a simple syllogism: a spiritual God cannot come in contact with corruptible and thus corrupting flesh; as the Son of God, Jesus is divine; therefore, Jesus could not have taken on flesh. But people had seen him and spoken with him in bodily form. No, said these converts. What they saw was a phantom, a nonphysical form the Son of God used to communicate with people. Jesus did not have a body but only seemed to have one. The Greek word for "seem" is *dokéo*, and historians call these Christians "Docetists." It may seem odd to us to call them "Christians," but, in their own way, they were, and at a time when being Christian was often unpopular and sometimes dangerous.

Possibly the Docetists got their idea from Paul himself, who spoke of Christ's "spiritual body" (1 Cor 15:44), but the apostle also spoke of his risen body and constantly emphasized the physicality of Jesus' body. In that same epistle (1:23) Paul said that he proclaims "Christ crucified," which meant that Jesus had to have a physical body.

The Docetist question echoes in the New Testament. The First Epistle of John (ca. 100–110) says, "This is how you can know the Spirit of God: every spirit that acknowledges Jesus come *in the flesh* is of God" (4:2; emphasis added). The Second Epistle of John complains, "Many deceivers have gone out into the world, those who do not acknowledge Jesus Christ as coming *in the flesh*" (v. 7; emphasis added). The First Epistle to Timothy says that Jesus "was manifested *in the flesh*" (3:16; emphasis added) but does not imply that some deny this. Many scholars think that the prologue to the Gospel of John (ca. 100) refers to Docetism when it insists "The Word *was made flesh* and dwelt among us" (1:14; emphasis added). In the second century, a number of Christian writers attacked the Docetists, most prominently Ignatius, bishop of Antioch, who died a martyr in Rome circa 117, making him a contemporary of the author of the gospel and epistles attributed to John.

What exactly was wrong with Docetism? This belief foundered on the redemption. From the first days, Christians taught that Jesus redeemed humanity from sin by his suffering and death, both of which required a physical body. Paul's speaks of Jesus' physical suffering; the gospels portray him walking, eating, even weeping. Imagine someone telling disciples who had physically touched Jesus that he was a phantom! Docetism itself survived into the early third century, and its basic premise, that Jesus was not fully human, would plague Christianity for centuries, but denying Jesus' physicality simply had no future in a church that accepted a redemption achieved by Jesus' physical death.

Docetism was clearly a heresy. It went against the accepted public teaching of the earliest disciples and of the apostle Paul that Jesus died a redemptive death on the cross to save humanity from sin, something he could not have done without a genuine physical body. To be sure, the forms of ecclesiastical authority were still coming into being, and not all of the twenty-seven books of the eventual New Testament had even been written, but the church's teaching about Jesus' physicality was clear.

So much for Docetism, but what of the Docetists? Were they truly heretics? Probably not. Rather, they were the first witnesses to an enduring problem in Christianity, taking the gospel message across various cultures. The Docetists believed in Jesus' divinity, but, products of Greco-Roman culture, for them divinity meant pure spirit untouched by contact with corruptible flesh, and they rejected Christian teaching growing out of another culture, that of the Jews, whose God had created the physical world and had even gotten his hands dirty (cf. Gen 2:7: the creation of Adam). Why, the Docetists asked, should Christianity privilege Jewish culture over theirs?

This problem has occurred endlessly. Sometimes Christians simply ignored the cultural problems, as when the European settlers in the Americas dismissed outright the native culture as pagan superstition and made little or no attempt to understand it. Other times Christians have worked to bridge the gap. For example, Pope John Paul II spoke sympathetically of animist beliefs held by primitive tribes in South America. This writer once met a Presbyterian missionary who had worked in the southwest Pacific among people who did not know what a lamb was. Trying to explain Jesus as the Lamb of God, he checked around to find out which animal played that role for this island society. It turned out the animal was a pig, and the missionary conceded that he just could not bring himself to say, "Behold the Pig of God!" But he did not abandon trying to bridge the cultural gap.

But is cultural openness dangerous? Will not adapting the message to various cultures water it down? Yet what happens when the original cultural expression or formulation loses its meaning for believers? In the Synoptic Gospels (Matthew, Mark, Luke), "Son of Man" is Jesus' favorite self-designation, and it has strong apocalyptic overtones deriving from the Old Testament book of Daniel (for example, 7:13). But the fourth- and fifth-century Greek-speaking and Greek-cultured Christians who provided the church with the doctrines of the Trinity and of Christ had little use for eschatological titles, and they typically interpreted "Son of Man" as biblical proof for Jesus' full humanity against opponents who questioned it as the Docetists had done.

To update the question, to what extent should contemporary African and Asian Christians have to accept European understandings and formulations of the faith? But can the church dispense with two millennia of understanding Jesus' life and message?

It is an enduring problem in dealing with heresy: to determine whether the "heretics" truly reject Christian teaching or cannot accept the cultural framework in which the teaching is presented.

* * *

This chapter will close with a return to the most formidable problem facing orthodoxy. Christians refer to the "mysteries of the faith." Recall that in Greek *mystérion* means something that we cannot and will not ever understand, something the book of Job made so marvelously clear: "I have dealt with great things that I do not understand; / things too wonderful for me, which I cannot know" (42:3). Our attempts to understand God can never enjoy total fruition. Yet people cannot worship or pray to "Whoever You Are" or "Whatever Is Out There." We need to have some notion of God even though that notion can in no way measure up to the reality. Faith continues to seek understanding.

But this leads to a very serious problem. If we acknowledge that no theological formula can encompass the divine reality, how can the church insist upon the orthodoxy of a particular formula, to say nothing of calumniating, expelling from the community, or, in the ancient and medieval worlds, executing those who could not accept the formula?

There is no definitive answer to this question. The church must stand for something. It must teach, and the best way to do so is to rely on Scripture, on the teachings of the church, and on the work of great thinkers of the church's tradition. If church leaders do this faithfully, then they have the knowledge and also the obligation to differentiate what they believe to be authentically Christian from what they believe is not, that is, heresy. But they must also do so in a sense of humility, recognizing that no formula can ever adequately convey, much less explain, the mysteries of the faith, and that those who express dissatisfaction with the current formula are not necessarily enemies of the faith but may be good Christians trying to express their own understanding of a particular faith stance.

Christians believe God to be beyond time, but we live in it. History impacts us endlessly. It shapes the world into which we are born, and it shapes how we understand that world, including our understanding of the church and its teachings, just as did the church of the earliest believers.

What follows are five chapters about heresies and the historical forces that shaped them. These chapters will try to demonstrate that historical forces and human beings of particular historical eras play a great role in how both orthodoxy and heresy come into being and how they are understood. The intent is not to reduce orthodoxy and heresy to historical forces but to suggest that an understanding of the historical circumstances of both is essential in understanding them and especially in determining what might be orthodox or heretical.

Montanism

The earliest church experienced diverse modes of authority, but by the early second century some of these modes had simply faded. Those who could claim a personal knowledge of the earthly Jesus had passed into history, as did anyone contending that a family relationship to him gave them authority. The charismatic ministries so praised by the apostle Paul flourished in an era of eschatological expectation, but as the Parousia faded into an indeterminate future, more regular ministries moved to the fore, especially that of *episkopos*. Scripture, in the sense of the Old Testament interpreted to support Christian views, always existed and enjoyed great authority, but by the early second century the Christians had concluded that they too had produced inspired books.

In the second century the church continued to expand geographically. We know of Christians in Gaul (modern France), Roman North Africa (modern Tunisia and Libya), Spain, and even faraway Britain. The Christians likewise expanded socially. That information comes from unusual sources.

A pagan historian named Dio Cassius (ca. 150–235) said that in the year 96 the emperor Domitian (81–96) brought a charge of atheism against two of his relatives, Flavius Clemens and his wife, Flavia Domitilla. The emperor also accused them of following "Jewish customs." Domitian executed Flavius and exiled his wife to a prison island. On the surface, this is a puzzling reference. How could one practice both Judaism and atheism, since the two were contradictory? Furthermore, Judaism was a *religio licita*, that is, a licensed religion, not just a set of customs. The answer may lie with the historian. Dio Cassius loathed Christians, even to the point of, where possible, not mentioning their name. Christians believed in one God but not in the pagan gods who protected the empire, who ensured the fertility of crops, animals, and people, and who resented it when people ignored their worship. Thus, the Christians, who did not worship the official gods, were denounced as atheists. There were also

Romans who had difficulty distinguishing the Christians from the Jews. If, as is likely, this couple had Christian sympathies, this means that the faith had reached the highest level of Roman society, the imperial palace.

The second example comes from a martyrdom. Circa 115 the Romans sent a Syrian bishop, Ignatius of Antioch, to the capital city for execution. Ignatius had an almost mystical view of martyrdom and very much wanted to die for the faith. Along the journey he wrote several letters, including one to the Roman Christian community. He genuinely feared that the Roman Christians would try to save him and thus deprive him of the martyrdom he so devoutly wanted. "If only you will say nothing in my behalf, I shall be a word of God. But if your love is for my body, I shall be once more be a mere voice. You can do me no greater kindness than to suffer me to be sacrificed to God while the place of sacrifice is still prepared. . . . Do nothing to prevent this new life" (*Epistle to the Romans* 2, 6). Since we can safely rule out some sort of commando-style rescue of the bishop who urged the Romans to "say nothing" on his behalf, clearly the Roman Christians must have had sufficient influence at court—possibly social, possibly financial, possibly both—to have saved Ignatius. No small feat.

About a decade later another piece of evidence shows how the Christians were moving into the higher levels of Roman society. Apologetics is a philosophical discipline by which one makes reasoned arguments for a position that she or he or the group holds. These arguments must convince someone who is doubtful if not outright skeptical, and so the apologist must use arguments acceptable to her or his opponent.

Around the year 125 an apologist named Quadratus wrote a discourse in defense of the Christians to the emperor Hadrian (117–38). We do not know if the emperor received the work or, if he did, took the trouble to read it. In general, Christian apologists had three goals: to refute the calumnies lodged against the faith, to show the weaknesses and irrationality of the pagan cults, and to present an accurate picture of their practices—for example, explaining that references to eating someone's body and drinking his blood did not mean that they were cannibals. Except for a sentence or two, Quadratus's work does not survive, but he set a pattern for later apologists who, wanting to win over cultivated Greeks and Romans, introduced some classical philosophical notions into their works to explicate some Christian beliefs.

The apologists demonstrate that the Christians accepted that they would remain in the world for some time to come and that they wanted to get along with those around them, albeit not at the cost of compromising their beliefs. The presence of prominent Christians at the heart of the empire suggests that they were succeeding. By the last quarter of the second century, definite proof exists that they did succeed. A Greek provincial from Syria or Palestine wrote a vicious attack on them. Little is known about Celsus, and his work, *The True Doctrine*, survives only in copious excerpts in a book written by a Christian to refute it. Celsus attacked on a wide front, even to the point of showing discrepancies in the gospel accounts of Jesus' career. But he also proved that the Christians had attained such influence in the empire that the pagans needed to be warned against them.

This impressive growth did not come without a price. Circa 136 Telesphorus, bishop of Rome, met a martyr's death; circa 165 an apologist named Justin met the same fate in Rome. But persecutions were mercifully few, and the vast majority of Christians died in their beds.

The larger movement was undeniable. The Christians had spread throughout much of the eastern Mediterranean, occasionally going beyond the Roman frontier, for example, into Armenia. The faith also spread west, penetrating Rome's western provinces. It attracted more and more educated Gentiles, and modern scholars believe that circa 150 the church had a Gentile majority, which had the partial effect of diminishing the influence not only of Jewish Christians but also of Jewish-Christian culture. As noted above, phrases like "Son of Man" had little relevance for Gentiles, and the title *Christós* ceased to mean "Messiah" since the Gentiles had little use for that essentially Jewish term. To these mega-issues can be added mundane ones. Some members of the community had to deal with the daily issues of a church, such as planning liturgies, offering instruction, preparing converts for baptism, visiting the sick, and the like. In sum, the church was becoming Westernized and institutionalized, both just consequences of history but, for some, threats to the true faith.

Why? Because many Christians, then and now, see the first, postresurrection church as an ideal for all time. The Protestant Reformers harkened back to the time before the popes had "corrupted" the faith, while one of the popes, John XXIII (1958–63), when calling the Second Vatican Council (1962–65), spoke of returning to "the smooth, clean lines of the early church." Anyone thinking this way should read Paul's First Epistle to the Corinthians to learn about factionalism, bickering, fighting for the best seats at the ritual meal, and even incest—not exactly the ideal era. But the notion persists and has a long history.

In this primitive church, spiritual gifts abounded, as Paul and Luke testify. Some of these gifts had simply disappeared; we do not read much about glossolalia after the first century. But many believed that prophecy still had a role to play, especially given its prominence in the Old Testament and to a lesser extent in the emerging Christian canon. But could those with charismatic gifts play a great role or even fit into the church of the mid-second century?

Clearly, charismatics, who could not predict the Spirit's actions or visitations to them, would not make good everyday leaders, and more stable ministries appeared. The New Testament books refer to them as *epískopoi, presbýteroi,* and *diákonoi.* These ministries soon predominated, providing the order and constancy required by a growing, spreading, and occasionally suffering church. The growing influence of the New Testament with its permanent text and its inevitable interpreters also weakened the charismatic element. Office replaced person, as the pseudonymous Third Epistle of John (ca. 100) proves. A revered elder named John complained to his followers that an institutional leader named Diotrophes, "who loves to dominate" (v. 9), would not allow him to visit this unnamed community, and the elder could do nothing about it.

To many believers this "institutional takeover" seemed unchristian, and they had a valid point. Ironically, the New Testament, itself part of the "takeover," contains a vivid account of how much religious people respond to charismatics, as when the gospels recount how "all Jerusalem" (Mark 1:5) went out to the Jordan River to encounter the prophet John the Baptist. Dissatisfaction with the new order was growing and spreading. Clement of Rome, writing on behalf of the Roman community to the one at Corinth, said his letter was prompted by the Holy Spirit. Ignatius of Antioch, the bishop martyred at Rome, claimed to have prophetic gifts and urged another bishop named Polycarp to be open to them. Circa 150 a Roman named Hermas wrote a visionary book entitled *The Shepherd.* Prophets were far from uncommon in the second-century church. A tense situation had arisen and was getting worse. Something had to happen, and finally it did. The Holy Spirit spoke to Montanus.

Montanism has long fascinated scholars, a fascination which has grown significantly in the last half century as archaeological research and novel approaches to history such as feminist exegesis of texts have opened new ways to understand this phenomenon. But our knowledge of Montanism rests largely on information provided by those who opposed or even hated the movement. Its enemies saw to the destruction of Montanist sites and literature. "Original sources," that is, the words of the Montanists themselves, are preserved primarily by its critics and opponents, most of whom wrote well after the movement's origins. Modern scholars worry about how accurately the material was preserved. Like the extant accounts of the Greek and Persian conflicts and of the Punic Wars, Montanism presents a classic case of the victor writing history.

A starting point for proving this is its very name, Montanism. The members of the movement called it the New Prophecy. Not until the late fourth century, two full centuries after the movement began, did it acquire its now common name when Bishop Cyril of Jerusalem (315–86) first used the term. In an intelligent and provocative book about heresy, *Voting about God in Early Church Councils*, Ramsay MacMullen points out that one of the ways those claiming to be orthodox battled presumed heretics was to create a name for their opponents—preferably one based on a person's name—so that the "heretics" would appear to be particularist and separatist, while their "orthodox" foes purportedly represented the entire church. This is an insightful and valid point, especially since later generations often bought into it simply because ecclesiastical usage had made the name common—thus Donatism, Pelagianism, and Nestorianism. The name Montanism caught on and has been used ever since, but it creates a problem because it suggests that Montanus was the main figure in the movement and that its teaching and discipline derived primarily from him when, in fact, they did not. In this case the traditional name alone distorts our understanding of the movement, but, for convenience and bowing to convention, we will use it.

Who was Montanus? When did he become prominent? And where?

The easiest question to answer is the last. The New Prophecy arose in Phrygia, a mountainous area of southwest Asia Minor (modern Turkey), and in that area it enjoyed its most successful and long-lived tenure. Most scholars believe the movement began around 156–57 and became well-known outside Phrygia by 170.

About Montanus himself, little can be certain. One ancient critic said he had been a priest of the religion of Cybele, the Great Mother, and had castrated himself to serve that goddess. But the source, the church Father Jerome (d. ca. 420), wrote more than two centuries after Montanus lived. Furthermore, Jerome was a vicious polemicist who often played loose with the truth. It would be more accurate to say that Montanus was apparently a Christian layman who had some kind of spiritual experience, which he interpreted as a new revelation. He soon claimed to be receiving prophecies from the Holy Spirit, and he started to preach and gather disciples, male and female. Soon after his career began, Montanus was joined by two women, Priscilla and Maximilla, who prophesied as much as he did and shared with him the leadership of the movement. As Rex Butler puts it, "The two women were not spiritually dependent upon

Montanus but contributed equally in prophetic activity while he not only prophesied but also organized the movement" (11). The ancient hostile sources (Heine, 23) say critically that the two women were married and left their families to participate in the New Prophecy, yet in the gospel of Luke Jesus says, "If anyone comes to me without hating his father and mother, wife and children, brothers and sisters, and even his own life, he cannot be my disciple" (14:26). So the two women prophets followed a gospel example when they left their families to make what they saw as the spiritually better choice. But on this point and several others their critics simply overlooked or ignored the biblical paradigm.

The organization worked, and the New Prophecy grew and matured. Maximilla and Priscilla engaged in missionary journeys. A small movement grew, and the New Prophecy even had a financial officer named Theodotus, suggesting that although the charismatic element predominated, some of the movement's followers took some practical steps.

The New Prophecy featured familiar apocalyptic themes, including an imminent end, a prominent element even of modern prophecy (remember Y2K). It also had a strict moral code, which emphasized fasting, celibacy (including forbidding a second marriage for those widowed), and martyrdom. Some of these attitudes would cause problems with the larger church, but many, such as forbidding second marriage, should not have done so. The ancient church favored women remaining as widows, a point made by the apostle Paul (1 Cor 7:8), and the forbidding of second marriages would not be a great difficulty in itself. Nor would the imminent end of the world. Throughout Christian history many people, including many prominent ones such as Pope Gregory I (590–604), anticipated and even predicted an imminent end. The elements of Montanist teaching presented no real problem.

Instead, the issue quickly became, who were the New Prophets to make such claims?

Like all prophets, Montanus, Maximilla, and Priscilla presented an insoluble challenge for church leaders. If the Holy Spirit indeed inspired them, then the rest of the people had the obligation to listen to what the Spirit had to tell them. But how could one be sure if the Holy Spirit had indeed spoken through these self-designated prophets? If one did acknowledge that the Spirit spoke through them, how could one disagree with the prophets' sayings, beliefs, and even their commands? And in back of these questions was a bigger one: How does the Spirit still speak to the church?

But whatever fears the bishops in Asia Minor might have had, the common believers of Phrygia flocked to hear the New Prophecy. Like those of the Baptist, the three New Prophets' revelations were not confined to a sacred book. The thrill of a living prophet became contagious in Phrygia. The bishops had to be careful; no one wanted to appear to be hostile to the work of the Spirit. But prudence soon overcame caution.

By the late second century the bishops understood themselves to be the guardians of orthodoxy. They had struggled mightily and with varying degrees of success against a group called the Gnostics, a group of Christians who probably originated in Alexandria, Egypt. Greek educated, the Gnostics followed the grand tradition of the Greek philosopher Plato (427–34 BC) that the body had little value. Plato had actually called it the prison of the soul (*Phaedo* 62b). But if the body had little value, how could Jesus have redeemed the world by the death of his body? The answer was simple—he could not have done so. Instead, Jesus brought saving knowledge, a special knowledge about the cosmos passed along in select circles because the average, ignorant Christian could not understand the message Jesus brought. The Greek word for knowledge is *gnosis*, and thus these Christians acquired the name Gnostics. Their rejection of the redemptive nature of Jesus' death put them outside the orthodox pale.

Some extremists went well beyond the Gnostics, considering the corruptible fleshly body to be unworthy of being assumed by the spiritual Son of God, so that Jesus simply did not have a body but only "seemed" to have one. These, of course, were the Docetists, but the Gnostics proved to be a stronger problem, and several great third-century theologians, such as Clement (d. ca. 220) and Origen (d. 254), both of Alexandria, wrote against them. But even if Gnosticism had not been dealt with completely by the time of the New Prophecy, the bishops still had the collective experience of standing up to threats against the church now governed by them.

But how could the bishops counter the New Prophecy? As noted above, the women's having left their families would not be amiss if the Prophecy were authentic. The ban on second marriages violated generally accepted teaching, but it could be understood as ascetic extremism rather than unchristian or antichurch. The personal lives of the prophets provided little ammunition for an attack upon them.

And so the bishops focused on authority. Later generations would focus on the authority of Scripture or of ecumenical councils or of the papacy, but none of that lay to hand for the second-century bishops. Ecumenical councils did not yet exist; the first one would not meet until 325, and its initial acceptance in the church at large was rocky. The papacy, the medieval solution, did not exist. Not until the late fourth century would

Roman authority become extensive even among the Latin churches. As for the Bible, it was there—sort of. The Old Testament existed, but no Christian group had yet pronounced on its canon or, for that matter, on the canon of their own Scriptures. Not only was there no canon, there was no formal New Testament to speak of. As we saw, the first person to use the phrase "New Testament" to mean a collection of inspired Christian books was Clement of Alexandria circa 200, yet his great pupil Origen could refer somewhat dismissively to the *so-called* New Testament.

The traditional remedies of later generations simply did not yet exist, but the bishops of Asia Minor still knew they had to do something.

Much of the bishops' problem stemmed from the Montanists' reluctance to accept episcopal authority, not only because they had the authority of the Spirit but also because they believed the bishops were betraying the ethos of the first generations of Christians, among whom prophecy had flourished. The Montanists pointed to the prophet Agabus, cited approvingly by Luke in Acts and accepted by the early Jerusalem community. They also pointed to the four daughters of the deacon Philip, not only prophets but women prophets, thus validating the role of Maximilla and Priscilla. (An early second-century church Father named Papias supported the tradition about Philip's daughters.) The Montanists also looked to the book of Revelation, relentlessly prophetic and written to churches in western Asia Minor, including churches where bishops now opposed the New Prophecy. To cite Butler again, "These men and women viewed the increase in ecclesiastical hierarchy as resignation to the delay in Christ's return, and they condemned the resultant decline in eschatological and extra manifestations of the Spirit" (21). In sum, "By their fruits you shall know them" (Matt 7:16), and the "fruits" of the bishops were simply not the works of the first generation of Christians, the generation of the Twelve, of Paul, and of the New Testament prophets. The bishops found themselves being denounced as innovators. (One is tempted to put an exclamation point at the end of that sentence.) Many modern scholars interpret Montanism as a conservative reaction by self-styled primitive Christians against the modernizing tendencies of the episcopate and possibly the intellectualism of the Gnostics.

By 170 another factor entered the debate. Montanism was spreading well beyond Phrygia. First it went to the cities of the Aegean Sea, including some evangelized by Paul, such as Ephesus, and others that received letters from the presbyter John who wrote the book of Revelation.

But Asian Christians were a mobile group. Many resided in Rome itself. Scholars have long noted that all the earliest Christian literature going to and from Rome, such as Paul's epistle and the letter of Clement to the Corinthians, was written in Greek. Most of the early bishops of Rome had Greek names, such as Anacletus, Evaristus, and Telesphorus. Many scholars think that part of the hostility toward the Christians there, such as Nero's persecution, resulted partly from the foreign character of the community. Montanism would soon impact the Asians resident in Rome and through them the larger Roman Christian community.

The Asians had also gone on to Gaul and not just to the coastal cities. Irenaeus (d. ca. 179), from the Asia Minor city of Smyrna, had migrated to Gaul and become bishop of the inland city of Lyons. By his episcopate the New Prophecy had reached the Lyons community. By no later than 200 it had crossed the Mediterranean into Roman North Africa. By the early third century the bishops faced an empire-wide movement.

Although scholars cannot say for certain that the movement's homeland of Phrygia was more open to prophecy than other areas, it soon became clear that the New Prophecy was meeting a far less enthusiastic reception outside Phrygia. These areas, especially Rome and western Asia Minor, soon provided the initial and then the longest-lasting and most effective criticisms of and resistance to the prophets and their teachings. Furthermore, Rome and western Asia Minor had strong episcopacies whose members certainly did not think that their current ministry constituted a betrayal of the original faith. Firm in their views, these bishops set out to defend them.

Only in Gaul did the situation differ somewhat. Irenaeus, a native of Asia Minor whose name means "peacemaker," wrote to the church at Rome to urge a diplomatic settlement of the differences between the prophets and their opponents. His own church of Lyons endured great pressure from the local pagans and became the center of a vicious persecution in 177. The last thing the church needed was more division. But Irenaeus's view did not prevail in Rome or even in Gaul. The New Prophecy presented too great a challenge to the episcopal order and also represented a return to an age that truly was lost in the diverse, widespread, and increasingly intellectual environment in which the church now found itself. The "new age" of the church, especially in urban areas, was not that of the Spirit but that of an extensive, complicated, and organized religion.

Compromise eluded both sides. The prophets would not turn back because they could not turn back. How could they when the Holy Spirit was urging them on? To turn back would be to reject the Spirit. The bishops were in a similar position. They could see how the episcopacy had benefited Christianity. They could also see that a church that already reached as far as Britain, that had traversed Roman boundaries in the east, that had to endure persecution, and that had to deal with the problems that did not exist in the apostolic era simply could not become the church that the prophets envisioned.

Like all religious enthusiasts (from the Greek *én*, "in," and *theós*, "god"), the Montanists counted upon the truth of their message and the power of the Spirit to carry them along. Like most people in power, the bishops organized, looked for weaknesses, and forced the issue. This would be a defining moment for the history of Christianity.

The bishops soon recognized the most effective method to win this struggle: raise doubts about the authenticity of the New Prophecy. Did Montanus, Priscilla, and Maximilla truly get their authority from the Holy Spirit?

Immediate assistance came from Irenaeus of Lyons, who in fact challenged not the Montanists but rather the Gnostics, who would have never have accepted the Montanist claims of possessing the Spirit. The Gnostics knew about the growing New Testament and its claims to go back to the apostolic age. They claimed that they also had books dating back to that age, but these books had been passed along secretly in the Gnostic conventicles. Like many later Gentile Christians, the Gnostics had little use for the books of the Old Testament, which some of them rejected outright, and many did not care for the Jewish character of the New Testament books. The Gnostic books claimed to possess the true knowledge that Jesus had imparted to his disciples, knowledge that "outranked," so to speak, that available to the bishops and the masses. The esoteric nature of this knowledge made it more attractive to its devotees.

But Irenaeus brilliantly realized that the secret aspect of this "knowledge" provided the means of routing the Gnostics. He hit them hard on the issue of proof. He could prove that what he believed was contained in the apostolic books, many of which he named. Could the Gnostics prove that their books could be traced back to the apostles? He also argued that he could trace his beliefs through a succession of bishops whose names he could provide right back to the apostolic age. Could the Gnostics do likewise for their teachers?

This method did not cause the Gnostics to abandon their beliefs, but it did provide for the episcopal party a now common method of doing theology, namely, Scripture and tradition. Scripture for Irenaeus meant the Old Testament but also the New Testament, whose books he cited, including the first reference in Christian history to the Acts of the Apostles.

As for tradition, unfortunately that word became caught up in Reformation and post-Reformation polemics, but Irenaeus's understanding of the word differs significantly from those. For him, tradition did not mean a collection of practices or documents passed down through the centuries and thus binding because of their age; rather, it meant a living link to the apostolic church. Tradition also included a line of bishops and teachers who had faithfully preserved what the apostles taught and those teachings that corresponded with or at least did not contradict what could be found in Scripture.

And thus the approach for the bishops to use against the Montanists: the Holy Spirit inspired the Scriptures and guides the church, and the Spirit cannot be self-contradictory. Any claim to authentic Christian teaching must be consonant with the teaching of Scripture and of this living tradition. If Montanism went against these, it could not be authentic.

The bishops soon responded to the Montanists and then went on the attack against them.

The first church historian, Eusebius, bishop of Caesarea in Palestine (d. ca. 340), wrote well after the early phase of the New Prophecy but still provided the most information about that era and about the initial episcopal challenges to the prophets. His most important early source was a bishop whom he never named, so scholars, who have suggested many candidates for identification, simply call him the "Anonymous against Montanism," a title they usually shorten simply to "the Anonymous." He knew the New Prophecy well and was clearly a bishop in western Asia Minor circa 190, although what Eusebius records is from a visit the bishop made to the city of Ancyra in central Asia Minor. The Anonymous did not outright reject the notion of new, postbiblical prophecy, but he did reject this prophecy. The New Prophets claimed to stand in the biblical prophetic tradition, but, the Anonymous asked, did they really?

The Anonymous and other opponents of the New Prophecy focused on what they considered to be the authentic nature of biblical prophecy. Montanus often spoke ecstatically (from the Greek *ék*, "out of" or "beyond," and *stásis*, literally "standing" but generally meaning the normal status of something). The Spirit seized Montanus so violently that he was carried away and did not truly know what he was saying; he stood outside himself. Did the biblical prophets do that?

The bishop's answer was no. The Israelite prophets had written, but one cannot write a book while in ecstasy. (In fact, modern scholars believe that most prophets did not write but rather that their disciples recorded some of their prophecies, including ecstatic ones, or the disciples themselves wrote in the name of the master; for example, at least three different prophets stand behind the book of Isaiah.) The Anonymous went on. Since the ancient prophets predicted many events in the life of Christ, they wrote down things that, in the divine plan, would be understood fully only by Christians. Starting with God's promise to Adam and Eve in the Garden of Eden (Gen 3:15), the divine writings pointed toward the redemption of humanity in the person of Jesus. So crucial an undertaking simply could not depend upon the senseless utterings of people in ecstasy. Maybe pagan "prophets" spoke that way, but biblical ones certainly did not.

Yet 1 Samuel 19:23-24 says that Saul, king of Israel, spoke ecstatically when "the Spirit of God came upon him." Daniel, after fasting, had an ecstatic vision that ended when he fell forward in a faint (Dan 10:2-9). Although Paul insisted that comprehensible speech had more value than simple speaking in tongues (1 Cor 14:5), he nevertheless described the babbling glossolalia of Christians as being uttered under the influence of the Spirit (14:2). Incoherence did not rule out the influence of the Spirit, nor did lucidity prove it. As a bishop, the Anonymous presumably knew of these biblical passages, but, if so, he just ignored them.

The Anonymous went on to accuse the New Prophets of simply spurting out whatever came into their minds. He claimed that Montanus had converted to Christianity from paganism, thus implying that he may have brought pagan notions with him. In front of crowds, he fell and became "possessed," the implication being that if he were not possessed by the Holy Spirit, then he might have been possessed by an evil one. From the early second century the Christians had believed that the gods of the pagans did exist, not as deities, of course, but rather as demons who seduced people, as Montanus may have been! The Anonymous further said that Montanus engaged in pseudoprophecy, just rambling on and spewing out strange sounds. The Anonymous drew his conclusions, which Tabbernee (*Prophets*, 37) sums up: "A false prophet, by definition, is a person in an extraordinary ecstasy in which he or she speaks without restraint and without fear—beginning with voluntary ignorance but ending up with involuntary madness of soul."

The opponents of the New Prophets used another tactic, the very one that carried much weight against the Gnostics: tradition. But tradition did not work against the Montanists because they had one of their own, going back to Agabus, the daughters of Philip, and more recent prophets honored in Asia Minor such as Quadratus and the woman prophet Ammia. But the Anonymous countered by denying that the New

Prophets stood in the biblical tradition because the earlier prophets did not prophesy ecstatically, which, as we just saw, is inaccurate, although anti-Montanist writers would not concede that.

Using biblical prophecy to refute the Montanists ran into another problem. Christians, then and now, focus on Old Testament prophecies that they believe relate to the life and career of Jesus or other New Testament events. This highly selective approach overlooks the literally hundreds of prophecies that lack relevance to Jesus or to the New Testament but instead apply to ancient Israel, as well as some of which did not come true. And what does one do when prophets contradict themselves as we saw with Isaiah, Micah, and Joel about the swords and ploughshares? But the Anonymous did not deal with that issue.

The Anonymous did not wish to win over the educated so much as the general congregation that might have been impressed with ecstatic prophecy and believe it to be the result of a genuine spiritual experience; thus, his assertion that biblical prophecy was not ecstatic was an effective tactic. Eusebius does not tell us if the Anonymous enjoyed any immediate success with this approach, but later opponents of the New Prophecy would also use it.

Subsequent opponents would also use a rumor that Montanus and Maximilla both hanged themselves in despair, an act that the Anonymous acknowledged as a rumor but one that effectively linked them to the death of Judas (Matt 27:5), further calling his account's veracity into question. He also disparaged those Montanists who died as martyrs, pointing out that martyrs from the true church (he named two of them) refused communion with the Montanists in prison. In this way the Anonymous hoped to deny Montanism the prestige that came with having martyrs from their community. All in all, the Anonymous proved to be a determined and dangerous opponent to the New Prophecy.

Fifteen years later, circa 205, another Asian bishop attacked the Montanists. In the city of Ephesus, Apollonius, a visiting bishop, recounted how Priscilla and Maximilla had left their husbands to follow Montanus. In an era when respectable women usually did not go out of their homes unaccompanied, leaving their families to follow an ecstatic prophet would be scandalous. Ignoring the women who travelled with Jesus (Luke 8:1-3) and Jesus' words (Mark 3:31-35) about the true family and using what today would be called a "family values" issue, Apollonius accused the Montanists of dissolving marriages. While he was at it, Apollonius went on to accuse Priscilla of accepting expensive gifts from her followers, wearing makeup, and gambling! In a particularly cheap shot, he rebukes Priscilla, who was a mother, for claiming to be a virgin, a title that Christian mothers, married or widowed, would assume when they took a vow to abstain from sexual activity, sometimes living with their husbands in a "spiritual" marriage. "The opportunity to slur both Priscilla's reputation and to question the credibility of the contemporary leadership of the New Prophecy, however, is too great for Apollonius to resist" (Tabbernee, *Prophets*, 90).

Slander often works, and it would be used again.

On another area, however, Apollonius stood on firmer ground. The earliest Christians had a rigorous attitude toward postbaptismal sins—not the everyday ones that people supposedly commit seven times a day (Prov 24:16) but the more serious ones, specifically idolatry, adultery, and murder, which many thought to be unforgiveable if committed after baptism (which washed away all sins). By the end of the second century some writers were referring to a second forgiveness. But if that were possible, who could do the forgiving? Only God, of course, but through whom would he work? The rising episcopal church restricted the administration of penance to regular ministers, but many Christians—possibly a majority—believed that confessors, those who had suffered for the faith but had not been martyred, could also forgive sins. (North African evidence of this is especially strong.) Making no mention of confessors, Apollonius did accuse an unnamed Montanist prophetess of claiming the power to forgive sins. Such a charge against the New Prophecy would alarm bishops, especially when made by a brother bishop.

The bishops in Asia Minor and other eastern Mediterranean churches kept up the pressure. Bishop Serapion of Antioch (d. ca. 211) circulated a letter signed by several other Eastern bishops supporting Apollonius and warning about the New Prophecy.

One of the strangest adventures of the New Prophecy was its extension into North Africa, particularly the city of Carthage, Montanism's first venture into Latin Christianity. Yet what we know of the New Prophecy there depends upon just one person, the theologian Tertullian (ca. 160 to ca. 220). The first great Latin theologian, he attacked the pagans endlessly, wrote against the Gnostics using solid exegesis, and solidified the development of tradition by creating the phrase *regula fidei* or "rule of faith," which he cited against those who brought up new ideas that he believed went against the Scriptures. Furthermore, he developed the theology of the Trinity, being the first Christian to use the word *trinitas* to refer to the relation of the "three persons" (another phrase created by him). He also converted to Montanism.

Bishops dominated the African church, and Tertullian was a layman. Yet his theological brilliance and passionate writing style played a great role in creating the ethos of that whole church. Modern scholars have seen the African church as a "gathered community," that is, a church that deliberately set itself off from the larger society in order to preserve its holiness. Bishop Cyprian of Carthage (d. 258) originated the fateful phrase *nulla salus extra ecclesiam*, that is, "no salvation outside the church." He also compared the church to Noah's ark: either you are on board or you perish.

This church breathed a spirit of defiance. The earliest Christian document from North Africa tells of the martyrs of the town of Scilli who openly confessed their Christianity to the local proconsul. When he gave them thirty days to think things over (translation: to escape by leaving town), they insisted to him that they were Christians and that was that! The proconsul then ordered their execution.

The next extant document is the *Passion of Saints Perpetua and Felicity* that tells of the martyrdom of two young women who were part of a larger group of martyrs. In a dramatic scene referring to eventual divine judgment, the martyrs in the area said to the jeering crowd, "Today, us. Tomorrow, you." Since the document also reports prophetic visions had by Perpetua and others, many scholars think it points to an early arrival of Montanism in Africa. Some even think that the author was Tertullian, the New Prophecy's chief African supporter. These points continue to be vigorously debated, but at the least the *Passion* demonstrates that a predilection for contemporary prophecy extended well beyond Phrygia.

Tertullian never explained what won him over to Montanism, but he did share the unrelenting rigor of the African church, so scholars believe the movement's asceticism appealed to him. Knowing that the larger church allowed second marriages, he vigorously supported the Montanist view of no second marriage. He accepted that prophecy continued in the church and, a great biblical theologian himself, saw no conflict between the Montanist prophecies and the biblical ones. We cannot be sure whether Tertullian domesticated the New Prophecy or his influence protected it, but it enjoyed acceptance in Africa that it received nowhere else outside Phrygia. Butler (25) sums it up well:

> In the early years, new prophets functioned within the orthodox (African) church as an enthusiastic community, who recognized the daily work of the Holy Spirit and expected miraculous *charistmata* (charismatic experiences) during worship. Tertullian described a

characteristic practice in his (local) church, in which a group of Montanists remained after a regular religious service to hear a prophetess share her charismatic revelations.

Although the Montanists would experience attack and condemnation in the larger church, they maintained themselves in Africa down to the fifth century. In 429 the great African theologian Augustine of Hippo (354–430) wrote a book about heresies in which he mentioned the decline of a group called the Tertullianists, a reference to the Montanists who, over time, had produced several local groups who were often denominated by their founder's name. For example, in Asia Minor was another Montanist group widely called Quintillianists after the second-century prophetess Quintilla.

Tertullian also provides evidence for some of the difficulty the New Prophecy would encounter in Rome.

Rome was a strongly episcopal church that by the late second century demonstrated its belief that other churches should follow its lead. Bishop Victor I (189–98) argued with bishops in Asia Minor over how to compute the date of Easter. The Asians cited their traditions, and Victor cited his, which he considered superior. When the Asians refused to back down, Victor threatened to excommunicate them. Scholars do not know if he carried out the threat, or if the Asians even worried about it, but later Roman bishops made peace with the Asians.

The Romans came to know Montanism very early on, as we know from the letter of Irenaeus of Lyons pleading with Bishop Eleutherius (174–89) to handle the matter peacefully. Tertullian reported that a bishop of Rome, whom he did not name, accepted that the three founders of the New Prophecy indeed had prophetic gifts. Was this Eleutherius? Whoever he was, he retracted his earlier view under the influence of someone Tertullian called Praxeas and whom he loathed for opposing the Prophets.

Rome and Montanism headed for a conflict. In the early third century, a Roman presbyter named Gaius debated a Montanist named Proclus during the episcopate of Zephyrinus (198–217). Gaius knew that his opponents had been collecting the sayings of the New Prophecy's founders—that is, they had written them down. He denounced the impudence of the prophets in composing new scriptures. We do not know if the Montanists declared their works to be on a par with the Old Testament or the emerging New Testament, but if they contended that the works had been inspired by the Holy Spirit, Gaius had every right to denounce the works as potentially spurious scriptures. He also attacked another element of the Montanist tradition, that of earlier prophets such as the daughters of Philip who supposedly had prophesied in Hierapolis, a city in Phrygia. Gaius countered this claim by citing the monuments of Peter and Paul in Rome, the first on Vatican Hill, the second on the Via Appia. This argument may not have convinced the Montanists in attendance, but it reflected the typical view of the Roman church: our traditions go back to the leader of the Twelve and to the apostle Paul themselves. (It was not until the fourth century that the Roman bishops dropped the emphasis on two founding apostles and focused solely on Peter.) Therefore, our traditions are superior to yours, and if yours disagree with ours, then yours must be wrong.

Impacted by the Montanists, by the growing acceptance of a New Testament, and by their own views of episcopal authority, the Romans came to a conclusion that pushed the Montanists out of their church: they expected no new revelations since prophecy effectively ended with the Bible. The Holy Spirit remains in the church but no longer speaks through prophets or at least not through prophets unwilling to submit their revelations to ecclesiastical scrutiny and approbation. As Christine Trevett sums it up, "The Prophets made appeals to prophetic succession, the catholic side laid increasing weight on apostolic succession and writings of times past, thus invalidating any new insights. . . . Reliance on the insights of time past was safer, especially if the church could keep a hold on the 'correct' interpretation of those insights. Present revelation was disturbing, brought problems of testing, and challenged established authority. . . . Probably first in Rome the catholic side began to close ranks on such issues" (134, 136–37).

The New Prophecy's diffusiveness also worked against it. As noted earlier, a group aligned to Tertullian arose just as a group aligned to Quintilla had. This process repeated itself. While it led to new insights and much freedom of expression, it also meant that groups going by the name New Prophecy could wander in many directions, some weakening or even threatening the larger cause. Their enemies soon pounced, and in an unexpected area.

The early Christians had struggled with two difficult beliefs, the Trinity and the divine-human tension in the person of Christ. These are mysteries of the faith and thus beyond understanding, but the Christians still had to affirm verbally what they believed.

The Trinity presented an obvious problem. If Father, Son, and Holy Spirit were all divine, would that not be polytheism? Pressing as this issue seems, the Christians did not deal much with it until the end of the second century, when Tertullian and his Alexandrian contemporary Origen began to speculate on the nature and functioning of the Trinity. They were not alone; many others did likewise, including some who adhered to a theory called Modalism, which gained prominence in the early decades of the third century at exactly the time when the Romans and Africans were dealing with the New Prophecy. "In [Montanism's] early stage many of what would be Christianity's major doctrines were not yet formulated. Then the Prophecy in Rome became embroiled in debates about Father, Son and Spirit which wove into the formulation of those doctrines. When the dust had settled more than a century later, Montanists were on the wrong side" (Trevett, 222–23). The wrong side turned out to be Modalism

Modalism explained the Trinity via a method designed to preserve the divine unity. There was one deity who acted in a variety of ways. To simplify, when God acts as a creator, we understand him as God the Father. When he acts as the redeemer, we understand him as God the Son. When he acts as a sanctifier, we understand him as God the Holy Spirit. There are no distinct persons in the Trinity or any kind of change. Father, Son, and Holy Spirit are basically transitory terms to express "modes" of divine activity.

The trinitarian debates convulsed Latin Christianity, and the New Prophecy's emphasis on the Spirit could not avoid the discussion of how the Spirit should be understood. Some unnamed Montanists in Rome apparently favored Modalism. This meant little to a disparate movement that literally could never be sure what the Spirit may say next, but in an environment as organized as Roman Christianity, people spoke about doctrine not on their own but rather as loyal members of their church. When some Montanists showed a partiality for Modalism, Romans believed or at least claimed to believe that this was the "official" trinitarian theology of the group. (Very ironically, in North Africa Tertullian denounced a Roman he called Praxeas for being both a Modalist *and* an opponent of the New Prophecy.) This accusation of heresy would haunt the Montanists for centuries.

By the mid-third century Montanism was almost a century old. It ranged quite far geographically but never achieved outside Phrygia the success that it enjoyed there. In the early fourth century Phrygia saw another prophetess, Quintilla, revive the New Prophecy as a living entity, providing some of the spiritual excitement of the second century. Like the larger Christian groups, the Montanists had established an order of virgins, that is, a sorority of women who had consecrated their lives to virginity, and evidence survives of Phrygian virgins prophesying. But there is little known about community structures outside Phrygia.

Although it did not enter the larger "establishment," Montanism had an ongoing prophetic tradition. Sources also speak of Montanist presbyters and even bishops, although we know little of their functions. Given Montanism's missionary predilections and the attacks upon it from other Christians, it is understandable that the movement would have to do some organizing. But as long as they kept themselves open to new prophetic revelations, they could never become truly "established."

By the late third century, the larger church had moved on without the New Prophecy, although occasional references survive. But all Christians now had bigger problems to deal with. In 250 the emperor Decius (249–51) launched the first empire-wide persecution, and, after that, Christians continued to feel imperial displeasure or worse. The emperor Aurelian (270–75) was planning a persecution at the time he was assassinated. The emperor Diocletian (284–307) and his associates launched what the Christians call simply "the Great Persecution" of 303–5 because of its duration, ferocity, and the number of its victims.

Then the impossible happened. Convinced that the Christian God had helped him to win the imperial title over a sizeable number of rivals, a pagan Roman emperor converted to Christianity. Constantine I (306–37) took the step that changed history.

His conversion instantly changed the church. Not fearing persecution, Christian missionaries worked to convert the empire's pagans. They built large churches in the cities to make the new reality visible to all. Intellectual life flourished, and some of the faith's greatest theologians lived in the fourth century. But this came at a price. The Roman emperors had acted as the people's representatives to the gods. As such, the emperors were sacred figures, and some of them even had themselves proclaimed deities. As a Christian, Constantine would never do that, but he made it clear that he would intervene (translation: interfere) in the church when necessary, and he would do it in his own way.

He ruled a huge, diverse empire that had teetered on bankruptcy in the third century. He worked hard to unify it, and he expected the Christians to help him. A united church would aid a united empire, and Constantine became enraged when the Christians disappointed him. In North Africa a schism had occurred between supporters of a bishop named Caecilius and those of another named Donatus. In 313 both sides appealed to the emperor, who then relied on some Western bishops to adjudicate the matter. Those bishops favored the Caecilianist party, and Constantine backed them. The Donatists, as their opponents called them, had appealed to the emperor and lost, so now, in Constantine's mind, it was time for them to give up their cause and unite with the Caecilianists. Standing on religious principles, the Donatists refused. The bishops hoped for reconciliation, but the angry emperor sent troops to North Africa to coerce the Donatists (316–21). The coercion failed, but it illustrated the new reality.

Ancient peoples did not separate church and state. Under Constantine and his successors (as in medieval Europe and czarist Russia), the emperors expected good citizens to be good Christians and vice versa. To be sure, the empire had too many pagans for Constantine to push too hard, yet he and his successors gradually and almost entirely eliminated paganism in the empire. Christianity would help unite the empire, but only if it were itself united, as the emperor quickly learned.

The struggle in North Africa soon became a side issue because a new heresy had arisen in the eastern Mediterranean, home to most of the empire's Christians and most of its important bishoprics. The heresy revolved around the teachings of an Alexandrian priest named Arius about the Trinity. The bishop of Alexandria quickly called an episcopal synod to condemn Arius in 321, but he refused to accept condemnation and fled to Palestine where several bishops were sympathetic to his teaching (to be discussed in the next chapter). The Christian East was splitting up, and no one knew what to do. Then the emperor had an imperial idea.

He announced that he was calling a council of all the bishops of the *oĭkouméne*, that is, the civilized world, which effectively meant the empire and a few areas outside it that had accepted Greco-Roman culture or Christianity or both. The bishops would come together in the imperial presence, discuss the Arian controversy, and vote on what to do. The emperor would see that the bishops' decisions, which he had to approve, were carried out.

The Council of Nicea met in 325 and dealt with the Arian controversy, concluding that Arius taught heresy about the Trinity. But as long as the bishops were meeting, this was a good opportunity to specify and condemn other heresies, by this time a constantly growing list. Given the reason for the council, the bishops anxiously dealt with other trinitarian heresies, one of which was Modalism. The Montanists avoided condemnation at Nicea, but they were mentioned in connection with Modalism; the third-century link had survived. A good theologian, Didymus the

Blind of Alexandria (d. 398), believed Montanus himself was a Modalist, a chronological impossibility since he had died in the second century and Modalism arose in the third. But Didymus shows how an offhand connection to *some* Montanists had become an enduring problem.

After the bishops returned to their sees in the fall of 325, Constantine decided to go beyond the decision of the council and just get rid of all troublesome sectaries. No later than 326 he had issued a decree that the "Cataphrygians," as the Montanists were sometimes called, had to give up their buildings and hand them over to the orthodox bishops. The emperor also wanted heretical books to be ferreted out and burned. With no buildings or books, how could the heretics survive? People would have to turn to the orthodox churches. Uniformity would produce unity.

The Montanists proved to be made of sterner stuff than the emperor thought, and they persevered, although they lost their influence in the more populated areas. Indeed, only in Phrygia did they continue to enjoy any popular support. But the issue they had raised—does the Holy Spirit still speak prophetically in the church?—would not go away, and some fourth-century theologians maintained the attack upon the New Prophecy.

Eusebius, bishop of Caesarea, an ardent admirer of Constantine, wrote about the Montanists in his *Ecclesiastical History* and preserved much valuable information about them, especially their early rise. He also told of the attacks upon them by the Anonymous, Apollonius, and Serapion, making clear his agreement with those critics.

Cyril of Jerusalem (d. 386) loathed the Montanists and gave them that name to demonstrate that they belonged to just a dissident group and were not true Christians. He passed on "information" about Montanus. He said openly that Montanus was out of his mind, proof of which was the prophet's identification of himself with the Holy Spirit (a false charge). Cyril went on, accusing Montanus of being sexually immoral. About that charge the bishop modestly said he could give no details so as not to offend the women in the congregation (leading Tabbernee [*Prophets*, 217] to suggest that the women were "working overtime" to fill in the libidinous details). Cyril also accused Montanus, most seriously, of committing infanticide. Frightful as this sounds, it was standard antipagan and antiheretical fare. If they do not have faith, then they cannot have morals—a tradition stretching back to the first century, for example, 2 Peter 2:1-3.

The Latin archpolemicist Jerome next joined in. He used the traditional tack that any prophecies recorded in the Bible were fulfilled in the apostolic age and that the Scriptures, upon which he was an expert translator and exegete, must be the standard against which the New Prophecy should be measured for truth. So far, so fair, but Jerome then turned to the accusation that the Montanists were Modalists. He also claimed that before his conversion Montanus had served a priest of the mother goddess Cybele, whose priests had to castrate themselves so as to cease being men and, in effect, to become boys for their mother Cybele. Jerome called Montanus a "mutilated half-man" (Heine, 158). While it is possible that Montanus was a priest of Cybele, can so hostile a source as Jerome be trusted? And if it were true, does that lessen the value of Montanus's conversion? After all, Luke records (Acts 15:5) that some Pharisees, members of the group that so challenged and questioned Jesus' message, had converted.

Quick upon the heels of Jerome came Bishop Epiphanius of Salamis (d. 403) in Cyprus, a self-appointed heresy hunter who cataloged thinkers and thoughts that he distrusted. He quotes much from an anonymous, earlier anti-Montanist source, apparently written not long after the original three prophets had died. His source, which he edited, uses the standard third-century arguments—that true prophets spoke logically and intelligibly while the Montanists did not, that true prophecy did not extend beyond Scripture, and that authentic prophetic gifts always serve the church, in this case the episcopal church to which Epiphanius belonged. He also quoted several prophecies attributed to Montanus and Maximilla. Naturally, scholars would prefer an unbiased source—for example, Epiphanius never allowed that the prophets may have spoken ecstatically at some times but not at all times—but we must make do with what survives. The prophets had proclaimed orally to congregants in Phrygia, and so by default Epiphanius has become one of the best sources for their words.

Here is a saying attributed to Maximilla: "After me there will be no prophet, but the end." Epiphanius attributed a similar statement to "either Quintilla or Priscilla, I cannot say precisely," but she said, "Christ came to me in a bright robe and put wisdom in me that this place [Pepuza in Phrygia] is holy, and that it is here that Jerusalem will descend from heaven" (Heine, 133). They were, of course, wrong, as Epiphanius gleefully pointed out, although he neglected to mention that the apostle Paul also prophesied an imminent end (1 Thess 4:9-18). It is, however, valuable to have the words of the prophetess that substantiate accounts of apocalyptic notions among the Montanists, even from a source like this (Heine, 29).

Montanus himself said, "Behold, man is like a lyre; and I flit about like a plectron; man sleeps and I awaken him; behold it is the Lord who changes the hearts of men and give men a heart" (ibid., 33). The "lyre" would be Montanus, and the Spirit played him like one, a vivid prophetic image. Later on Epiphanius quotes him as saying, "I am the Lord God, the Almighty dwelling in man" (ibid., 43). This, too, the prophets would understand as the divine speaking through Montanus. Further on, "this miserable little Montanus" said, "Neither angel nor envoy, but I the Lord God the Father have come" (ibid., 45). Along these same lines is a quote attributed to Maximilla: "Listen not to me but to Christ" (ibid., 47).

Epiphanius cites these as proof that the prophets identified themselves with God and Christ, yet how often do the biblical prophets, such as Isaiah, Jeremiah, and Ezekiel, begin their prophecies not with "As I say . . ." but with "The Lord God says . . ."? In the Old Testament, God sometimes takes over the prophet's voice to express a message, so a fairer explanation would be that Maximilla and Montanus considered themselves to be instruments of the divine. As Butler points out about many of the sayings, "The ecclesiastical establishment did not consider the possibility that these statements emphasized only instrumentality in God's revelation, not superiority to it" (34).

Trevett sums up the treatment of the Prophets: "Many of [the critics'] claims about Montanism's unacceptable characteristics were based on copying and reiteration of earlier writers, either adding nothing new or compounding half-truths and errors" (215).

By the fifth century Montanism largely disappears from the radar, relegated to one more in a long list of early Christian heresies and surviving in small communities that kept their views and allegiance secret. Only in the Phrygian town of Pepuza, where Montanus had predicted Christ would descend, was there a shrine to the Prophets, maintained by miserably poor and humble people. But even that was too much for the emperor Justinian I (527–65), who issued legislation "to convert, by force if necessary, pagans, heretics, and Jews to Orthodox Christianity" (Tabbernee, *Prophets*, 299). Sometime in the emperor's reign, the Prophets' shrine met its end, having been destroyed by Justinian's agents.

This is a sad but fascinating story, and one that modern scholars have tried to understand not only by presenting the facts but also by using newer methods. For example, recent study of Montanism has included a strong feminist element, best exemplified by Trevett but also by other scholars.

Montanus may have originated the movement, but Maximilla and Priscilla joined him very early on. Since the Spirit spoke to all three of them, none could claim prophetic precedence over the other two, which in turn means that two of the three equals were women. To this can be added the presence of subsequent women prophets, such as Ammia and the two Quintillas and other unnamed women, as well as women ministers. We must also recall that the Montanists constantly appealed to the example of the four prophetic daughters of the deacon Philip (Acts 21:8-9). To what extent did a prophetic/religious movement with prominent if not sometimes dominant women energize and shape the opposition?

Paul's epistles make it clear that women in his communities had spiritual, even prophetic, gifts, and Acts tells us of Philip's daughters, an account repeated by an early second-century Asian bishop named Papias. The Hebrew Bible also speaks of women prophets, such as Deborah the judge (Judg 4:4) and Huldah in the time of monarchy (2 Kgs 22:14). But by the time of the New Prophecy, these biblical figures were conveniently dead and had become part of a historical period duly being enshrined as unique and therefore unrepeatable (and usually unmentioned). Yet women continued to play a role in visionary works. The mid-second-century Roman writer Hermas had a vision of the church as a woman, now a commonplace (Mother Church) but then a new understanding.

Although the earliest writers did not criticize the women more than Montanus, "the catholic side systematically blackened the Prophets' reputations, especially those of Priscilla and Maximilla" (Trevett, 155). Ironically, the standard criticism of ancient women by ancient men, namely, sexual misconduct, did not appear in the early diatribes, probably because the Montanists so strongly emphasized asceticism and celibacy. Instead, the women prophets received condemnation for leaving their husbands, although, as noted above, later generations of Christian women who told their husbands that they wanted to lead a sexless life were usually praised, especially if they could convince their husbands to join them in sexual abnegation. Sometimes both partners agreed; for example, Bishop Paulinus of Nola (d. 431) and his wife Therasia lived a life of continence later in their lives.

But Plato had denigrated women, wondering why, if not for sex and children, men needed women at all? Aristotle claimed women were biologically inferior, the products of an impregnation gone wrong (the notorious "misbegotten male"). Jewish tradition saw the good woman as one who married the man her parents chose and then gave birth to a son so that her husband's name would continue. Those like Elizabeth (Luke 1:24-25) who could not produce sons were disgraced. The Alexandrian theologian Origen lamented that the Montanist prophetesses violated another sacred custom, that women should stay in their homes, but even that great exegete ignored Luke 8:3 about the women who travelled with Jesus. Origen tartly pointed out that biblical women prophets did not speak in public, because such an open display violated ancient standards of modesty, a patently false claim that the career of the Judge Deborah (Judg 4–5) proved and that he would have known. Other Christian writers fretted that women would be "easy prey for seducing heretics" (Trevett, 155). Few elements of second-century Greek, Roman, or Jewish culture prepared the Christians for the women of the New Prophecy.

Knowing that the devil was behind such a horror, Christian clerics tried to exorcise Maximilla and Priscilla, only to be prevented by the prophets' supporters. "Here was war: male against female; . . . cleric . . . against laywoman" (ibid., 156). The process continued. An Asian bishop, Firmilian of Caesarea (d. 268), reported successful exorcism of a woman prophet. But such efforts had no real success, and later writers would claim that the devil himself spoke through the women.

The critics simply could not accept the idea that women could prophesy or even that they could play a leading role in the New Prophecy. When Cyril of Jerusalem coined the term "Montanism," he did so partly to make it clear that only a man could have spawned such villainy; the poor deluded women played only a secondary role.

But Montanism continued to have women prophets. As we saw, the fourth-century polemicist Epiphanius spoke of a prophetess named Quintilla and of her followers, the Quintillans, proof not only of the continuing role of women but also of the movement's gradual devolvement into local groups and leaders. Regrettably, Epiphanius provided no chronology for her.

As Montanism became somewhat "established," at least in Asia Minor, women began occupying clerical offices at a time when the mainline communities had begun to forcefully restrict women's roles. The New Prophecy offered examples of women's roles in the church that would not be replicated until the twentieth century. Trevett offers evidence—but does not push the point—suggesting that in some parts of Asia non-Montanist women did play significant roles, at least partly because they had seen the example of the women New Prophets (Trevett, 187).

Inevitably, the traditional, sleazy criticisms of aggressive women surfaced. A seventh-century writer named Timothy of Constantinople accused Montanus of procuring two prostitutes as his associates, taking the anti-Prophecy polemic to a new and repulsive nadir (Heine, 177).

Since *all* the writers who attacked the New Prophecy and its women leaders were men, and since they manifested the traditional ancient attitudes, prejudices, and misconceptions about women, we must allow that *part* of the opposition to Montanism was not to its teachings or prophecies but to the freedom and respect that it gave to women.

But, as noted earlier, the prevailing scholarly view is that Montanism was mostly a conservative reaction, a desire to reproduce the "good old days" of prophecy and charismata, both now being marginalized or even eliminated by the growing influence of the bishops, the nascent New Testament, and still-active Gnostics.

* * *

Was Montanism a heresy? As noted in the first chapter, heresy depends upon what is orthodoxy. As we have seen, "correct belief" took a long time to develop, and rarely was it clear. The apostle Paul believed Christ wanted him to bring the faith to all peoples, not just the Jews, yet Peter of the Twelve and James of Jerusalem did not accept this. Yet Paul himself misunderstood the Second Coming, being convinced that he and most of his converts would be alive to see it (1 Thess 4). The initial "orthodoxy" of James and Peter disappeared as the Gentiles converted and became the majority of Christians. The initial "orthodoxy" of Paul had faded by the time (ca. 120) a pseudonymous author wrote 2 Peter and made the argument that with the Lord a thousand years is like a day, an attempt to prop up the faltering belief in an imminent end.

Fortunately for Christianity, its earliest leaders brilliantly realized that some development—although they would not have used that word—was inevitable. To their great credit, they created a New Testament that contained books showing a christological development by accepting Matthew and Luke's revisions of Mark's portrayal of Jesus and then accepting the Gospel of John with a Christology (the divine Word descending from heaven) that Matthew and Luke never dreamed of.

But as the Christians moved into a Greco-Roman-thought world, they accepted the Platonic notion that the true reality, the spiritual reality of the divine, is unchanging (strongly contrary to the Old Testament image of God as a deity always acting in history and even changing his mind—cf. Gen 6:6). They also became wary of change, instead idealizing and idolizing the apostolic age and making that the fixed reference point. Ironically enough, the Montanists swallowed this apostolic age view wholesale, and their struggle with the episcopacy was over which group had more fidelity to that age, a phenomenon that had a long future—for example, in the medieval religious groups that wished to imitate the supposed poverty and communality of the apostles (based on Acts 2:42).

At this distance, can we tell if the New Prophecy was a heresy or not? For all Christians, orthodoxy lies in the Scriptures, but the New Testament was still developing in the mid-second century and could not have been an irrefutable response to the New Prophecy.

To the Scriptures, many Christians would add episcopal teaching authority. Yet many church historians, including Orthodox, Anglican, and Roman Catholic ones, question whether such an authority had actually emerged very widely by the mid-second century. Clearly, the bishops thought so, and the Asian bishops said so quite early, but could Montanism have spread so far geographically or maintained itself against withering hierarchical opposition if the bishops' teachings had been commonly understood and acceptable as authoritative?

Yet Montanism certainly hastened that process of acceptance.

Why? Because Montanism proved that prophets cannot lead a church in which 99 percent of the believers have no personal experience of prophecy and cannot fathom how it functions. Prophecy inserts a discordant note into religious life. In a demanding and often threatening world, people look to religion for some sense of continuity, and they cannot respond well to the notion that a particular belief or moral practice might be modified—with no warning—by a new revelation given to a person they had never known about before the supposed visitation to her or him by the Holy Spirit. Along these lines, the image of absolutist ecclesiastics suppressing free-thinking prophets should be abandoned because the prophets could be just as absolutist. If someone declared to you, "The Holy Spirit says . . . ," on what grounds could you differ? To phrase it a bit differently, what source could be more absolute than the Holy Spirit? (This would be true even today when churches have guidelines for the discernment of spirits.)

We must also remember that prophecy always exists within a functioning, that is, nonprophetic, society. The Israelite prophets certainly denounced the kings and nobility, but the monarchy and society did not disappear, and the prophets continued to benefit from the order and stability that they provided. Paul may have valued glossolalia as a gift of the Spirit, but he governed and even dominated his communities with his powerful and direct teaching and authority. Recall that he saved his harshest comments (castration) for those who challenged him (Gal 5:12). That was not a man to be moved by someone else's supposed revelation.

A community of prophets well demonstrated the need for steady, quotidian authority of the kind exercised by permanent ministers. Indeed, prophets could not function or even survive without more pedestrian believers to oversee the community. Somewhat ironically, the strong rise of episcopal authority in the third century derived partly from the Montanist challenge.

Historically, however, we cannot call the Montanists heretics. Montanus, Maximilla, and Priscilla lived in a century when doctrines, the New Testament, and ecclesial organization were being formed, and that formation took a long time. Heresy requires orthodoxy, which was too unformed in the late second century.

What then are we left with? Without portraying the Montanists as innocents being victimized by evil, scheming bishops, we can say that the New Prophecy was indeed a conservative reaction against new developments in the church—partly against growing clericalization, partly against the increasing authority of another testament whose canon would be determined by bishops and which would present a standard for evaluating prophecy, partly against the increasing restrictions on women's roles, and, although not mentioned in any Montanist source, partly against the growing power of Greco-Roman culture that steadily eclipsed the Jewish culture in which biblical prophecy had flourished. The New Prophets felt threatened, and rightly so, as their ultimate demise proved.

In the words of Edward Arlington Robinson's "Miniver Cheevy" or, if one prefers, the Poni-Tails' early (1958) rock classic, the Montanists were just "born too late."

Monophysitism

The Montanist controversy had made it clear that the episcopal mandate would play the dominant role in questions of heresy. Aided by the books of the Bible, Old and New Testament, which moved to full canonization by the late fourth century, the bishops had basically triumphed over prophetic, charismatic authority by domesticating the Spirit within a regular, ordained ministry. The collective episcopal authority that emerged in the third century would take a giant step forward in the fourth with the advent of new forces in Christian doctrine and life: the ecumenical council and the appropriate wording of doctrinal issues.

Third-century Modalists had asked what belief in the Trinity really meant. Their answer, one deity who acts in different modes, did not win acceptance in the larger church, but it did bring the main issue to the fore: how to reconcile a belief in the Father, Son, and Holy Spirit with monotheism.

Most third-century theologians had an answer: subordinationism, the belief that the Son of God, although divine, was somehow inferior the Father (surprisingly, not until the late fourth century did theologians focus on the Spirit as well). Subordinationism became third-century orthodoxy, advocated by Origen of Alexandria among others. But about 319, Arius, an Alexandrian priest with a very acute mind, finally argued what many had probably been thinking: Can a divine being truly be subordinate? His answer was an emphatic no. To be divine, the Son would have to be the equal of the Father, but that would be polytheism or at least ditheism. Arius would have none of that, and thus he came to a logical conclusion: the Son had to be a creature, a created being of such perfection that other created beings like us could not even imagine what he is like, but nonetheless a creature. Arius has the image of archetypal heretic, but breaking through subordinationism was no small achievement.

Arius had many talents, including preaching and song writing. He preached his doctrine widely in Alexandria, and he wrote hymns to go along with his views. He also created a brilliant catchphrase to summarize his views: "There was when he (the Son) was not." The bishop of Alexandria eventually excommunicated him and ordered him to stop preaching, but Arius fled to Palestine, where a sizeable number of bishops sympathized with his views. The see of Alexandria's prestige guaranteed that most eastern Mediterranean bishops would oppose Arius, although he had enough support to cause serious division. But he had not counted on the emperor Constantine.

As we saw in the last chapter, Constantine used force against the Donatists, but that was in a matter of ecclesiastical discipline. This matter dealt with the very nature of God and so was itself dealt with at the ecumenical council called by the emperor that met in the city of Nicea in 325. Almost all of the attending bishops came from Greek-speaking areas.

The Arian controversy, Nicene trinitarianism, and the struggles for the Christian doctrine of God are extraordinarily complicated and have generated thousands of scholarly papers and books. What follows is a sketch that will get us to Monophysitism.

The vast majority of the Nicene bishops believed Arius to be wrong, but they did not know exactly how to reply to him. Naturally, they turned to the Scriptures for proofs of their own position, only to find that Arius and his supporters, using exegetical methods common in Alexandria, could reinterpret to their own cause any text advanced by the bishops. At the suggestion of Constantine, who was advised by a Spanish bishop familiar with Greek theology, the council adopted the word *homooúsios* to describe the relation of Father and Son. Most understood the word to mean that the two persons of the Trinity shared the same "essence" or "substance," just as humans share "humanity." But *homooúsios* presented two great problems.

First, it had a checkered past, having been used by several theologians the bishops considered heretics, such as a third-century Syrian bishop named Paul of Samosata. Indeed, the word *oúsia* or "substance/essence" could also mean "individually existing being" or, more simply, "person." In that case *homooúsios* would mean "one and the same *person*." Some Eastern bishops wondered if the word was not a smokescreen for Modalism or other theologies that denied the distinction between Father and Son.

Second, *homooúsios* appears nowhere in the New Testament or in the widely used Greek translations of the Old Testament. Many conservative bishops feared using nonbiblical terminology as too radical a step.

This second problem proved the easier of the two to solve. Its supporters, especially Athanasius of Alexandria (deacon at Nicea, bishop from

328 to 373), claimed that *homooúsios* represented the essence of Scripture; that is, although not scriptural, it represented what Scripture taught about the relationship of the Father and Son. This sounds audacious, but ever since the second century when Christians took Jewish books into a Greek intellectual environment, theologians had been creating new words—such as "Trinity"—to express their faith.

Solving the first problem proved far more difficult. After the council many Greek-speaking bishops felt that they had been pressured by a Latin-speaking emperor, his Latin-speaking Spanish advisor, and the Alexandrian party into accepting a dubious if not heretical term. Their doubts helped Arianism to survive in various forms for a half century and even to receive support from some of Constantine's imperial successors. The tireless efforts of fourth-century Nicene theologians finally convinced the bishops that the term *homooúsios* had an orthodox meaning. In 381 another Western emperor, the Spaniard Theodosius I (379–95), called the second ecumenical council at his capital of Constantinople, which confirmed the teaching of Nicea and affirmed that the Holy Spirit was *homooúsios* with the Father and Son. Arianism did not disappear and actually lived a long life among barbarian tribes and Western academics, but the fourth-century bishops had soundly rejected it. They argued effectively that Arianism was not consonant with Scripture and with ecclesiastical tradition.

The establishment of trinitarian orthodoxy quickly impacted another area of theology, Christology, the theology of Christ. This, of course, is the theology that dominates the New Testament, especially the gospels, and it had been developing for centuries. An essential message of the gospels is that Jesus had come from God to redeem the world and was himself the Son of God in a unique way, that is, not as all people are God's children. By the early second century Christians had come to believe that the Son of God was himself divine. John's gospel opens with a prologue (1:1-14) that identifies Jesus with God's Word (*lógos*) and ends the gospel with the disciple "Doubting" Thomas identifying Jesus as "My Lord and my God" (20:28). About 115 Pliny the Younger, Roman governor of a province in northwest Asia Minor, wrote that the local Christians "sang hymns to Christ as a god" (Pliny, *Epistle* 10.96). The belief in Christ's divinity gained wide acceptance throughout the second century.

But the understanding of the "Son of God" depends upon how one understands "Son" and "God." The trinitarian councils (as Nicea I and Constantinople I are known) had generally settled these questions, strongly affirming the divinity of the Son. Now theologians would try to explain how the divine son could be human. This effort would be far more divisive and long lasting than the effort to create a trinitarian doctrine.

Surprisingly to the modern mind, the issue was not Jesus' divinity but his humanity. The Old Testament had portrayed a very materialist God. He rewards Abraham not with heavenly peace but with land, slaves, livestock, and an heir; he rewards David with kingship and a promised line of successors; he battles alongside the Israelites during their invasion of Canaan. The Bible firmly links the deity to the created world of matter. But Greek intellectual tradition had strenuously separated the physical and the spiritual, and many bishops and theologians treaded carefully around a link between a spiritual being and a material creation.

As we saw, the Docetists and Gnostics took their reservations about Jesus' having a body to unorthodox lengths, but the Gnostics had focused on the main issue of early Christology: How can a divine person also be human? Would not the divine swallow up the human? Would not the human taint the divine? As Monophysitism would prove in the fifth century, the early Christians never really came up with an answer that satisfied everyone, but, with faith seeking understanding, they did arrive at a formula.

Besides the Gnostics' question, the Nicene controversies focused on another almost intractable problem in achieving orthodoxy: theological terminology. How can such terminology possibly address something that theologians admit is beyond comprehension? And if no words can ever correspond to the reality, how can any formula be truly heretical? To what extent must orthodox belief be tied to specific language? For example, if a fourth-century Christian believed that Father and Son were both distinct, equal, divine persons—the orthodox position—why must she or he express that belief as *homooúsios*? Even in our well-educated world of today, how many believers have even heard of *homooúsios*? Yet somehow they manage to believe in the doctrine of the Trinity, even if they could not explain the theology supporting it. The christological controversies of the fourth to the seventh centuries plunged the issue of terminology to a low and depressing level.

The final element in understanding patristic (that is, of the Fathers of the Church) Christology is one that played a role in the Nicene controversies, albeit a minor one compared to what would happen later: politics, both imperial and ecclesiastical. To be sure, no doctrine has ever come into being independent of nontheological factors, and that continues today. But in the christological controversies, nondoctrinal and nontheological issues played an overwhelming role.

By the late fourth century, Christian theologians had focused their attention to Christology. A Nicene bishop named Apollinaris of Laodicea (d. ca. 390) maintained his lifelong concern to refute Arianism and preserve the divinity of Christ by advocating a Word-Flesh Christology. By this he meant that the eternal Word took on human flesh to accomplish redemption. Apollinaris did not downgrade the physical; Jesus truly had a body. For Apollinaris, there was a genuine union of flesh and Word. He did not believe, as some opponents claimed, that the Word put on flesh like clothing. But Apollinaris did not see any need for a complete human nature. For example, the divine Word would vivify the body, and Jesus had the perfect knowledge enjoyed by the Word, and, as such, he did not really progress in human knowledge. These overwhelming divine qualities made the human ones superfluous.

For many bishops, this inventive theology resurrected the specter of Docetism. For them Apollinaris's denial of Jesus' full human nature thus called Jesus' very humanity into question. Many theologians wrote in opposition to Apollinaris, and they based their arguments on Jesus' redemptive death for our sins. Specifically, they claimed that if Jesus did not have a complete human nature, he was not fully human and thus could not effect our redemption. The Asian theologian Gregory Nazianzus (ca. 329–90) phrased it best: "What was not assumed could not be saved" (*Epistle* 101). If Jesus had not assumed a complete human nature, he could not save our complete human natures. Against Apollinaris, Gregory and others advocated the Word-Man Christology—that is, the divine Word was a true human in his earthly life and is a resurrected human now.

This initial problem seemed to be solved, but soon other theologians pushed into new areas, asking how the divine and human were related in the person of Christ. Unfortunately, what should have been a scholarly debate involved the two great rival theological schools of the ancient world, Antioch and Alexandria.

In the earliest centuries Alexandria established itself as the theological leader of Christianity, especially in the eastern Mediterranean. Its bishops were the most powerful churchmen of the age, and they expected and usually received deference from other prelates, especially in Egypt. They also maintained a strong connection to the premier Western see, Rome, a connection that strengthened considerably when the Nicene hero Athanasius sought refuge in Rome when some Arians had driven him from his see. The theological school of Antioch, influential in Syria and parts of Asia Minor, had occasionally challenged the Alexandrians, especially on matters of biblical exegesis, but the Alexandrians confidently enjoyed their primacy.

But when Constantine became emperor, everything changed. As we saw with the Montanists, he expected to play a major or if not determinative role in the church. He lived in the arrogantly named Constantinople, the *pólis* (city) of Constantine, which he made his functional capital, the New Rome, and he left Old Rome behind. Constantinople was a thoroughly Christian city, filled with churches but without pagan temples.

The imperial city also had a bishop.

During the Montanist controversy, the New Prophecy's episcopal opponents argued that their sees had apostolic foundations and that the bishops taught truths passed on to them from the apostles and would in turn pass those truths on to their successors. Dedicated in 330, Constantinople had no apostolic foundation, but its bishop had the ear of the divinely chosen emperor. Slowly but surely, the bishops of Constantinople gained power and prestige in both theology and the church at large. By 381, at the First Ecumenical Council of Constantinople, the bishop of the imperial city succeeded in getting the council to teach that Old Rome had the primacy of an apostolic foundation, but the New Rome stood second to it as the emperor's own city. The bishops of Rome never accepted that particular teaching of the council and always insisted that a city's political status did not determine its ecclesiastical status, but the council's decision carried much weight in the eastern Mediterranean.

"Old" Rome's attitude meshed well with that of Alexandria, whose bishops resented the Constantinopolitan bishops' rising power in the East. Alexandria's opportunity to put the *nouveau* see in its place occurred in 398 when the emperor Arcadius (395–408) chose an Antiochene monk named John to be bishop of Constantinople (398–407). The Alexandrians could not allow a representative of their theological rival Antioch to use his authority as bishop of their ecclesiastical rival Constantinople against them. Theophilus, patriarch of Alexandria (385–412), set to work to destroy him.

As it happened, Theophilus had to do very little. The Constantinopolitan bishop John, known to history as John Chrysostom or Golden Tongue because of his remarkable preaching abilities, brought his monastic attitudes with him to the wealthy, sophisticated, and powerful capital city. The Antiochene John had a strong righteous streak along with a horror of the machinations and open lust for power and money so blatantly evident at the imperial court. In a scathing series of homilies, he attacked the court lifestyle, criticizing luxury and intrigue and actually suggesting that the male nobility had the moral obligation to be faithful to their wives! He survived some initial criticisms and continued his moralizing sermons, sparing no one, not even the empress Eudoxia (395–404). Aligning himself with the imperial critics of John, in 403 Theophilus of Alexandria presided over a meeting of bishops known as the Synod of the Oak, at which John was deposed and banished. But when a strong earthquake hit the city, the people and even the empress thought it sign of God's anger at the treatment of John. The emperor recalled John, who saw no need to make peace with the emperor or the Alexandrians. He preached even sterner sermons than before. The imperial court could endure no more, and in 407 Arcadius sent John into an exile so harsh that he soon died. With the fall of John, Alexandria had triumphed over both Constantinople and Antioch.

But the machinations against John had caused great scandal among the many bishops who lamented the split between the two great sees. Eastern and Western prelates urged reconciliation, suggesting that Theophilus restore John's name to the diptychs—that is, the list of worthy orthodox bishops, living and dead, with whom Alexandria previously or currently maintained communion. He refused. Upon his death in 412, he was succeeded by his nephew Cyril (412–44). The bishops now asked Alexandria's new patriarch to restore John to the diptychs. Cyril had been at the Synod of the Oak with his uncle Theophilus, and so he replied that he would rather restore Judas to the company of the apostles than restore John to the diptychs.

A ruthless autocrat, Cyril was also a great theologian, especially in Christology. Like most Alexandrians, he emphasized the unity of human and divine in Christ. He did not deny their separateness, but that mattered less than their unity, especially since Antiochene theologians traditionally stressed the independence of the divine and human. This would have remained a theological debate had not another Roman emperor, Theodosius II (408–50) appointed another Antiochene monk to be bishop of Constantinople in 428. This monk's name was Nestorius, who, thanks to Cyril, would gain infamy as an archheretic.

Although a personally devout monk, Nestorius was also a tactless, outspoken heresy hunter who in a very short time found abundant doctrinal deviance in Constantinople. With the approval of the clergy, the populace of the imperial city venerated Jesus' mother Mary as *Theotókos* or "God bearer." This old title had gained the support of some earlier theologians and, more importantly, enjoyed tremendous popularity among the people for whom the Virgin represented a compassionate, loving female figure, often quite different from a deity seen as judgmental and swift to action (for example, people usually saw floods and earthquakes as divine punishment for their sins). Enraged believers soon put the new bishop on the defensive.

Nestorius argued logically that a human woman could not be the mother of the eternal, omnipotent, omniscient, omnipresent creator of heaven and earth. She gave birth to the *man* Jesus Christ and should thus be called *Christotókos* or "Christ bearer." This purported theological solution failed to assuage popular discontent, but, more dangerously, it gave Cyril a theological opening for attack.

Cyril believed that Nestorius had committed the classic Antiochene theological sin. He had separated Christ from God. Nestorius had spoken of Christ's being one person but separated the human and divine natures in Christ in such a way that Cyril thought he separated the two far too strongly. Cyril stressed the unity of the two natures in a single *hypóstasis*, a term for "person" that indicated the strength of the union of the two natures. But he also spoke of "one single nature of the incarnate Logos" because Alexandrians could speak of two natures before the union within the Logos but one nature after it. By "one nature" Cyril meant a single subject and a single center of will and activity, something corresponding to *hypóstasis*. Unfortunately, Alexandrian terminology did not always carry well beyond Egypt, and theologians in Antioch and Constantinople wondered if Cyril meant that Christ had just one nature, the divine, and had thus denied Christ's human nature and with it his true humanity.

But discussion about Cyril's theology would wait because the Alexandrian had set to work to destroy Nestorius. Calling upon the traditional Roman-Alexandrian axis, Cyril wrote to Celestine I (422–32) of Rome to complain about Nestorius. Knowing that Celestine could not read Greek, he diplomatically wrote in Latin. Now Nestorius also had to write to the pope, which he did in Greek. Historians cannot be sure how well Celestine understood the theological issues involved, but he did know that Nestorius had given shelter to some papally condemned Western heretics. The pope eventually concluded that Nestorius did not teach what Rome believed about Christ, and in 430 he called a Roman synod to condemn Nestorius's teachings.

Nestorius appealed to the emperor Theodosius II, who promptly advised Cyril to stop causing trouble. He would have been better off asking the sun not to rise. Cyril pushed Nestorius hard with a series of letters outlining his own theological position. In his second letter (429) Cyril insisted that the Word had to be united in an ineffable (inexpressible) manner, but that even though the Word remained fully divine, the two natures of Christ were perfectly united in the one person to whom Mary gave birth, thus justifying the title *Theotókos*. Surprised and threatened by Cyril's theological offensive, Nestorius sensed he was losing control of the situation and asked the emperor to call an ecumenical council to settle the matter. Theodosius agreed and summoned a council to meet at Ephesus in western Asia Minor in 430.

Before the council met, Cyril wrote an important third letter in which he referred to the "one *hypóstasis* of the Incarnate Word" (*Epistle* 3 to Nestorius), here using *hypóstasis* in the sense of "nature," a term that, as we noted, usually meant for Alexandrians an individually existing being. In some other writings, Cyril actually used the phrase *mía phýsis*, or "one nature," a belief that could also be expressed as *monóphysis*. This was acceptable in Alexandrian theology to express the unity of divine and human in Christ, but to Nestorius with his Antiochene theology of distinction of the divine persons, Cyril had proved himself to be no better than Apollinaris, denying the reality of Christ's humanity by merging it with the divine. At the end of this letter the Alexandrian appended a list of twelve propositions to be anathematized or condemned. The Twelve Anathemas, as they came to be called, insultingly included the main points of Antiochene Christology.

As the opening of the council grew near, Celestine of Rome had a problem. By the fifth century the popes considered themselves the heads of the entire church whose word decisively settled all matters, a view not held in the East, then or now. A Roman synod had condemned Nestorius's teaching, so for Celestine the matter had been settled and the upcoming council was superfluous. But the emperor wanted it, and so it would be held. The pope could do nothing except deputize Cyril to speak for Rome. The Alexandrian promptly accepted the pope's offer, but, of course, he did not feel bound to the decisions of a Latin council, promptly ignored the papal mandate, and created an ecumenical council in his own image and likeness.

When the council began on June 22, 431, Cyril presided, partly because the bishops from Syria and Antioch itself had not yet arrived to support their fellow Antiochene Nestorius, who wisely chose to skip the first session, correctly fearing a theological lynching. Cyril promptly opened the council, which just as promptly condemned Nestorius and his teaching. The council had opened, met, and closed on a single day and had provided Cyril with a great triumph. On June 27 the Syrian bishops, led by John of Antioch (429–41), arrived and asked when the council was to begin. When they learned that it had already met and closed, they promptly denounced Cyril and called a council of their own, which supported Nestorius and declared Cyril deposed. On July 10 the papal legates arrived and asked when the council was to open, only to learn that two competing councils had already been held. Following Celestine's instructions, they sided with Cyril, who diplomatically called a new session into existence at the residence of the local bishop of Ephesus. The legates made the Roman case, the assembled bishops reiterated their condemnation of Nestorius, and the assembly then went on to condemn John of Antioch and other Syrian bishops. To further accommodate Celestine, the bishops confirmed the papal condemnation of a Latin heresy known as Pelagianism, which supposedly taught the possibility of a sinless life.

The scandalous proceedings at Ephesus infuriated Theodosius, and both sides worked to win him over. Through outright bribery of imperial officials, family members, and even the emperor's favorite mistress, Cyril secured the emperor's support. Seeing the writing on the wall, Nestorius dramatically offered to resign and return to his monastery. Somewhat to his surprise, Theodosius accepted his offer. For a second time in a quarter century an Alexandrian bishop had driven a Constantinopolitan bishop from office and vanquished his Antiochene theology. Cyril had apparently won a significant victory, both theologically and politically, while poor Nestorius was sent into a rigorous exile, first in Palestine and then in Libya.

But, paralleling the reaction to the Alexandrian Theophilus's triumph over John Chrysostom, many bishops were horrified by Cyril's conduct at the council. Many who were not well versed in Alexandrian theology also had concerns about Cyril's formula. Had his emphasis on the one nature of Christ obliterated the distinctions between Christ's humanity and divinity? But first and foremost for the bishops and the emperor came the ecclesiastical scandal of a break between the churches in Egypt and Syria, which, as a frontier province bordering Rome's ancient Persian enemy, raised political as well as religious concerns for the emperor.

"Two years later (433), despite their deep mistrust for each other, and after painstaking negotiations, harmony was formally restored between (the bishops of) Alexandria and Antioch" (Frend, 21). They agreed to a Formula of Reunion as "of two natures" in one person. As Frend observes, "It was as far as Cyril could be fairly expected to go and much further than any of his supporters went" and "without, however, Cyril's favourite terminology, *mía phýsis*," (22) that is, "one nature," which had been replaced by the Antiochene one *prósopon* (person).

The Eastern bishops expressed satisfaction with the outcome since it apparently had clarified the often uncertain terminology. The Romans also praised the formula because Latin theologians were comfortable with the notion of two natures, human and divine, in the one person, Jesus Christ. By all rights, this reunion should have been the end of the controversy, but, in fact, it was just the beginning.

In Alexandria many thought that Cyril had compromised too much. While he lived, they could do nothing, and Cyril managed to convince a sizeable number of his supporters that his teachings had remained unchanged. But after Cyril's death in 444, the new patriarch Dioscorus (444–51, d. 454) would take a harder line, and, astonishingly, like the first two controversies, the next one would also begin in Constantinople.

And again it would begin with a monk.

Monasticism began in Egypt in the third century and grew significantly in the fourth in both numbers and geographical spread in Palestine and Syria. The monks renounced society and moved into the deserts of the Near East to practice lives of rigid asceticism. For Christians the martyrs had always been the heroes, but in a Christian empire martyrdom had thankfully ceased. The monks became the new martyrs, devoted to mortification (literally "making dead") of their physical bodies, which they saw as endless sources of temptation. An Egyptian *abba* ("father") named Dorotheus once said of his body, "It kills me, so I kill it" (Palladius, *Lausiac History* 30). The monks feared more than just their bodies and the temptations to sex and fine food that came with them. They also feared a church that, in their view, was being co-opted by the empire as bishops became important social and religious leaders. Monastic writers would sometimes tastelessly compare monks in their cells to bishops on their thrones. One Egyptian monk said he went to the desert "to flee women and bishops"! (John Cassian, *Institutes* 11.18).

The monks soon became heroes to the people who often considered them living saints who struggled viciously with Satan on a daily basis and who frequently performed miracles. The great Nicene theologian Athanasius wrote a life of Antony (251–356), the father of Egyptian monasticism. It is a vivid, florid account of Antony's battles against demons and his miraculous victories over them. Like the patriarch of Alexandria that he was, Athanasius stressed that Antony avoided heretics (the Arians) and obediently listened to his bishop in Alexandria.

Monks began writing about their heroes, putting much stress on their spirituality as well as their miraculous achievements; this literature made them even better known. As monasticism became more important in church life, the monks involved themselves in theological controversies. Some few monks were well educated; most were illiterate. Bishops tried to mobilize them for support, and no bishops did that better than the patriarchs of Alexandria.

Eutyches (d. 454) was the archimandrite (leader) of a powerful, three-hundred-member monastery in Constantinople, and someone who loathed Nestorius and his theology. In opposition to the now deposed bishop, he developed a Christology that basically argued that Christ had two natures before the Incarnation but only one after it, namely, the one nature (*monóphysis*) of the incarnate Word. While this was not exactly what Cyril had taught, it could easily derive from his use of the phrase "one nature." Eutyches's theology differed from Apollinarianism but echoed it with its double acceptance of Jesus' full humanity and the conjoined divinity that somehow overwhelmed it. Like Cyril, Eutyches believed that Jesus had a real human nature, but Eutyches expressed himself in such a way that he implied that Jesus' flesh differed from that of other humans, his flesh being that of the Word Incarnate, a difficult phrase that he never really defined.

The Alexandrian tactics at the Council of Ephesus had not been forgotten in Constantinople or Antioch. Since the council, Antiochene theologians had been strengthening the case for a two-nature Christology, and they did not hesitate to point out that much in Cyril's writings supported the notion of just one nature (not always allowing for how the word "nature" could be understood in Alexandria). The Antiochenes went on to suggest that the great Alexandrian had at least implicitly taught heresy. Angered by this and loyal to Cyril, "by 447 he [Eutyches] was openly proclaiming the one nature of the Word Incarnate but attributing to the Word itself sufferings of the Passion" (Frend, 27–28). His bishop, Flavian of Constantinople (446–49), rebuked him, an appropriate but disastrous step.

Eutyches's godson was the emperor's grand chamberlain, and monks in Syria and Egypt revered the elderly archimandrite. Soon monastic complaints about Flavian's supposed mistreatment of the venerated Eutyches, as well as his criticisms of the archimandrite's theology, were reaching Bishop Dioscorus in Alexandria. Sides were quickly drawn. Both Eutyches and Flavian wrote to Leo I (440–61) of Rome for support. Cool to Eutyches, Leo supported Flavian with a christological treatise known as the *Tome* in 448. But events in the East soon moved well beyond anything the pope could do.

As he did in 430 at Ephesus, the emperor Theodosius II wanted a council to solve matters, and he again chose Ephesus as the location. Like his predecessors in Alexandria, Theophilus and Cyril, Dioscorus had strong political instincts, and he moved quickly to control the council and to put down Flavian and his Antiochene supporters. The council opened on August 8, 449, with 135 bishops in attendance, including Flavian and the Constantinopolitan episcopacy, many Egyptians and their supporters, and representatives of Rome who brought a copy of Leo's *Tome* to read to the bishops. Dioscorus could have acted decorously and maybe won a compromise, but his arrogance prevailed. He was happy to quote the anti-Nestorian (that is, anti-Antiochene) sections of Leo's work, but he forbade the reading of the *Tome* to the disappointment and anger of the Roman legates.

Dioscorus asked the heavily Cyrillian bishops, "Two natures before the union but only one after it. Is that not our faith?" The assembled bishops agreed. The council declared Eutyches to be orthodox and then voted to depose Flavian from his see. As he began to protest, imperial troops suddenly appeared and arrested him, abusing Flavian so brutally that three days later he died of his injuries.

In spite of this, the council met for a second session, which the Antiochenes and papal representatives avoided. At this session the bishops deposed Bishop Domnus of Antioch for his supposedly Nestorian views, and they then proclaimed as orthodoxy not the Formula of Reunion between Cyril and the Antiochenes in 433 but rather the Twelve Anathemas that Cyril had sent to Nestorius before the Council of Ephesus, that is, his virtual condemnation of Antiochene theology.

Dioscorus had become the third Alexandrian patriarch to depose a bishop of Constantinople in less than a half century; he topped off his victory by having Anatolius, his choice for patriarch of Constantinople, chosen by the emperor Theodosius to fill that office.

Yet many bishops, East and West, reacted with repulsion to what had happened at Ephesus II. Leo of Rome gave the council its permanent Latin name, *latrocinium*, or "council of robbers." But the emperor supported the council, and the bishops could only protest.

And then everything changed.

On July 28, 450, Theodosius II went hunting. His horse stepped in a hole and threw the emperor to the ground, killing him. He had no heir, so his sister Pulcheria (450–53) succeeded him as empress. Realizing that most citizens could not accept a woman ruling on her own, she promptly married Marcian (450–57), a senator who had risen through the military, to be her consort and thus emperor. Both of them opposed Eutyches, Dioscorus, and their council, and they set out to overthrow all three.

Eutyches disappeared quickly from Constantinople, sent into an exile from which he did not return. The imperial couple next arranged for a suitable funeral and burial for the patriarch Flavian, who had suffered at the hands of the council. The imperial couple also made clear their desire for a new council to make up for what had happened at Ephesus.

Encouraged by this, Leo tried to get the council held in Italy, but the imperial couple wanted it in the East and especially near Constantinople, and the pope could only accede to their wishes. They chose the city of Chalcedon, across the Bosphorus from the capital. They made it clear they would attend, thus making Chalcedon (451) the first ecumenical council to be called by a woman. (Nicea II in 787 would be the second.)

The council president, Anatolius of Constantinople (449–58), owed his position largely to Dioscorus, but he could see which way the political winds were blowing. Furthermore, like the imperial couple, he saw Constantinople as the major see of the East and resented the endless Alexandrian interference with it. He would not support Dioscorus. Nor would the Roman legates or the bishops from Syria, and so other bishops, such as those from Palestine, also declined to support Dioscorus. Soon even the Egyptian representatives realized that their cause was hopeless. The council quickly deposed the isolated Dioscorus.

The *Tome* of Leo was read to the council, and the Greek-speaking bishops found this clear and thorough statement of Latin Christology to be a general match for their own views. Leo spoke of two natures inseparably join in one *persona*, while the Greek-speaking bishops spoke of two *phýseis* joined inseparably in one *hypóstasis*. This last term helped to clarify the terminology but went against the common teaching of Cyril that Christ was "of" (*ek* in Greek) two natures but not "in" (*en* in Greek) them. Chalcedon had thus enshrined a Diophysite (two-nature) Christology, the one still accepted by Roman Catholics, most Protestants, and most Orthodox.

Chalcedon proved to be a great victory for the papacy, the patriarch of Constantinople, and the imperial couple, who made it bluntly clear where the final authority in doctrinal matters lay. Yet, although they could determine doctrine, they could not make people accept it, especially in Egypt, as they, the Eastern bishops, and even the popes were about to learn.

What follows is an incredibly complicated story, so only the outlines can be provided here.

The imperial couple expected all their subjects to accept the Council of Chalcedon. To replace Dioscorus as patriarch of Alexandria, the council chose an Alexandrian priest named Proterius. He proved acceptable to the imperial couple and in 452 was acknowledged by the leaders of the Alexandrian community. Proterius followed Chalcedon's teaching, but other Egyptian bishops temporized, fearing the people as well as the many monks who had an undying love for Cyril, whose teaching, they believed, had been at least compromised if not outright rejected at Chalcedon. A conscientious bishop, Proterius stood up for his see in many matters, but the people's fury at Chalcedon trumped everything he could do. By January of 457 both members of the imperial couple, the protectors of Proterius, had died. Two months later the Alexandrian mob lynched their Chalcedonian bishop. The Monophysites, as we shall call them from here on, chose their own bishop, Timothy, who held his see until 460 when the emperor Leo I (457–74) banished him. After Leo's death, Timothy returned in 475 and died in Alexandria in 477.

The emperors at Constantinople found themselves in an impossible position. The Egyptians simply would not accept Chalcedonian bishops. The few whom the emperors appointed feared constantly and justly for their personal safety. The emperors clearly could not tolerate a major province ignoring their authority, and when Monophysitism spread into Syria, again supported by monks, the emperors now had a second troublesome province and, as noted earlier, one that bordered the empire's traditional enemy, Persia. When emperors did move against Syrian Monophysites, the Monophysite leaders found a welcome just over the Persian frontier, as the Persian kings knew keeping Monophysitism alive in Syria would distract their Roman enemies and make their border provinces more secure. (Ironically, the Persians had also provided refuge for Nestorian Christians fleeing persecutions. Persian patronage proved so accommodating that no later than 489 a Nestorian church had come into being in the city of Nisibis near the Roman border, one more eastern thorn in the empire's side.)

Could not the Christian emperors just tolerate the Monophysites? No, and for three reasons. First, the emperors headed the church, and, as such, they had to promote true beliefs. Second, in an era when church and state were inextricably linked, the emperors could not just let their citizens openly hold beliefs contrary to those officially espoused by the state. Third, no one in that era, Monophysite or Chalcedonian, believed in religious toleration, much less religious freedom.

Soon another problem complicated matters for the emperors. The Western emperors, those ruling in Old Rome, had lost all their authority by the mid-fifth century. They had a policy of aligning themselves with some barbarian Germanic leaders in hopes of keeping out other potentially worse menaces. No fools, these barbarian Germanic generals soon seized unofficial power and then made and unmade emperors, who usually reigned for four or five years and sometimes only for one. In 476 a barbarian general put an end to the ongoing charade by deposing the infant emperor Romulus Augustulus (grandiosely named for the founders of the city of Rome and of the empire) and by announcing he would rule on his own. Now the emperors at Constantinople were the only Roman emperors and, theoretically, rulers of the western Roman provinces such as Italy and Gaul. That meant they had to deal as best they could with the heavily Chalcedonian western provinces where, as the emperors did not sufficiently realize, the bishops and especially the popes did not always recognize imperial intervention in ecclesiastical matters.

But for the emperors, the heart of the empire lay not in the West but in the East. No emperor could avoid the Monophysites. Hoping to win them over, the emperor Zeno (474–75, 476–91) fell back on every politician's best friend, the compromise. Like many nonfanatics, Zeno recognized that the beliefs of the Chalcedonians and Monophysites were not that far apart, since both believed in the true divinity and true humanity of Christ. Surely some formula could be devised to bridge the gap.

The emperor turned to Acacius, the Chalcedonian patriarch of Constantinople (471–89). In 482 the patriarch produced a document called the *Henotikon*, an attempt at compromise with the Monophysites. Basically, this document taught that the creed of the Council of Nicea (actually, the "Nicene" creed emerged from the First Council of Constantinople of 381) was the only true and binding creed and that later statements, even ones of other ecumenical councils, did not have Nicea's authority. Acacius condemned Nestorius and Eutyches, an obvious attempt to appeal to both sides, and, in a direct reach to the Monophysites, claimed that Cyril's Twelve Anathemas were virtually canonical for christological discussions. In a very audacious gamble, he simply ignored the Council of Chalcedon in the *Henotikon*, hoping in this way to be seen as neither approving nor condemning that controversial synod. The emperor Zeno embraced the *Henotikon*, which soon became his instrument for uniting his religiously divided subjects.

Some Egyptian Monophysites announced they could accept the document, but the Chalcedonians could not; indeed, many rejected it outright. As so often happened, monks played a role. In Constantinople a monastery housed a large group of monks who, in relays, prayed twenty-four hours per day, earning them the title "Sleepless Monks." Strongly Chalcedonian, they turned on Acacius immediately. Knowing the emperor supported the *Henotikon*, they looked for help from someone beyond the emperor's reach, Felix III (483–92), bishop of Rome. The two bishops of the imperial sees opened negotiations, which failed miserably because the Romans, like the Sleepless Monks and other Eastern Chalcedonians, considered the 451 council to be authentic and binding. The Romans also objected to the *Henotikon*'s failure to mention the teaching of Leo the Great, whose *Tome* the Eastern bishops had accepted at Chalcedon and which gave the council much legitimacy in Rome. In 482 the frustrated pope called a Roman synod to excommunicate Acacius, beginning what the Roman See called the Acacian Schism (484–519). Possibly ignorant of conditions in Egypt, Felix also wanted to know why the emperor tolerated the presence of a Monophysite bishop in Alexandria. Although the Western rejection of the *Henotikon* disappointed Zeno, he could live with it, having no real interest in trying to impose imperial authority on barbarian-ruled Italy, to say nothing of Frankish-occupied Gaul and Saxon-occupied Britain. Better to focus on the East.

But the situation was not much better there. A group of Alexandrian monks rejected the *Henotikon* for not condemning Chalcedon and Leo's *Tome* outright, while the bishop of Antioch objected that the document was too strongly anti-Chalcedonian. Even worse, the Monophysites had begun to disagree among themselves about some points of doctrine, making unity with them and the Chalcedonians more elusive. Yet Zeno never abandoned the *Henotikon*.

Neither did his successor Anastasius (491–518), a high-ranking palace official who gained the throne by marrying Zeno's widow. Religiously, he tried to walk a middle line, although he personally opposed Chalcedon. He wanted religious peace, and he realized that neither the Monophysites nor the Chalcedonians could provide it. He also wanted to end the schism between Constantinople and Rome, but he could not accept the papal view that a Latin-speaking bishop in a frontier province ruled by Germanic barbarians (the Ostrogoths) had the right to tell the Eastern Christians what to do. He wrote angrily to Pope Hormisdas (514–23) to let him know that a pope could not command the emperor, even in matters of doctrine.

While the *Henotikon* floundered in a dogmatic limbo, other events would make it expendable.

Severus of Antioch (ca. 465–538) was born in Asia Minor. Educated in Alexandria and at Berytus (modern Beirut) in Syria, he was initially a monk in Palestine. He quickly picked up anti-Nestorian views, which soon translated into anti-Chalcedonian ones. A natural organizer, he moved to Alexandria and became the leader of many anti-Chalcedonian monks and was soon held responsible by the secular authorities for some trouble they had caused. In 509 he moved to Constantinople, where he much impressed the emperor Anastasius, a supporter of Monophysitism. But the capital was strongly Chalcedonian, and Severus had much difficulty there until the emperor appointed him bishop of Antioch in 512. Since by then Syria had become largely Monophysite, this was a good opportunity for man of Severus's abilities. Indeed, the appointment proved a great gift to the Monophysite cause.

Severus was an immensely attractive man to his followers. He led a very ascetic life, which impressed all who knew him. He also used his considerable education to do theology, producing some of Monophysitism's most important works and giving the movement an intellectual strength it had previously lacked. The organizer in Severus impelled him to insist that the non-Chalcedonian bishops in Syria and even in Egypt should be in communion with him. This move occurred too soon historically, but it pointed to what would eventually become a separate Monophysite hierarchy and church.

When the emperor Anastasius died in 518, he was succeeded by Justin I (518–27), a pro-Chalcedonian who intended to combat Monophysitism. The new emperor forced Severus to give up the see of Antioch. The deposed bishop moved to Egypt, where he focused on theological writing and worked against Chalcedon in any way he could. In 535 the emperor Justinian I (527–65), hoping to win back the Monophysites, invited Severus to Constantinople. But negotiations failed, and the emperor ordered the burning of Severus's books. Severus quickly sought refuge in Egypt, where he died sometime in 538.

Severus's life demonstrated how much Monophysitism had changed and developed. He was not an Egyptian but a native of Asia Minor who was a monk in Palestine and a bishop in Syria—all proof of how Monophysitism had spread geographically and had become a major force in the Roman Empire. His unsuccessful attempt to become a regional bishop still pointed toward an eventual Monophysite church. He was also a brilliant theologian whose works demonstrated that theologically Monophysitism offered more than just a refutation of Chalcedon and a reiteration of the works of Cyril of Alexandria. He proved his abilities as a theologian against the writings of Julian of Halicarnassus (d. ca. 527), another Monophysite from Asia Minor who resided in Egypt from 518. Julian headed an Alexandrian group called the Aphthartodocetae, who claimed that the historical Jesus had an incorruptible body. Severus denounced this as heresy, contending that it was incorruptible only after the resurrection.

This theological falling out had great historical significance. First, it showed the movement's intellectual and theological vitality, something often overlooked by the Chalcedonians and occasionally by modern scholars. Second, it demonstrated that the Monophysites had become strong enough to survive splits in their own ranks. Third, it meant that the emperors who wished to win back the Monophysites could not win back all of them with just one document like the *Henotikon* because of diversity within the movement. Indeed, it indicated to the emperors that only force would work, and the imperial persecutors would find out that an entrenched population, geographically widespread and backed by the certainty of their faith, would make a formidable opponent.

And then things got even worse for the Chalcedonians.

Another great Monophysite leader appeared. Jacob bar Adai's (ca. 500–578) early life is somewhat uncertain, but he came from Syria and was originally a monk (again the monks!). In 527 he went to Constantinople as an ambassador for the Syrian Monophysites, knowing that the empress Theodora (527–48), Justinian's wife, was a Monophysite sympathizer. Jacob stayed in a monastery in the imperial city for fifteen years until Theodora convinced her husband to appoint him to be bishop of Edessa in Syria in 542. The emperor quickly regretted the appointment when Jacob showed himself adept in winning over others to the Monophysite cause and arranged for Monophysites to occupy vacant bishoprics in Syria, some of which had previously been held by Chalcedonians. The government moved promptly to arrest him, but Jacob fled from Edessa to engage in almost ceaseless wandering. From 542 to 578 he worked as a Monophysite missionary, strengthening the church wherever he went. Disguised as a beggar, he sometimes traveled thirty to forty miles per day, no mean feat in the sixth century. One of the greatest and most heroic missionaries in Christian history, Jacob was never betrayed by any of his people, despite government bribes, offers of rewards, and intimidating threats.

When he arrived in a new area, Jacob the bishop ordained clergy and helped to establish a local Monophysite church, which in turn led to a larger separatist church throughout the eastern provinces of the Roman Empire and even into parts of Persia. This separate church was probably inevitable. More than a century had passed since Chalcedon, and the initial split not only had continued but had significantly widened. Emperors had tried to end it by theological compromise, clemency offers, threats, and persecutions; volumes of abstruse and polemical theology had been written but had converted almost no one; national identities had been forged as Monophysitism became the faith of Egypt and of much of Syria while Chalcedonianism prevailed in Asia Minor, the Balkan provinces, the Latin West, and, most importantly, the capital city of Constantinople. The dispute about theological terminology had solidified into a permanent schism, as Jacob correctly realized. Indeed, so influential was he that the churches founded or influenced by him are sometimes called the Jacobite churches.

The ongoing schism disheartened religious people who less and less expected the eastern provinces to again be religiously united, but the political rulers still hoped for a settlement.

In 518 the emperor Anastasius died without an heir. As we just saw, succeeding him was Justin I (518–27), a native Latin speaker from the Balkans who rose to prominence in the military. He naturally looked to the West and hoped to end the split between Rome and Constantinople over the *Henotikon* and then to deal with the Monophysites. Although a Latin, he believed firmly in imperial control over the church, an issue that fortunately for him did not come up during his dealings with the popes. He plunged right into the controversy, driving Severus of Antioch out of the capital and making it clear that a Chalcedonian now ruled. He approved of Leo's *Tome*, which had the advantage of being written in a language Justin could read. Clerics who did not agree with the emperor had no future in his reign.

Pope Hormisdas responded positively and forcefully. He wanted the name of Acacius and some of his supporters removed from the diptychs of the Constantinopolitan churches, meaning that they would no longer be recognized as true bishops. He also wanted the condemnation of the emperors Zeno and Anastasius for supporting the *Henotikon*. Since Rome's position on Chalcedon had not changed since the days of Leo the Great, doctrine did not play a great role, but the authority of the Roman see did. Yet Hormisdas could achieve none of his goals without the emperor's support, and he needed Justin to follow the Roman line. But Justin quickly realized that he ruled in Constantinople, not in the West. Reluctant to condemn emperors posthumously, and especially Anastasius, who had made him a general, and equally reluctant to embarrass his own patriarch to assuage the anger of a Western bishop, Justin provided some but not all of what the pope wanted, seeing to it that only Acacius was condemned by name. The Acacian Schism had ended, and the emperor hoped for good relations with the papacy.

As usual, reality soon intervened. The Byzantines (as we will call the eastern Romans from now on) had little political authority in Italy, and, as for the papacy, Gelasius (492–96) had told the emperor Anastasius (whom he patronizingly addressed as "my son") in 494 that there were two powers in the world and that the power of bishops exceeded that of emperors because only the bishops would be judged by God for what they did. Subsequent popes took the same line. Justin wisely concluded that he could not succeed as emperor in Constantinople if he worried too much about the West, where he governed neither church nor state, while ignoring his eastern provinces, where chaos often reigned and where the hostile Persians always watched and waited. The Monophysites continued to occupy first place in imperial policy.

Like all the Byzantine emperors, Justin saw himself as the guardian of orthodoxy, and in 521 he launched a persecution against all the dissident bishops—that is, Monophysites and the occasional Nestorian cleric who had wandered over the frontier from Persia—but, significantly, the emperor attempted no persecution in Egypt. In this effort he had the support of his nephew and heir, Justinian. The two persecuted every heretic they could find, especially in Constantinople: Nestorians, Monophysites, Manichees, and even a few surviving Montanists. (For good measure, in 529 the younger man would also close the Academy of Athens, which had existed since the time of Plato. Pagans were as unwelcome as heretics.)

When Justin died on August 1, Justinian I (527–65) ascended to the throne. With the new emperor, the history of Monophysitism took an extraordinary turn and actually would generate one of the most controversial of all the ecumenical councils.

Justinian had a sense of his own greatness. It infuriated him that Germanic barbarians ruled what had been the western half of the empire, and so he set out to reconquer it. His armies enjoyed immediate success, easily retaking much of North Africa from a tribe called the Vandals. This encouraged him to invade Italy, which he did in 532. The Ostrogoths there fought hard, but the Byzantines made steady progress. Naturally, they saw themselves as heroes to the Italians, restoring them to the empire and the empire to them. The Italians, including the clergy, initially welcomed them but soon discovered that their Byzantine rescuers brought different notions of church and state (along with higher taxes). Justinian expected the Italian bishops, popes included, to tow his line, and he became infuriated when they insisted on the traditional rights of their church vis-à-vis the state.

Justinian had another problem—his Monophysite wife, Theodora, whom, in spite of her religious views, he loved very deeply and with strong appreciation for all that she had done to help him reign. She worked to keep her coreligionists safe but also urged her husband to solve the schism if he could. The invasion of Italy was bogging down and proving very costly, and Justinian did not need the Monophysites added to his problems. But then, ingeniously, he thought about solving both his Italian and Monophysite problems at the same time.

Nestorius, the bane of the Monophysites, had been Antiochene in his theology, as had been most of Cyril's opponents. Justinian hoped to mollify the Monophysites by condemning the writings of three prominent Antiochene theologians whom they considered heretical. These were Theodore of Mopsuestia (d. 428), Theodoret of Cyrrhus (d. ca. 466), and Ibas of Edessa (d. 457). Since the emperor's court theologians had isolated three parts of their writings for condemnation, this process became known as the Three Chapters. Justinian wanted to get papal support for this controversial move because many Chalcedonian bishops strongly objected to posthumous condemnations of people who had died in the faith. The emperor assumed that he could count on Vigilius, an ambitious Roman deacon whose accession to the papacy had been arranged after Theodora had obligingly engineered the deposition and exile of the reigning pope, Silverius (536–37).

Initially, Vigilius (537–55) worked with Justinian, condemning the Three Chapters in 548, only to find serious opposition among the Latin bishops, who, like many Greek prelates, did not like condemning theologians who been considered orthodox during their lifetimes. A chastened Vigilius actually retracted his condemnation. Furthermore, the papacy had an imperious quality of its own. Becoming accustomed to his office, Vigilius saw himself as the successor to Hormisdas and began to have second thoughts about accommodating the imperial couple in Constantinople. But that did not stop the emperor, who considered the popes to be under his authority, especially since the Byzantines now governed the city of Rome.

Knowing how much the Monophysites loathed Chalcedon, Justinian decided that only another ecumenical council condemning the Three Chapters would suffice. He would call it—as was his imperial right—but he wanted Vigilius to attend and, of course, to support the emperor's preordained decision. To the emperor's surprise, Vigilius opposed the council. But no bishop, not even a pope, could oppose Justinian. Dropping the diplomacy, he had Vigilius kidnapped and brought to Constantinople, where in 553 the emperor opened the Second Ecumenical Council of Constantinople. Vigilius was brutalized and forced to attend the council and then to approve its decisions, which, of course, dutifully condemned the Three Chapters. (That one sentence summarizes an incredibly complex series of events.) Finally allowed to return home, Vigilius died on the way, thus avoiding the fury of many North African and northern Italian bishops who felt he had betrayed both them and the Council of Chalcedon.

Justinian had his council, which both Roman Catholics and Orthodox accept as ecumenical because theologians of both churches have found heretical teachings in the writings of the three Antiochene theologians, that is, the Three Chapters. But did the council win over the Monophysites? In a word, no.

Too much time had passed. Thanks to Severus of Antioch, the Monophysites had a good theological base, one strong enough to support an increasing number of theological differences, and they had an episcopal organization to go along with this. Thanks to Jacob bar Adai and other missionaries, their church had expanded in the East and gained independence. Perhaps most importantly, the majority of Monophysite leaders had concluded and accepted that they would never win over Constantinople and those provinces loyal to Chalcedon. A separate, independent Monophysite church had come into being.

Amazingly, the persecuted Monophysites had managed to do even more. The Ethiopian church had accepted missionaries from Alexandria in the fourth century. As Egypt became more Monophysite, so did Ethiopia. In 640, after the Muslim invasion, the Monophysite patriarch of Alexandria moved to Cairo and made the Ethiopians dependent on his see. To this date the Ethiopian church is Monophysite.

While still an independent kingdom, in the third century Armenia became the first country to make Christianity its state religion. The Armenians stayed out of the Chalcedonian controversies (they were not even represented at the council), and the church became Monophysite in the late fifth century, causing the Romans to lose another frontier province to an outlawed faith. But Armenia's geographic isolation from the other Monophysite areas prevented it from playing a serious role in the controversy.

The church in Nubia (more or less coterminous with modern southern Egypt and northern Sudan) had also been evangelized from Egypt, and in the sixth century it accepted Monophysitism, although there is evidence for some diversity of views. Helping the Nubians finalize their conversion was a missionary named Julian whose journey was heavily financed by the empress Theodora.

Also in the sixth century the Ghassanids, a tribe of Christian Arabs living just south of the Roman province of Syria, had a Monophysite king named Al-Harith who invited a Monophysite missionary named Theodosius to convert his people to the "true faith."

But what of Justinian and his grandiose plans? Still focused on returning the western provinces to the empire, he reluctantly abandoned his hopes of winning back the Monophysites, and if he did not grant them freedom of worship, he definitely toned down his attacks upon them. His war in the west eventually went well. In 554 the Byzantines won a final victory over the Ostrogoths. Fortunately for Justinian, he did not live to see his life's work in the west destroyed when a new group of Germanic barbarians, the Lombards, invaded Italy in 567, conquered most of the peninsula, and reduced the Byzantine holdings to seacoast territories.

But there was more. In the mid-seventh century one of the great fears of the emperors came true.

In the early seventh century the Persians invaded the eastern province, capturing Jerusalem and Damascus. The Byzantine emperor Heraclius (610–41) waged a holy war against them, and in a struggle that lasted two decades, he routed the Persians in 627 and drove them completely from Roman territory by 629. Heraclius had permanently weakened the Persians' army and exhausted their treasury. But unfortunately for both the Persians and the Byzantines, a new power was arising to the south in the Arabian Peninsula. Inspired by a new faith and led by brilliant commanders, out of the Arabian Desert came the armies of Islam that ended forever the Persian empire. They then turned on Byzantium's eastern provinces, thoroughly destroying Heraclius's army in 637 and opening up the provinces for conquest. The embittered Monophysites saw little reason to help the Constantinopolitan emperors who loathed them, who had persecuted them, and whose many misdeeds, true or alleged, were chronicled and repeated in Monophysite churches and monasteries. Once the Byzantine armies had been defeated, the Arab armies met little resistance. The early Islamic rulers gave the Monophysites what they had always wanted from the Byzantines, freedom to practice their faith.

Most big dreams die slowly. Into the seventh century some Byzantine theologians sought a formula for reunion with the Monophysites, suggesting as a starting point Monoenergism, the belief that there was but one activity (*enérgeia* in Greek). This quickly evolved into Monothelitism, the belief that Christ in effect had one will since the divine and human wills could not disagree—that is, Christ the man could never make a moral choice that the divine Word would not make. Many theologians, Greek and Latin, heard echoes of Apollinarianism, which had denied that Christ had a human intellect. But the emperor Heraclius supported this theory, and in 638 his theologians produced a temporizing document, the *Ecthésis*, which, as Frend says so bluntly, "was doomed to failure" (352). Many Byzantines saw Monothelitism as just one more blatant attempt to compromise Chalcedon, and the Western bishops were unanimously against it. As the Muslims consolidated their hold on Egypt and Syria, the emperors asked themselves if it was worth all the trouble to try to win back religious separatists in areas the empire no longer even controlled. Their collective answer was no, and in 681 the emperor Constantine IV (668–85) called the Third Ecumenical Council of Constantinople, which dutifully condemned Monothelitism as heretical.

One might observe here that the practical, commonsense approach the later emperors took might have been taken by earlier emperors. In an era of sacred rulers, an intelligent, well-intentioned emperor could have used his political power to settle ecclesiastical issues or at least to moderate the harm being done. Regrettably, this was not the case.

A vast conglomeration of historical, nationalist, ethnic, geographic, and, of course, religious forces combined to make sure that Monophysitism survived into Middle Ages. In fact, it survived throughout the Middle Ages and is today represented largely by the Coptic Church in Egypt, the Armenians, and Jacobites of Syria, and by several churches in other countries, including the United States, founded by immigrants from those areas. Today, ecumenically minded Monophysites and Chalcedonians (to use the classical terminology) dialogue and debate and put more emphasis on what unites them than on what divides them.

* * *

Were (are) the Monophysites heretics? Certainly by the standards of Chalcedon, which means by the standards of Roman Catholics, most modern Protestants, and most Orthodox. But one has to wonder how much of this separation had to occur. The modern believer has a simple solution, freedom of religion. If the ancient churches and governments had not been so eager to stifle debate and to excommunicate and even to persecute those who disagreed with them, possibly a mutually acceptable christological formula or some kind of settlement might have been achieved. How could two groups of Christians, both anxious to express their belief that Jesus is both divine and human, not have found a way to come together?

There is a branch of theology called apophatic or "negative" theology that argues that the only things we can say *definitely* about God is what he is not—for example, evil. Apophatic theology denies that any human category can be affirmed of God and that the deity is unknowable. The first Christian theologian to advocate this was a man known as Pseudo-Dionysius the Areopagite because he wrote under the pseudonym of an Athenian converted by the apostle Paul (Acts 17:34). Ironically, Pseudo-Dionysius lived in the sixth century at exactly the time when Chalcedonians and Monophysites were attacking and even killing one another over how to speak about the divine.

The Monophysite controversy strongly raises the question of language. Since doctrinal formulas can only approach the divine mystery, would not theologians and religious leaders look for verbal formulas that would embrace the largest number of believers rather than formulas intended to set rigid boundaries? George Bernard Shaw reworked the old saying "Britain and America: two countries separated by an ocean but united by a common language" into "Britain and America: two countries united by an ocean and separated by a common language." Snide, but correct. The same word can have different meanings in different environments. Even in the same environment, words can change. "Icon" has gone from being a Byzantine image to being a symbol on a computer screen. Translations can be misleading, and many exegetes have disagreed and argued over the exact meaning of a biblical word. Even concepts change. The ancient councils referred to Jesus as a human "person," but since the rise of psychology and sociology, the notion of personhood has moved far beyond the ancient meaning. Indeed, some scholars have attempted to do a preliminary psychological profile of the human Jesus, while others have tried to understand his public career in its social setting (Galilean carpenter trying to win over educated Jerusalemites). Moderns simply do not understand the word "person" the way the early Christians and their Greek and Roman sources did.

We can only wonder how the Chalcedonians and Monophysites could not have realized that when discussing a divine mystery, no formula could ever have been adequate, and thus how can anyone be so infuriated that devout believers do not all approach the mystery in exactly the same way? This should especially be so when such fury led to arrest, exile, torture, and execution. Recall that for the Monophysites, Christ was "of" (*ek*) two natures, while for the Chalcedonians, he was "in" (*en*) two natures. Should people really have been burned alive for a preposition?

Believers need to know what to believe and to know it as precisely as possible, and verbal formulations inevitably play a crucial role in that. But believers also need to know and should be taught by those in ministry and education that those who disagree with their particular formula are often true believers who are also searching for the truth. If good, devout Christians believe that Jesus is both human and divine, why does it matter if their shared belief, which is what is really important, is expressed in different formulas? To be sure, some formulas can negate what appears to be a shared belief, but as much as possible the emphasis should still be on the belief and not on the formula.

Let us also note how the struggle over Monophysitism so clearly demonstrated another important point: how fruitless coercion usually is in matters of belief. Formulas can be condemned; churches can be destroyed; "heretics" can be imprisoned or executed; books can be burned. But no tyrant can ever control what people believe. They may have to hide what they believe, as did the Christians in feudal Japan and many more Christians in communist Europe during the Stalinist era, but they continue to believe. Ultimately, belief flourishes in minds and hearts.

The Cathars

The most difficult and enduring issue for Christianity and for virtually any religion is the problem of evil. God is good and so does not wish evil to occur. God is omnipotent and so could prevent evil. Yet evil occurs. Why?

Christians attempting to solve this problem must deal with monotheism. There is only one deity, so, unlike in polytheism, there is no one else to hold responsible for the existence of evil. "Theodicy" is the term created by the German scholar and mathematician Gottfried von Leibniz (1646–1716) for the *attempt* to reconcile the coexistence of God and evil, which, like the Trinity, is a mystery. Christian theologians have generally argued that God must give his creatures free will, which they will sometimes abuse by choosing to sin, which *God must allow them* to do. Most Christian churches also posit the existence of a fallen angel called Satan who goes about the world seeking the ruin of souls, but Satan does not solve the problem of evil. As a created being, he could be restrained or even destroyed by God, so the problem becomes, *why does God allow Satan* to do what he does to us? This brings us back to why God permits evil.

The favored Western approach to the issue was created by the African theologian Augustine of Hippo (354–430), who accepted—as did virtually everyone of his era—that two prehistoric people named Adam and Eve, after serpentine temptation, defied God by taking a bite out of a piece of fruit, thus introducing sin into the world. Augustine went much further, creating the term Original Sin and arguing that all humans are born with the guilt of that sin and so will be damned to hell for all eternity unless they receive Christian baptism, which removes the guilt. All unbaptized people, including not just pagans and Jews but also stillborn infants, go to hell unless God, in his unfathomable mercy, decides to save them. As for those who are baptized, they are free of the guilt of Original Sin but not its baneful effects. Original Sin corrupted human nature, a phenomenon most visible physically (we become ill, we grow old, we die), but it also had spiritual consequences. On our own, we have no ability to choose the good unless God gives us the grace to do so. We are further plagued by another consequence of Original Sin, namely, concupiscence, or the strong desire to do what is evil to get what we want. Although normally thought to apply only to sex, Augustine believed concupiscence applied as well to money and power. For example, he claimed the ancient Romans had a *libido dominandi*, an inexhaustible desire to conquer and rule others.

This stunning, original, and comprehensive theory explained daily evil for a millennium and a half (and, as we shall see in chapter 6, still claims many adherents), but it did not explain why God permitted the serpent to tempt the primeval parents, why he did not give them the power to overcome the temptation, or, to repeat the famous question asked by Carl Jung in his *Answer to Job*, why God did not just forgive Adam and Eve? The bottom line remains the same: God could have prevented evil but did not, and so the problem of evil rests with how we understand God.

But some religious traditions took a very different approach called "dualism," the belief in two divine beings, one good, one evil. No one knows how old such dualism is. Elements of it appear as far back as early Egyptian religion, but it surfaces most clearly in the ancient Persian Empire in a religion eponymously called Zoroastrianism after its founder Zoroaster, whose life historians place somewhere between the tenth and seventh centuries BC. The founder's original texts do not survive, and scholars dispute what his exact teachings are and what those of his followers are, but basically Zoroastrianism posited the existence of two divine beings, the good Ahura Mazda (Wise Lord) and the evil Ahriman (Hostile Spirit), who struggle eternally for the souls of humans.

Regrettably, the available sources do not clearly state the outcome of this cosmic battle for the Zoroastrians, but basically two kinds of dualism are possible: *absolute dualism*, the belief that the two spirits have equal power, and the *moderate dualism*, the belief that the good one will eventually overcome the evil one, often at the end of time. Although Christians never taught that Satan was a second deity, Christian belief in Satan is a form of moderate dualism since he has unlimited opportunities to harm people but will meet his comeuppance at the Last Judgment so vigorously described in the book of Revelation.

Absolute dualism has poor theological credentials for Christians, whose definition of God derives from the Old Testament as interpreted by Greek-thinking Christians, themselves much influenced by Platonic and, to a lesser extent, Aristotelian thinking on the deity. Christianity postulates one omnipotent, omniscient, and all-loving being. To the Greek Christian mind, any other understanding of the deity would be nonsensical and absurd. How could God be God if there were a second deity?

Yet this did not completely solve the problem of evil for Christians, not even in the great age of Greek and Latin patristic thought.

Christianity is an aggressively missionary religion, and it evolved in a Mediterranean and western European world that constantly changed in the first millennium. As the Roman frontiers collapsed in the west and became difficult to maintain in the east, barbarian tribes, first Germanic and Celtic, then central Asian, entered imperial territory and often converted to Christianity, by this time heavily influenced by Greco-Roman culture, as the controversies over Christ's person and nature proved. But just as the Greeks and Romans put their imprint on the faith, so would the barbarians, with values sometimes almost deliberately in opposition to those emanating from Rome and Constantinople. These values sometimes included dualism.

Sometime in the tenth century in Bulgaria, at that time ruled by the Byzantine Empire, a priest named Bogomil—possibly a pseudonym—organized some kind of rebellion,

> born, in part, of the sufferings of the peasants at the hands of their masters, of reaction against an alien Byzantine-trained higher clergy imposed on a recently converted people, and in part on the doubts and tensions of an imperfectly instructed populace still close to heathenism and possibly influenced by preexisting dualist beliefs in the country.
>
> The heresy was marked by a profound hostility to the beliefs and practices of Byzantine orthodoxy, its priesthood, liturgy, churches and [the church] Fathers, which it replaced by a simple community of believers. (Lambert, *The Cathars*, 23–24)

Dualistic Bogomilism spread in Bulgaria and thence to Constantinople itself, where its chief proponent was a physician named Basil who, circa 1090, was betrayed to the authorities and burned alive. (Recall that Nestorius had been deposed and exiled in 430. By the eleventh century penalties for heresies had increased significantly, with burning thought to be most appropriate since burning purified the church of an evil and sent the heretic, via earthly fire, to the eternal fires of hell.)

By the time of the Bogomil infiltration of Constantinople, the First Crusade to the Holy Land had begun (1095–99), and for the next centuries Western Christians would be going on through Byzantium to

Palestine and then home again. For obvious reasons, heretics kept much of their teachings and activities as secret as possible, ironically at the same time they were spreading their beliefs; and because of this secrecy, scholars cannot trace the movement of Bogomil dualism into the West, for example, via Crusaders, merchants, or pilgrims. Nor can scholars be sure about Bogomil missionary activity in the West. But by the mid-twelfth century Bogomilism had arrived in Mediterranean France and probably in northern Italy. It soon penetrated to southern France and on to Languedoc, home of the Cathars.

Earlier we considered Ramsay MacMullen's pointed observation that one of the ways to turn one's enemies into heretics is to give them a name (for example, Montanists) that makes it clear—at least to the "orthodox"—that they represent a *hairésis*, a group, while one's own group represented the *ekkelsía*, the church as a whole. The inquisitors who destroyed the Languedoc dualists referred to them as Cathars (among other titles), which is thus the name by which they are known. The heretics referred to themselves as "the good men" or "the good women" and not once as Cathars. But the name has stuck, and we will use it here. It means "the pure ones."

The Cathars suffered a destruction rarely experienced by other religious groups. They left little of their own writings behind, and so historians must work from documents prepared by their enemies, as with the Montanists, another disappointing case of the victor writing history. Historians contemporary with the Cathars show constant hostility toward them, yet, allowing for the historians' bias, their works are considered generally reliable. But material gained from inquisitors provides more controversy.

The inquisitors had the power to execute heretics, imprison them for life, destroy their communities, and tear down their towns, so scholars wonder about the Cathar testimonies preserved in the Inquisition's records; that is, in describing their beliefs, did the heretics say what they thought the inquisitors wanted to hear? Furthermore, scholars have proven that the inquisitors had read much on previous heresies, especially dualistic ones, and they shaped their views of Catharism along those lines so that they fit Cathar dualism into an existing intellectual pattern. For example, there was a Bogomil church in Bulgaria, and the inquisitors spoke of a Cathar "church" in Languedoc. Scholars cannot be sure if such a church actually existed or, if it did, how exactly was it organized.

Yet enough material survives to allow us to create a picture of the Cathars and of the forces that destroyed them.

Languedoc is the name now given to much of the Mediterranean coast of France. It is sizeable, stretching from the Spanish border to where the Rhone River empties into the sea. In the twelfth century this was not part of France but rather a collection of counties and duchies (areas ruled by counts and dukes) that stretched along the Mediterranean littoral and over the Pyrenees into what is now northeastern Spain. Contemporaries called this area Occitania. The residents on what is now the French side spoke not French but a language called Occitanian, which had more in common with dialects in Pyrenean Spain and far-northern Italy. Languedoc comes from the French phrase *langue d'oc*, that is, the language of Oc or Occitania. Unlike France, a feudal, heavily agricultural country, Languedoc, like northern Italy, had many towns with educated mercantile populations.

The medieval French kings had long desired to conquer this area, not just to enlarge their domain, much of which was contested by the French-speaking Norman kings of England, but also to give themselves a sizeable presence on the Mediterranean. But three forces kept the French monarchy at bay. First, the Occitanians would certainly defend themselves, and their commanders, the counts of Toulouse, had a distinguished military history. (Raymond IV of Toulouse (1042–1105) had been one of the leaders of the First Crusade.) Second, the English kings occupied much of what is now modern France, and border disputes and even armed conflicts were common. Having an army tied up in Languedoc might invite Norman aggression into central France itself. Third, across the Rhine lay the Holy Roman Empire, ruled from 1152–90 by Friedrich Barbarossa, an able and aggressive ruler who even set up a rival papacy when the legitimate popes resisted his domination. "If only," mused the French kings, "we could invade Languedoc with forces sufficient to conquer it and not have to worry about the English and the Germans." Thanks to another European power, the papacy, such musing would become reality.

In the twelfth century the papacy had arisen to a previously unimagined level of political power. The popes exercised unquestioned authority over the Western, Latinized churches, although they often had to take into account the attitudes of the monarchs, especially the forceful ones like William the Conqueror and Friedrich Barbarossa. The popes lived in an era when no one separated church and state, and all rulers wanted at least nominal papal support because no one gained by petty crown-versus-tiara struggles. Besides, the popes and rulers understood one another: all were monarchs not just accustomed to getting what they wanted but believing that sole, even absolute, rule was the best kind, reflecting the one divine Ruler of heaven and earth.

But the popes could play a trump card that the monarchs could not. Everyone would die and face divine judgment. The monarchs could prepare no one for that, but the papacy could. Many medieval people believed that those whom the popes excommunicated, that is, expelled from the earthly church, would be denied entry into the heavenly community. Dying while excommunicated would mean eternal damnation.

This sounds like an unbeatable weapon, but the papacy had a serious weakness, its involvement in politics. In the eighth century, thanks to a donation by a Frankish king named Pepin, the popes had become the political rulers of a sizeable chunk of central Italy known as the Papal States, which survived until 1870 (see chapter 5). This made the popes secular rulers, and so the popes had to engage in political activity—especially in Italy—which made some rulers—especially in Italy—wonder if some papal pronouncements and actions were more political then religious in nature and thus liable to resistance and even rejection.

Additionally, since no one separated church and state, inevitable papal activity in churches in other countries brought equally inevitable involvement in political affairs, which no secular ruler questioned, although the nature and extent of papal involvement could raise concerns. Like the Italian nobility, medieval rulers looked warily at papal activities, and this could sometimes weaken acceptance of the papacy's spiritual role. Yet the secular rulers accepted the church-state link, and, whenever possible, they worked harmoniously with the popes and their representatives, as the French monarchs would do against the Cathars. But attacking heretics involved more than just aiding church authorities. Heretics threatened the church, and so they also threatened the state, which in turn meant that both spiritual and physical means could be used to suppress and, if considered necessary, to destroy them.

* * *

By 1143 Cathars had appeared in Germany, professing dualistic views. They soon crossed the Rhine, and in 1167 there was a meeting—a "council"—at the French town of Saint-Félix-Lauragais, where a Bogomil missionary named Nicetas put in an appearance. About this time the Cathars apparently accepted, to the extent that they were organized, a radical dualism with two opposing principles.

They associated God, the good principle, with the spiritual realm and the evil principle with the material world, echoing Gnostic ideas, although it is unlikely that twelfth-century Cathars in Languedoc knew anything directly about second-century Greek Gnostics in Alexandria. Since the opening verses of Genesis say that God created the material world and saw that it was good, the Cathars concluded that the Old Testament could not be divinely inspired, since a good deity would shun anything material. We do not have firsthand evidence of their explanation for the creation of the material world, but inquisitorial evidence says that they considered a lesser deity or even Satan to have effected the creation.

An attitude at such variance from medieval Catholic belief would naturally manifest itself in multifarious ways, such as the rejection of the Eucharist since eucharistic theology identified the material bread with the material body of Christ. And how could material objects like bread and water (for baptism) sanctify a spiritual soul? For the Cathars, the sacraments—outward, usually material signs of spiritual realities—could have no meaning.

But in fairness to the Cathars, much orthodox spiritual writing seriously downplayed the body. As we saw in chapter 3, the monks of Egypt practiced mortification, a gradual killing of the body. Even great theologians like Augustine had difficulty avoiding the traditional Platonic view of the body as the prison of the soul. Mandatory celibacy and constant praise of virginal saints were central elements of twelfth-century piety.

The danger the body presented to the soul often manifested itself in sex, and so the Cathar leaders idealized a rigorous celibacy, although they accepted that not all of their followers could observe that. The Cathar leaders, known as the *perfecti* or "perfect ones," also practiced a strict vegetarianism, refusing to eat anything that came from the flesh, not just animal parts but even things like eggs and cheese. The mass of believers, the *credentes*, were also supposed to abstain from meat and dairy products, from violence, and from swearing oaths. They were not, however, expected to be celibate. Against these views, the Catholics had to defend the goodness of the body since the Son of God had assumed one, but their teaching often conflicted with the ascetic tradition of the body as a threat, especially in sexual matters. The Catholics also had to uphold the Augustinian teaching that intercourse between wife and husband was a venial sin unless procreation was the intent, which, of course, meant that couples who knew that procreation was impossible (infertility, postmenopausal wife) committed a sin whenever they had relations. Cathar asceticism, similar to that of rigorous Catholics, presented a problem to their critics, who sometimes fell back on an old argument, namely, that good works done by heretics do not really count, similar to devaluing the deaths of Montanist martyrs.

Their opposition to matter caused the Cathars to reject worldly wealth and honors, a view also promoted by their Catholic opponents who claimed to idealize poverty and humility. Yet the church owned enormous amounts of land in an era when land meant wealth, and in every era wealth means power. The church also owned nonportable property such as buildings as well as portable property such as jeweled chalices. In fairness to the medieval hierarchy, business schools and the like did not exist in the Middle Ages, and so the only way one learned to deal with land and property was to grow up with it, so choosing bishops from the noble ranks made sense to monarchs and popes. Unfortunately, most of the bishops, upon ordination, could not abandon the wealth, power, and finery to which they were accustomed or the aristocratic attitudes that went with them.

The Cathars found the bishops' materialist lifestyles to be scandalous and contrary to Christian principles, and they did not hesitate to say so. Nor were they alone in doing that. The two greatest spiritual figures of this period were the Spaniard Dominic Guzman (ca. 1174–1221), founder of the Order of Preachers or Dominicans, and the Italian Francis of Assisi (1181–1226), founder of the Order of Friars Minor or Franciscans. These two saints initially wanted their orders to be mendicant, that is, to own nothing and to beg for everything. Francis so feared wealth that he would not allow the friars to accept money when they begged; that is, rather than beg for money for food, they were supposed to beg for food directly. The mendicants' lives provided a strong witness against episcopal wealth and power, just as the Cathars did, but the heretics took the final step of rejecting the structure of the Catholic Church, while the mendicants worked within it, although both orders abandoned their strict mendicancy within a generation of their founders' deaths.

One scriptural passage favored by both Catholics and Cathars is Acts of the Apostles 2:42-44, which spoke of the earliest Christians living a communal life with no individual possessions. Indeed, the apostle Peter struck dead two people who sneakily tried to keep some goods for themselves (5:1-11). Groups following this passage in Acts were said to live apostolic lives, yet another contrast to the lives of the aristocratic members of the hierarchy.

Their association of the Catholic clergy with the material world and its wealth caused the Cathars to keep their own organization, such as it was, very simple. Many historians speak of Cathar bishops, but others consider the title inaccurate if not inappropriate. In place of an elaborate hierarchical structure, the Cathars had a very straightforward organization, dividing themselves into the *perfecti* and the believers. Since perfection is difficult to achieve, the *perfecti* never numbered very many, possibly only a few thousand in the early thirteenth century. As noted earlier, only they had to lead lives of rigorous celibacy and physical austerity. Few were educated, and so these leaders hardly filled the role of an episcopal magisterium, and their "theology" remained simple. All the evidence demonstrates that the Cathars won people over by the apostolic quality of their lives.

One of the most important tasks of the *perfecti* was the *consolamentum*, an initiation ritual that granted redemption and liberation from the material world via a laying on of hands and the transfer by which the recipient became a *perfectus*. The new *perfectus* had to demonstrate commitment to this new life by surrendering her or his worldly goods to the community and dressing simply. Often the perfecti would perform the *consolamentum* for the *credentes* who were dying so that they might receive liberation from this world as they were about to enter the next. There is evidence that *credentes* who received the *consolamentum* but did not die soon after refused to eat or drink, that is, to nourish their bodies. This practice was called the *endura*. The Cathars' opponents criticized them for starving people to death. We must note that some scholars have doubts about the very existence of the *endura*.

If the Cathars shared so many ideals of the Catholics, why could the two sides not reconcile? Issues like dualism made union impossible, but many historians think another factor played an equally great role.

By the late twelfth century the popes accepted and espoused the belief that they and they alone had the final say on matters of doctrine and morals and that all other bishops as well as all clergy and laity had the obligation to follow them or run the risk of excommunication. "Those who were searching for the consolation of heaven or the forgiveness of sins could not secure these benefits without the intervention and interposition of the church and its authorized ministers. Salvation had been institutionalized" (McGrath, 206).

The popes now claimed the final authority to interpret the Bible. No more did emperors call ecumenical councils; the popes now did that and had the power to approve or reject the council's decisions. Heresy still meant the conscious disagreement of a public teaching of the church, but the popes would decide when heresy had occurred, that is, when heresy had become a deviation from teachings the popes had approved.

Such a situation can work within a highly organized church, as it does in modern Roman Catholicism, but in the Middle Ages how could one know which papal statements carried such importance that disagreeing with them would be heresy, especially since the popes pronounced on such a huge variety of topics, not all spiritual and religious? Suppose someone disagreed with the popes on political matters? In general, the popes could not brook any disagreement, and "many movements were branded heretical for political reasons" (McGrath, 208).

But the popes did not achieve their power by abusing it, and they often preferred a practical and preferably pastoral approach where feasible.

By the mid-twelfth century the Cathars had become such a problem that papal action was necessary. In 1145 Pope Eugenius III (1145–53) dispatched the great spiritual writer and preacher Bernard of Clairvaux to Languedoc to learn what was going on and to try to win the Cathars over not just with his preaching but also by the witness of his apostolic life. But this Cistercian monk's mission failed.

In 1179 Pope Alexander III (1159–81) called the Third Lateran Council (recognized as ecumenical by Catholics), and this council warned against unrecognized, unordained preachers, a description that fit the Cathars, although not just them, and urged bishops to regulate them or discipline them.

But the movement kept growing in Languedoc, not least because the local nobility did not wish to hunt the Cathars down. This reluctance derived partly from fear of the social dislocation such action would cause, partly from a resentment of orders coming from the bishops of Rome who claimed authority over the churches of Languedoc, whose prelates were traditionally appointed or at least controlled by the nobility, and partly from the nobility's agreement with the Cathar teaching, including one important aspect of it.

The Cathar *perfecti* included women, and many noble women held that office. We must not consider the Cathars to be medieval feminists, but noble women, accustomed to prominence in secular life, could now find it in religious life as "good women." They could influence their male relatives to go easy with the heretics, and in many cases they could win the men over to Catharism to become "good men."

Some scholars saw this tolerance as typical of the whole area of Languedoc, and they may be right. The towns, which often vied for power with the nobles, often welcomed and sheltered the Cathars. But tolerance had no place in the medieval church or state.

In 1198 Innocent III, a thirty-seven-year-old Italian aristocrat, became pope, and he reigned until 1216. A short, thin man, he had the youth and energy to reform the church, which he combined with an extraordinarily high view of the papal office. By the third century the bishops of Rome had emphasized the primacy of their see because they succeeded the apostle Peter; Stephen I (254–57) was the first pope to cite Matthew 16:18 ("you are Peter, and upon this rock . . .") to support Rome's claims, a citation that set a future pattern. Siricius (384–99) was the first pope to speak to other bishops not in his own name but in that of Saint Peter; he also addressed other bishops patronizingly as "my son" rather than the traditional "my brother," and he expected his "sons" to obey their "father."

Innocent took the imagery to a new level. The medieval popes had adopted the title Vicar of Saint Peter; that is, they stood in place of Peter the apostle, but Innocent styled himself Vicar of Christ; that is, he spoke not in Peter's name but in that of Christ himself. To disagree with him was to disagree with Christ. (Subsequent popes have kept the title.)

In the early fifth century the African church Father Augustine had written a justification for the use of force in matters of religion. This was hardly a new idea; Constantine had used force—unsuccessfully—to bring about uniformity in the North African church, and, of course, pagan emperors had persecuted the Christians. But a great theologian like Augustine could give the practice a soundness and legitimacy that others could not.

This theory was often linked to the notion of a "just war." This is an important theory in Christian morality, setting up standards by which a state can justly go to war, such as self-defense. By the High Middle Ages the *iustum bellum* had been expanded by scholars to embrace other causes, most prominently the liberation of the Holy Land from the Muslims by crusading armies. This was important because the Seljuk Turks had not attacked the western European Christians, and they lived in (an uneasy) peace with the Byzantines. But canon lawyers and religious leaders, starting with pope Urban II (1088–99), who had called for the First Crusade in 1095, had justified the crusade as a battle between true Christians and their enemies, who were routinely demonized.

This interpretation of just war was based in the medieval papal insistence that in matters of religion, error had no rights because such error would threaten people's souls. All non-Christians, heretics, and schismatics were by definition in error and therefore represented a threat to both church and society.

Once views like this had gained acceptance, it did not take long before "crusades" were called to justify attacks on pagan, Baltic lands in northeast Europe for no other reason than that their inhabitants were pagan. This appealed strongly to German Christians who saw no reason to travel to Palestine to fight unbelievers when they could do so with their pagan neighbors and, as in the Holy Land, take over their lands. Spanish Christians decided to fight Muslims in Spain rather than Palestine, and some "Crusaders" attacked the Rhineland Jews who, labeled as Christ killers, were justifiable targets, a practice strongly denounced by the hierarchy who, unfortunately, did not also tone down the rampant anti-Semitism of the era.

For Innocent, heretics threatened the church more than unbelievers did because, unlike the Muslims and pagans, they looked and acted like believers and thus could deviously mislead others. As threats to the church, they too could be dealt with violently. "A just war was fought by a faithful warrior with an inward 'precept of patience' that compassionately guided and legitimated his outward bellicosity. An act of violence against a heretic was actually an act of benevolence that lovingly released the sinner from his sin. . . . Legally, ethically, the epitome of a *iustum bellum* was a holy war against heretics within Christendom" (Pegg, 57).

Innocent III strongly supported crusades throughout his pontificate, although his main concern was the Holy Land, where things had gone badly for the Christians. The Third Crusade (1189–92) had failed to recapture Jerusalem from Saladin, in spite of the participation of three monarchs, Richard I Lionheart of England, Philip III Augustus of France, and Friederich I Barbarossa of Germany (who did not even make it to the Holy Land, drowning in a river in Asia Minor along the way).

Innocent called a new crusade, the ignominious Fourth Crusade (1202–4), in which the Venetian navy and a French army attacked and captured Constantinople, driving out the legitimate Byzantine emperor, giving the Venetians major trading rights in Byzantium and providing several French nobles with sizeable new territories, including the Latin empire of Constantinople. This perversion of his intended crusade infuriated Innocent, who never forgave the Venetians but was willing to accept the French rule in the East (it lasted till 1261) because now a papally appointed Latin hierarchy ruled Constantine's city.

At the time the Cathars became prominent in Languedoc, the notion of using force in religious matters was, if not commonplace, at least widely accepted.

Like all successful rulers, Innocent did not believe in force as an initial tool. Dominic Guzman had traveled through Languedoc and had been appalled at the poor quality of the Catholic clergy and the inadequate if not nonexistent preaching. He believed that effective preaching by virtuous men who led apostolic lives could win over the Cathars. This method would directly challenge the Cathars' strongest point, the appeal of their virtuous "good men." Innocent agreed, and in 1206 Dominic and other well-educated preachers went into Languedoc, supported by papal legates who dealt with the local bishops and nobles. By this time the university system in Europe had developed a new type of theology called scholasticism, and Dominic and other preachers constantly tried to debate Cathar preachers, hoping to show that their dualistic teaching had little intellectual or, more importantly, biblical support. But no matter their success, the Dominicans still represented a church that many local people resented. Furthermore, Languedoc was a large area, and the preachers often had to move on from one locale to another. When they did, the Cathars routinely reasserted themselves.

At this point, we must consider an important question: How widespread were the Cathars in Languedoc? For periods before the age of printing, demographics is a challenging discipline. Regarding the Cathars, scholars' best guess is that they comprised about 10 percent of the population. To be sure, that is a sizeable percentage, but the Cathars were nowhere near being a majority of Languedoc's population, although there were probably small towns in which they were. Yet scholars have determined that even many people who remained Catholic still had esteem for the Cathars and opposed the attacks upon them. These people also resented—and came to resent far more—external interference in their affairs. But Languedoc was definitely not a Cathar country.

Innocent let the preachers do their work, but he did not forego other harsher methods. "Innocent detested heresy, and especially Catharism. It was an enemy to be destroyed" (Lambert, *The Cathars*, 97). "Innocent was not a gentle man: he rejoiced uninhibitedly over military triumphs, and when he used such terms as '*exterminare*' and '*animadversio debita*' (due penalty) for the treatment of heretics, his meaning was not restricted simply to canonical sanctions or the expulsion from cities—he had in mind the death penalty" (ibid., 98).

The pope did not trust the Languedoc bishops because of their proven indolence in dealing with the heretics, and during the first decade of the thirteenth century, he worked to replace them. He also sent legates to look into matters, to encourage or force the bishops to act, and to urge the local nobility, especially Raymond VI, count of Toulouse (1194–1222), to act as well. The legates wanted bishops, municipal officials, and nobles to take an oath to repudiate heresy. This was serious business because an oath was taken before God, who presumably would be offended if the oath were broken. In Toulouse the legates dealt directly with the city councils, bypassing the authority of Count Raymond, who naturally resented the legates' approach. The papal representatives also involved the Spanish king Peter II of Aragon (1196–1213), who in 1204 presided over a debate between Catholics and Cathars. Since Occitania spilt over the Pyrenees, Peter's presence was reasonable, but the Languedoc nobility understandably resented the Spanish king's presence in their territory. The papal representatives offended many Occitanians.

The legates focused on heresy wherever it threatened. They represented an international institution, and they routinely crossed local borders since they took their authority to be universal and not beholden to the wishes of the local nobility and episcopacy. The Languedoc leaders at first took this as an affront to their honor; they soon realized it represented a threat to their authority.

The two most effective legates were both French Cistercians, Arnauld Amaury and Pierre de Castelnau. Since Languedoc was not part of France, the locals saw an international institution, the papacy, subjecting them to men from a powerful country that wished to annex their territories. But by 1207 the legates had succeeded in getting the local town councils along with Peter of Aragon to agree to fight heresy, an agreement supported by oaths. Raymond of Toulouse refused to go along. The local bishops, resentful of being ordered around by Frenchmen representing an Italian pope, cautiously sided with their count. Pierre de Castelnau had had enough. He excommunicated Raymond, which put him in both spiritual and political danger since a ruler not supported by the church could be legitimately opposed by others, such as French monarchs, and even by his own subjects. Loathe to be excommunicated, Raymond worked to reinstate himself in the pope's good graces, but he could not bring himself to accede to de Castelnau. In January of 1208 an officer of the count murdered the legate. No proof exists that Raymond ordered the murder, which would have been a remarkably foolish step, but he made no pretense at grief that his tormentor was dead.

The murder of a papal legate outraged Innocent, who now saw no reason not to resort to force. He had been thinking of a crusade against the heretics for some time, and the time had now arrived. Innocent had previously asked the French king Philip IV Augustus (1180–1223) to intervene in Languedoc, but Philip, recently victorious in a conflict with John of England over that monarch's territories in France, did not think it advisable to leave his realm until matters had settled. He also wanted to keep his son Louis with him in France, and so the king declined the pope's request. Innocent next thought of Peter II of Aragon, who knew the area and had strong interests there, but he knew that the French government, whose support he needed, would not tolerate a Spanish king bringing an army into territory adjacent to France.

But the murder of the legate changed everything. The French king knew that the pope had to avenge the death and, in the process, to destroy the heretics who had occasioned it. Philip allowed papal representatives to preach the crusade in France; Arnauld Amaury would organize it; French nobility would provide the troops. Some of France's most powerful, bellicose, and/or avaricious nobles joined. Thus began what history calls the Albigensian Crusade.

Raymond of Toulouse watched with great apprehension as the crusade was organized. Concluding that he could not hold out against the invading army, he made a number of concessions to Innocent, and, after a humiliating public penance, he had his excommunication lifted. He joined the Crusaders, signing up, as almost all of them did, for forty days. Forty days for a crusade that would ultimately last for forty years.

There are several good accounts of the crusade, especially the one by Mark Pegg, and what follows is an outline.

Medieval sources speak of an army of twenty thousand knights and one hundred thousand foot soldiers, but those are impossible figures. Since people joined or left the crusade after it had begun, exact figures are uncertain, but scholars know that the Crusaders initially had much larger forces than their opponents, partly because the aristocrats and cities of Languedoc did not unite initially against the Crusaders, or as they called them, the French. Also their natural leader Raymond of Toulouse had sided with the Crusaders.

The French knew little about their opponents, assuming that Languedoc abounded with heretics, although, as we saw, the Cathars made up at most 10 percent of the local population. Most people were Catholics, many of whom tolerated the Cathars and all of whom feared the consequences of a foreign invasion.

The Crusaders advanced first into the territory of a viscount named Raymond-Roger Tranceval who had rejected the opportunity to join the crusade, thus marking him off as a supporter of heresy. They arrived at the walled town of Béziers. The Crusaders camped in front of the city and planned a siege, but some youthful camp followers began an attack that attracted soldiers who, without orders, joined the attack that, to everyone's surprise, succeeded. The French army quickly rushed into the city. The inhabitants flocked into the cathedral and other churches, but the Crusaders, believing they were attacking Cathars who, as heretics, had no right of sanctuary, invaded the churches where they engaged in a massacre, not only of the defenders but also of the clergy, women, and even children. When the slaughter had finished, the French looted and burned the town. A medieval historian, Caesarius of Heisterbach (1170–1240), says that when one soldier with a conscience asked the papal legate how he could distinguish Catholics from Cathars, Arnauld Amaury replied, "Caedite eos; novit enim Dominus qui sunt eis" (Kill them all; the Lord will know his own). The story may be apocryphal, but it summarizes the Crusaders' attitude. They reported their triumph to Innocent, who did not condemn the massacre. It would not have made much difference. The French had decided upon terror tactics to crush resistance.

The tactics worked. The crusading army moved on to Carcassonne, reaching the city on August 3, 1209. The local lord, Raymond Roger, stayed in the city to organize the defense. Then, surprisingly, the king of Aragon arrived to act as a mediator. Peter II had no sympathy for the Cathars but feared a sizeable French army so close to his territory. Mediation failed, and the attack began. But Carcassonne soon ran low on water, and then Raymond Roger negotiated with the Crusaders, who took him as a hostage. City leaders agreed upon capitulation. The Crusaders allowed the citizens to leave the city wearing only their underwear—some men and women were actually naked—and carrying none of their goods. Since the city had not been damaged in the siege, the Crusaders occupied a town full of supplies and loot.

At this point some "Crusaders" concluded that since they had twice vanquished heretics and piled up some loot, they had fulfilled their forty-day obligation and would return to France. But the great nobles wished to continue the crusade, although not under the leadership of a cleric, because they wanted a secular ruler for the conquered territories, a move that the prelates accepted. Initially, the great nobles made the offer to two of their own, who declined, to the relief of the French king, who did not want powerful nobles becoming more powerful. Then the Crusaders turned to Simon de Montfort, a count from a noble family but "relatively poor, so that he posed less of a threat . . . than other great men and must have been reasonably acceptable to King Philip" (Costen, 129).

De Montfort had fought with the king against Richard the Lion-Hearted of England and had taken part in the Fourth Crusade. His rule began with a serious problem, an army that steadily shrank as the forty-day Crusaders returned home. But he was a superb soldier and an indefatigable campaigner who believed strongly in terror tactics and in the harshest treatment of heretics. Under his rule, Cathars were burned at the stake whenever a town surrendered.

In the spring of 1210 new Crusaders arrived from France, and Simon began his assault on the areas still supporting or at least sheltering the Cathars. Accompanied by the papal legate Arnauld Amaury, he captured town after town. When the Crusaders captured Minerve, "the result was a great pyre on which the crusaders burnt some 140 *perfecti*, men and women. This was the first of the mass executions which were to be a feature of the Crusade throughout the Languedoc" (Costen, 131). Simon did not limit mass executions to heretics. On one occasion, he hanged a nobleman who had resisted him along with ninety of his knights, an unheard of practice (noblemen and knights usually ransomed their way to freedom) that Simon justified by saying they were traitors.

As Simon's power grew, Raymond, count of Toulouse, rightly feared for his own county, in spite of his having made peace with the pope. In June of 1211 Simon besieged the city of Toulouse, but the size of the city and the increasing resistance of the Languedoc leaders caused him to lift the siege and return to already-conquered territories. Raymond of Toulouse now found more and more help, including troops sent by Spanish rulers worried about Simon extending his power to the Pyrenees and also by King John of England (1199–1216), who knew that Simon's success would bolster the French crown. Formal opposition to Simon would soon emerge.

In the summer of 1212 the pattern of "summer Crusaders" recurred, and Simon went on a vigorous offensive, capturing and recapturing towns, massacring the garrisons, and burning all Cathars unlucky enough to be caught. As he brought more territory under his rule, Simon began transforming it, introducing French feudal customs previously unknown in Languedoc. Pope Innocent also helped transform the area by appointing a host of new bishops to replace those whom he felt had not worked hard enough to root out heresy.

The threat of French rule in Occitania became so great that Peter II of Aragon felt forced to act. In 1212 he had been a leader of a Spanish Christian army that inflicted a devastating defeat on the Spanish Arabs at Las Navas de Tolosa, a defeat so great that the Arabs remained on the defensive from then until 1492 when Ferdinand and Isabella expelled the Muslims from Spain. Rome lauded Peter for routing the infidels; his star had risen in western Europe.

Using his prestige, Peter gathered a sizeable army and joined with Raymond of Toulouse to oppose Simon near the town of Muret in

September 1213. Although badly outnumbered, Simon won a total victory, and Peter died in battle. Peter's death and the extension of Simon's power now alarmed Innocent III, especially since so many Occitanian Catholics had died in the wars. The pope could not deny Simon's power, but he could control it. In 1214 he proclaimed that Toulouse should be spared further attacks. In January of 1215 the papal legates called a regional council that acknowledged Simon as ruler of Languedoc but told him that the pope must confirm their decision. At the Fourth Council of the Lateran (recognized by Catholics as ecumenical) in 1215, the pope and assembled bishops declared that Simon could keep the land he won from the heretics, diplomatically overlooking the fact that he had also taken much land from Catholics, but Simon would do so as a vassal of the king of France, whose support was essential for the success of the council. The assembled prelates also declared that the Occitanian lands Simon did not rule would be governed by the church on behalf of Count Raymond's son, who would become Raymond VII of Toulouse on reaching his majority. The Cathars and other heretics were condemned. Less than a year later Innocent III, the driving force behind the council, was dead.

The council had settled much theoretically, but things remained different on the ground. The people of Languedoc did not want French rule, and the count of Toulouse negotiated with Rome, made submission, made offers, and generally bargained in any way he could to keep his lands. Finally, Simon had enough of negotiations and delay, and in June of 1218 he besieged Toulouse again. The entire population labored on the defense of the city, including women and little girls who worked catapults, sending heavy stones at the besieging army. One of the stones shot out by the women hit Simon in the head, killing him instantly. His army soon abandoned the siege.

Simon received universal plaudits for his work on behalf of the church. "Extraordinary holiness and extraordinary cruelty were never incompatible during the crusade—indeed, more often than not, they were regarded as necessary. The redeeming majesty of [God's] love was revealed only through wholesale slaughter honoring Him" (Pegg, 161).

But a corner had been turned. Simon's son could not maintain his father's conquests, and the Occitanians continued to resist. In 1215 Philip II of France had sent his son Louis to tour Languedoc with Simon, just to remind the conqueror whose vassal he was. In 1219 Prince Louis returned with a crusading army, staying only for forty days but making it clear who would be the ultimate ruler of the land. In 1223 Philip died, and the prince became Louis VIII (1223–26). A French bishops' council meeting in 1225 excommunicated and thereby deposed Count Raymond VII of Toulouse, paving the way for the new king to legally occupy his land. Louis returned to the south with a crusade in 1226, now a ruler chosen by God and, if not independent of the church, at least powerful enough to make bishops obey him and popes move cautiously. Louis besieged Toulouse, but that city led a charmed life. Like Simon on two occasions, Louis also failed to take it, not for military reasons but because political matters required his return to Paris. On the journey home the king died from dysentery and was replaced on the throne by his nine-year-old son Louis IX (1226–79), known to history as Saint Louis.

A new era for the Cathars would begin.

After Simon de Montfort's death, Cathar fortunes improved somewhat. The confusion of the invasions had weakened authority in many places. Local resentment of French Crusaders and the new, papally appointed bishops along with the willingness of the *perfecti* to risk their lives to provide the *consolamentum* for the poor and lower classes made the Cathars, if not more popular, at least more acceptable, even among the southern nobility. Some *perfecti* even organized and met while local nobles shielded them. But Louis VIII's 1226 campaign had demonstrated that French power, when led by a king, would be irresistible, especially since nobles who opposed the king and lost would have their lands taken from them and often from their heirs and then given to others or retained by the crown, a process that eliminated the southern nobles' hereditary rights and power and also made it economically difficult for them to resist. The question facing the French was how to get the job done once and for all.

During Louis IX's minority, his part-English, part-Spanish mother, Blanche de Castille (d. 1252), continued the conquest of Languedoc but saw no reason for her young son to become too personally involved. French generals could finish the job, and they did, conquering the land and killing the Cathars. They even subjugated Toulouse. French Catholic occupation reduced the Cathar *perfecti* to fugitives, skulking about darkened urban lanes, hiding in safe houses, forced into the wilderness, and endangering everyone who sheltered them. In what would be the last great military contest of a forty-year crusade, a sizeable group of *perfecti* fled to a mountain fortress called Montségur where they lived in peace among a largely Catholic population. But heretics had no right to protection, and the king's local seneschal along with the bishops demanded the lord of Montségur to surrender to them. He refused, contemptuously telling the French they would never take his castle. In a ten-month period between 1243 and 1244 the French proved him wrong. Accepting the eventual outcome, the lord and his family, his soldiers, and the Catholic civilians were allowed to leave. Two hundred male and female *perfecti* and some supporters were captured and burned alive. After this no Occitanian noble gave open support to the Cathars, and few gave even covert support.

The Cathars had been vanquished, but the threat was not completely gone.

Heretics emerge from within the church. In the Middle Ages they were considered traitors, and thus they deserved the fate of all traitors, namely, extinction. But they presented an additional threat. As Innocent III had perceived, unlike other religious people loathed by the medieval Christians, such as Jews, Muslims, and pagans (in the Baltic regions), heretics did not look different or act in a discernibly unorthodox way on a daily basis. Church and royal leaders knew that heresy dwelt in the mind and in the heart, and until it was rooted out from those, it remained dangerous. But if it could be not rooted out peacefully, then anyone holding those views, no matter how discreetly or even secretly, must be destroyed. Languedoc would be the testing ground for the first wide-scale operation of a new church organ, the Inquisition.

The word Inquisition summons up lurid imagery, even today. When Pope Benedict XVI was elected, some media outlets quickly pointed out that he had served as prefect of the Congregation for the Faith, "the successor to the Inquisition," as if that fearsome word had any relevance in 2005. We must also note that the search for heretics did not begin with the Inquisition, nor was it limited to the church. As we saw, the Christian Roman emperors worked to destroy heresy and exiled or executed dissidents. Throughout the Middle Ages, the local dioceses had courts through which the bishops could investigate charges of doctrinal deviance, although in a society so marked by illiteracy, even among the lower clergy, many nonorthodox views derived from ignorance or a misunderstanding of preaching; for example, many medieval sermons portrayed the devil as so menacingly powerful that it was hardly a surprise that some form of dualism made sense to the unlettered. In 1232 the worst enemy of the medieval popes, the emperor Frederick II of Sicily (d. 1250), issued an edict that imperial officials must ferret out and punish heretics, proof that heresy hunting did not necessary go along with allegiance to Rome. Also, contrary to popular perception, the Inquisition did not exist to execute heretics but rather to win them back. For the inquisitors, every execution marked a failure. But, even allowing for that, the Inquisition in Languedoc proved to be a gruesome, cruel, and very bloody organ of repression.

Pope Gregory IX (1227–41) created the Roman Inquisition and in 1232 entrusted it to the Dominicans. Both French churchmen and royal officials feared that Languedoc would never become a part of France as long as Catharism existed. They were not alone in thinking so; the external enemies of France also entertained the idea/hope that the Cathars might continue to be troublesome. To the French authorities and the popes, the Inquisition seemed the most effective way to eliminate Catharism and guarantee the southerners' acceptance of—if not loyalty to—the crown and the church. They turned out to be right. "It is . . . in the spring of 1233 in Languedoc that we may fairly speak of the birth of the Inquisition as historians understand it" (Barber, 125).

The popes preferred the Dominicans as inquisitors, right down to the Protestant Reformation. Why? When universities came into being in the twelfth century in western Europe, starting with Paris circa 1134, the Dominicans quickly realized the tremendous potential of the universities and so became involved in them. As inquisitors, the well-educated Dominicans focused on beliefs and their formulations: that is, they knew what orthodox teaching was and were able to distinguish it from heresy as well as from simple ignorance. They truly wanted to win people back to the faith and preferred to do that with preaching, but, starting with their founder Dominic (canonized in 1234 by Gregory IX, the Inquisition's founder), they would not hesitate to use force—torture, imprisonment, execution—to destroy heresy.

How did the Inquisition work? Michael Costen provides a succinct account:

> From the start the Inquisition was conceived as an emergency measure against an overwhelming danger. The inquisitors, with the aid of the secular authorities, could arrest whom they pleased on suspicion of heresy. The suspect had no rights and could be held in the bishop's or inquisitor's prison indefinitely. But the most repressive and tyrannical measures were the denial of legal assistance and the denial of a right to appeal. Lawyers were threatened with the loss of their legal status if they assisted the accused. The old bishop's inquisition was a public affair, attended at least by a number of interested clergy. The new Inquisition was essentially a closed administrative procedure, by which the accused was questioned about beliefs and actions by the inquisitor and his assistants who did not reveal the evidence to the accused. Accusers were never brought before the accused, and the proceedings could be adjourned at will for indefinite periods by the inquisitor. Only at the end of the process would a final statement of

guilt and of punishment be made in public. Thus the Roman Law characteristics which had become the normal practice in Church courts were extended into an administrative procedure which had no element of public justice and which left the accused with no safeguards. . . .

It was the prototype of the numerous secret police forces which have plagued Europe throughout modern times. (166–67)

Costen does not exaggerate. For example, even as Catharism had reached its end in the early fourteenth century, having been reduced to a handful of fugitive *perfecti*, the inquisitors did not let up. In Albi, the town that gave its name to the crusade, some suspects arrested in 1300 were still in prison in 1306 without ever having been brought to trial.

Using their almost unlimited authority, the inquisitors moved very methodically. Unlike the Crusaders, who relied upon slash-and-burn techniques that often took Catholic lives, the inquisitors thought out the process. They focused upon the aristocrats and other secular leaders who gave the Cathars shelter, correctly realizing that if the Cathars lost this kind of support, they would be less physically safe and would lose prestige among the peasantry who respected those favored by the aristocracy. The inquisitors saw to it that not only were nobles who supported the Cathars dispossessed of their lands, but so were their children. (Recall earlier that Innocent III had punished Raymond VI of Toulouse but preserved his lands for his son.) This step literally guaranteed the extinction of noble families whose wealth resided in land and whose title "count" depended solely on a specific tract of land.

After the nobility, the inquisitors focused on the cities and towns among whose populations the Cathars could hide. The inquisitors would sometimes arrest the entire adult populations of small towns and then question everyone. They knew what kind of questions to ask, and evasive answers pointed if not to actual guilt then at least to some kind of support for Cathar ideals. The *perfecti* all took oaths never to lie, and thus when they were arrested, to their enduring credit, they confessed to their status, knowing that it would lead to their execution by fire. Very few *perfecti* escaped.

Cathar believers could be sentenced to life imprisonment, which meant life in a small, dark cell, always chained to a wall, never being allowed out for any reason, and being fed on bread and water, unless the imprisoned had relatives willing to bribe a guard and smuggle in some food. In such dank, unsanitary conditions rife with vermin, malnourished prisoners did not survive very long.

Those who had been heretics but abandoned Catharism received a variety of sentences, the most common being required to wear yellow crosses on their clothing, usually on the shoulder. While this would often lead to discrimination and embarrassment, they lived. Other penalties for converted heretics included pilgrimages, a common religious practice but one that was often dangerous, financially ruinous, and could take several years to complete.

In their desire to be thorough, the inquisitors actually had the bodies of dead heretics exhumed and then burned. This was not a useless step but one with great symbolic value. The inquisitors wanted to purify the land of Languedoc, literally.

With the *perfecti* usually on the run, the Dominicans could turn to something they did very well, namely, preaching. They dominated the churches and the city squares, and they did win back many people to the Catholic Church.

Not all went smoothly. Many Cathars fled either to Italy or to the Pyrenees or to remote areas of Languedoc. Sometimes they fought back. In 1242 a noble supporter of the Cathars murdered eight members of an inquisitorial party and stole their records, an event that produced widespread rejoicing but also provoked the French to attack the Montségur fortress in the following year to make clear what would happen to nobility who supported the Cathars.

More serious opposition came from the local bishops, even those appointed by the popes. As diocesan bishops, they resented the enormous role given to an order of priests who operated in their diocese and usually without episcopal approval or involvement. The bishops also wanted more leniency. Executed or imprisoned or deliberately impoverished people could contribute nothing to church life. People driven from their land often became bandits. Episcopal complaints often brought results, although the Inquisition continued to work in Languedoc well into the fourteenth century.

The trials of the Cathars produced a great deal of information about them because many people confessed and in the process recounted their beliefs and practices, which the inquisitors recorded. Since many Cathars had no learning and explained their religion in disordered or fragmentary form, the Dominicans organized the material and made it comprehensible. Much of what historians know about Cathar beliefs and practices comes from inquisitorial records and reflects the views of those doing the recording. (Recall that the Cathars did not even call themselves by that name.) But a problem quickly arose and has not yet been settled.

The Dominicans as a group had superb theological educations, and they quickly related the Cathars to other heretical groups—some rather logical matches, such as the dualistic Manichees, others rather a stretch, such as the Arians because the Cathars' rejection of medieval trinitarian teachings aligned them with other trinitarian heretics. That material was probably too organized. But historians have been able to sort through the material and to largely separate what the Cathars believed from the parallels drawn by the inquisitors.

In a word, the Inquisition succeeded. Towns were won back for the church by effective preaching that no one could challenge. The nobility avoided the Cathars in order to hold on to their lands. The end of the wars in the late 1240s brought peace and some prosperity, and few people wanted a renewal of the crusading days. Catharism clearly had no future in Languedoc, and fewer and fewer people wished to risk their lives for it.

But there were always some who would. In the early fourteenth century, the *perfectus* Pierre Authier attempted not to revive Catharism but to keep it alive. His family supported his efforts as he went from farmhouse to village to administer the *consolamentum* to believers, whose gratitude was endless, knowing what a chance he was taking for them. He made some converts but, very significantly, not among the nobility or even among the town gentry, that is, among people who had much to lose materially. Even those who welcomed him had family members who feared the consequences of having the "good men" among them, and the Authiers found fewer and fewer supporters whom they could trust.

The inevitable happened. In 1308, when the notorious Dominican inquisitor Bernard Gui had coordinated a search, an informer told the police where some *perfecti* could be found. Several *perfecti* were arrested, including Authier's son. All were interrogated, convicted, and burned at the stake. Pierre Authier remained on the loose until 1309, when he was captured. After a year of imprisonment, Gui had him burned at the stake in Toulouse. "Between 1308 and 1321, 25 believers were burnt to death, almost all in Toulouse. Three more were burnt to death at Carcassonne in 1329. The last *perfectus* to be burnt was Guilhem Belibaste, who was captured in 1321" (Costen, 177). Technically, that was not the end of the Cathars, since some in prison survived for years, and no doubt many other Cathars maintained their religious anonymity for decades. But Catharism had ended.

With the heretics and their noble supporters gone and with towns clamoring for peace, Louis IX, twice a rather unsuccessful Crusader against the Muslims, had no need to crusade in Languedoc. The inquisitors and the royal governors had pacified the land, but with, of course, royal approval. The southerners resignedly accepted French rule. Even the persecuted Cathars knew that they would have to survive in a territory ruled by northern French Catholics and not by sympathetic local supporters. Occitania as an independent region had come to an end. It would continue to play an important role in Mediterranean and even European cultural affairs but would do so as part of a much larger country.

The church had won a resounding victory over the dualistic heretics, but at an appalling price. The Inquisition had claimed a prominent place in ecclesiastical life, one it would maintain for centuries and whose values would be exported to Protestants, as Calvinist Geneva would prove. The Inquisition made the charge, not the proof, of heresy a weapon to be used against anyone. For example, in 1277 Étienne Tempier, bishop of Paris, labeled as heretical six propositions from the works of the great and recently deceased (1274) theologian Thomas Aquinas. Historians have also demonstrated that the techniques used against heretics (who, at least, existed) were applied in the fifteenth, sixteenth, and seventeenth centuries against "witches," who, of course, did not exist but who came into existence via "confessions," often extorted by torture and abuse, again a practice used ecumenically and one exported by Spanish Catholics and English Puritans to the New World.

The Roman church had established itself as the guardian and determinant of medieval orthodoxy. The papacy had done what the local bishops and even the Crusaders could not do; it had destroyed a dualistic heresy, no small achievement when one considers that dualism went back, in form or another, to ancient Egypt and had manifested itself repeatedly in Christian history. The papacy had also established a mechanism to deal with future heresies. The popes had given a big boost to mendicant orders and to theological training. Monks sequestered in monasteries could not outpreach, so to speak, the Cathars or locate heretics in the towns or countryside. In an era when an appalling number of parish priests were illiterate (only in 1546 did the Catholic Council of Trent establish the seminary system), the popes supported the mendicants, especially the Dominicans, who had the knowledge to discern heresy and to correct it. As noted earlier, the inquisitors wanted to win people to orthodoxy, not to execute them. In a large measure, they succeeded against the Cathars but also raised the doctrinal awareness of many Catholics in Occitania.

But a price that the church and much of western Europe paid for the crusade and the Inquisition in Languedoc was the rise of France to unrivaled prominence in western Europe. The Crusaders did the dirty work, but the French monarchs took over Languedoc in the end. Territory under French royal rule had significantly increased, as did the French population in an era when a large population was an economic and military asset. The French monarchs could use these new resources against the English kings who claimed dominion over much of France. The Hundred Years' War, which began in the fourteenth century, would end in the fifteenth century with the English holdings in France reduced to the channel port of Calais and some territory surrounding it.

This increased strength also gave the French monarchy more clout with the Germans over the Rhine and even with the papacy. Philip IV (1285–1314), grandson of Louis IX, bullied and attacked the popes and was much responsible for the decision of the French Pope Clement V (1305–14) to move the papacy from Rome to Avignon, where it stayed for seventy years and often served French interests.

The Albigensian Crusade also gave France an increased, indeed major, presence on the northern shore of the Mediterranean, never quite the presence of Spain or Turkey or the Italian seafaring city-states, but a major presence nonetheless, and one that the other Mediterranean states could never ignore.

Rarely have the secular rewards for upholding orthodoxy been so obvious or so plentiful, and rarely has the impact of historical forces in exaggerating a heretical threat been so clear.

But the Occitanians never forgot the Cathars. In religiously free modern Languedoc, the locals, using websites inter alia, welcome tourists to *le pays cathare*. One can even purchase *vin des Cathares*, presumably with some irony, given Cathar asceticism.

* * *

Were the Cathars heretics? Absolutely. As dualists, they consciously went against the Scriptures and more than a millennium of church teaching. The opening verses of Genesis say that the one God of Israel created the material world and "saw that it was good." In the second century, before the canon of Scripture had been established, it may have been understandable for the Greek-thinking Gnostics to repudiate the Jewish Scriptures, but by the twelfth century the books of the Old Testament had become Christian Scripture that no Christian could renounce.

But the Cathars, like the Montanists and Monophysites, were caught up by powerful historical forces that often had little or nothing to do with their beliefs.

The eleventh-century popes made great claims for the ecclesiastical and secular powers of their office, but they could rarely make good on those claims. The twelfth-century popes, however, did make good on many of those claims. Papal government grew enormously, almost exponentially, in the twelfth century. The popes made use of Roman law, which far better suited a strong monarchy than the various Germanic and feudal codes that plagued the medieval monarchs who tried to promote central government. More and more the popes were drawn from the ranks of canon lawyers who could handle the new government structure.

Innocent III was one of those. He genuinely believed that all Christians needed to subject themselves to his authority for their spiritual good. "All" meant "all." Using a sort of medieval Christian "domino theory," Innocent could not tolerate the idea that anyone would disagree with his understanding of the faith. If one person disagreed, she or he might infect someone else, who would infect someone else, and so on. To his credit, Innocent hoped to solve the problem pastorally by using effective preachers, a method that enjoyed some success. But he could not bring himself to ask if Catharism had any validity at all or why the Cathars held on to their beliefs and values. He could not see that the care that the *perfecti* exercised for the poor meant more to the people than doctrinal correctness or that a sect that allowed women to play important roles and even to lead men would appeal to women, who endured second-class status in every area of medieval life.

Catharism arose in Languedoc just as the papacy was extending its control over the church, as Christianity became more legalized, and as the secular rulers would gladly use church concerns for secular goals. Since church and state were united, a crime against the church was also one against the state, and secular rulers applied secular punishments to heretics, but often for secular ends.

The Cathars were a small group of people, no more than 10 percent of one Mediterranean province, and they were mostly poor and uneducated. They hardly represented a threat to the church at large, but even so, their existence as those who differed with the church could not be tolerated.

In the last chapter, we will consider heresy today and the responses to it. As Alistair McGrath has pointed out, modern Christians feel very uncomfortable with the term "heresy," but, scholar that he is, McGrath points out that this cynicism results largely from what people know about traditional ways of dealing with heresy, especially with attacks focusing less on the heretical notions than on those who held them. Modern cynicism about heresy hunting arises partly from a reaction against the medieval principle that "error has no rights." We resent and repudiate the attitude that no one has the right to hold any opinion contrary to that of governmental or ecclesiastical authorities. To moderns, the destruction of Catharism demonstrates heresy hunting at an appalling and immoral level. Costen's comparison to modern police states is not far from the mark.

Sometimes apologists for force in religion will claim that what we see as unacceptable violence against defenseless people was a regular part of medieval life. That is true, but only to a point. Historical situations do impact people for better or worse, but human nature has shown much consistency over the centuries. People want to be happy, to love and be loved, to have material possessions, to feel secure, and to have some dignity. Historical circumstances can excuse just so much.

When the Crusaders, the "army of God," captured Béziers, "all the men, women and children crowded inside [the church of] Saint-Nazaire were beaten to death" (Pegg, 76). Did no one wonder how *infants* could be heretics who deserved to be executed? Does living in the thirteenth century mean that people really thought babies held dualistic views? Why did not the local bishops condemn this as murder? Why did not Rome do so?

When Carcassonne fell to the Crusaders, the inhabitants were expelled and allowed to wear only their underwear or less. A famous medieval illustration of the event in the British Library shows women fleeing bare breasted. Given the endless medieval sermons about the evils of sexual temptation, did it bother no cleric that the "soldiers of Christ" got to watch the wretched, seminude women in public? When the Crusaders raped women prisoners, why did no one complain about the immorality? When Simon de Montfort blinded prisoners, could no one recognize sadism?

Nor can historical circumstances excuse the Inquisition. If someone told a medieval man, "I heard someone call you a thief," his natural reaction would be, "Who said that?" When suspected Cathars were not given a chance to know who accused them (a business rival? a love rival?), did they think that was fair because they lived in the Middle Ages? Did no accused person ever think it unjust that the tribunal consisted of lawyers but that she or he could not have legal representation?

Historical circumstances can explain many things but not everything. Medieval people could see that the "army of God," "the soldiers of Christ," the Inquisition, and the secular and religious authorities unleashed a vicious flood of brutality and terror upon the population of Languedoc.

* * *

Heresy exists in every age and must be combated in every age. Yet when modern clergy and theologians attempt to counter heretical ideas, they find themselves pilloried in the media as enemies of free speech, as bigots, as petulant nitpickers, or, even more demoralizing, as subjects of humor. They will object that this is unfair, which it is, but they will just have to accept that resentment of heresy hunters is partly the legacy of the appalling medieval approach to dealing with dissidence, an approach that set the stage for the persecution of witches, of differing religious groups in the Reformation, and of those who disagreed with modern "orthodoxies" such as communism.

The modern Occitanians are right to remember the Cathars.

Roman Catholic Modernism

In his 1907 encyclical *Pascendi*, Pope Pius X (1903–14) condemned a heresy that he called "modernism," a condemnation that would impact Roman Catholic intellectual life for a half century. This was not the first but perhaps the most pronounced confrontation between traditional religious authority and the forces unleashed by the modern world.

It is difficult to define the ostensible subject of this chapter. In one sense, modern*ism* has never existed anywhere. The suffix -*ism* implies a belief system, in religious forms such as Buddhism or Confucianism and in secular modes such as capitalism or communism. Thus modern-*ism* would mean an absolute belief in the modern, and no one has ever thought that something is good just because it is modern. Every modern person can see the wonderful things done by computers and the internet by making enormous amounts of knowledge available literally at one's fingertips. But computers also brought us identity theft and have enabled hate groups to go online to increase their memberships. So too with theological "modernists," Catholic and, as we shall see in the next chapter, Protestant. They never advocated abandoning all church traditions for newer ones, but rather abandoning those that they believed modern biblical scholarship and modern science had shown to be impossible to maintain.

Scholars debate whether Catholic modernism ever existed, arguing that Pius X in his condemnation of modernism effectually defined the term, so that it means what he defined it to mean (Jodock, 1), while both Lester Kurtz (9) and Harvey Hill (*The Politics of Modernism*, 195) say that Pius caricatured the scholars who offended him as modernists when he condemned the supposed movement in his 1907 encyclical *Pascendi*. Paul Misner says, "The Modernists comprised those Catholics whose ideas of reform did not set much stock in updating medieval Thomistic thought" (80). The Augustinian priest Gerald Daly points out that "Rome did much to create the monster it slew. Allowing *Pascendi* to define Modernism leads to the intrinsically awkward business of deciding who was and who was not a Modernist by reference to an artificial criterion; there is a considerable measure of agreement among scholars that no single Modernist conforms to the systematic profile depicted in *Pascendi*" ("Theology and Philosophical Modernism," 89).

The modernists did not comprise a movement, like the Montanists, but were a group of scholars who had similar views. The two most prominent ones, Alfred Loisy and George Tyrrell, never met one another, and the "movement" was linked, to the extent that it was, by a peripatetic nobleman who knew all the major players, visited them, and sometimes gave them copies of the others' writings.

But, like Montanism, the name "modernism" has stuck, and we will use it here but with the understanding that the "modernists" worked for the most part on their own and what chiefly connected them was a concern that the church was going the wrong way intellectually in the modern world. The modernists were hardly the only Catholics who thought that way, but they were the ones who did the writing and whom Pius targeted in his encyclical.

Although the modernist controversy broke out in the first decade of the twentieth century, its true beginning can be found in the eighteenth century. The Constantinian link of church and state persisted. Most European countries had established churches; that is, the government recognized the church, gave it favorable status, issued laws to protect it, and provided it with financial support. This applied in Orthodox Russia, Lutheran Prussia, Presbyterian Scotland, and Catholic France, inter alia. Nonbelievers living in those countries saw their tax money going to these churches, which also controlled schools, banned books, and saw to punitive measures against heretics. Grudgingly or not, most people took this situation for granted, even those not belonging to the established church.

The Scientific Revolution changed much of this, although few people recognized it at the time. Throughout the Middle Ages, the few educated people had looked for authority to the Scriptures, traditional church teaching, and the clergy, which in Roman Catholicism more and more meant the authority of the popes. But none of these religious authorities could tell anyone anything about the circulation of the blood or about optics. Scientists did not work against religion but did work outside it, and their continued and astonishing discoveries demonstrated what the power of reason could do when no external authority interfered with it. Many religious leaders felt uncomfortable with this development, even if scientists tried to pacify them. Isaac Newton knew that parts of Genesis could not be literally true, and he speculated that Moses deliberately wrote a creation account that would appeal to the illiterate people whom he led. The Catholic Inquisition in the Papal States censured and silenced the Italian scholar Galileo Galilei in 1633 and sentenced him to perpetual house arrest, but by 1700 even Catholic universities were teaching the new understanding of the cosmos.

The scientific proof of the power of reason started a religious earthquake. Recall that the Augustinian theory of Original Sin claimed that it had corrupted human nature, including our minds. Since we could not think as clearly as we should, churches argued, we must trust religious authority. But the scientists from Copernicus to Newton had presented a new cosmos, and one difficult for people to accept. Humans and their world no longer occupied the center of the cosmos but had to cede that honor to a lifeless ball of fire. Scientists had changed the way educated people understood the very world they lived in, and they had done it with corrupt, fallible reason and without ecclesiastical authority. To be sure, scientists made plenty of mistakes as all scholars do, but no one could ignore, much less deny, what they had achieved.

During the eighteenth-century Enlightenment, intellectuals began to apply reason to all areas, including religion. Not fearing church authority, they asked questions such as, why do the various gospels disagree in several passages if they were reliable biographies of Christ? The most effective attack fell on Original Sin: Why does a loving God condemn to eternal suffering the 90 percent of the human race who through no fault of their own did not receive baptism? And why would God do all this because two prehistoric people took a bite out of piece of fruit? Jean-Jacques Rousseau simply asserted human goodness, not bothering to refute the doctrine of Original Sin. Furthermore, as the western Europeans learned more about other civilizations, especially in the Americas, they found flood narratives, virgin births, and ascensions into heaven, leading intellectuals to conclude that the ancient Jews and Christians had just made use of traditional mythical material that later generations took literally. This was not yet the science of comparative religion, but these parallels were difficult to ignore.

The churches insisted on the historicity of much of the Bible but especially of the gospels, which record many miracles. But Enlightenment intellectuals pointed out that no objective empirical evidence existed for miracles; all the gospels really preserved was the faith of the first Christians that Jesus had performed miracles. Thomas Jefferson produced what he considered to be an authentic gospel by going through the four gospels and deleting what he thought was the nonsense believed by ancient, uneducated people. Even today it is strange to read an account of Jesus' life with no nativity account and no miracles. The Scottish philosopher David Hume (1711–76) snidely observed that the only miraculous thing about miracles is that people believe in them.

The churches responded as best they could, and the great majority of Europeans continued to believe in the literal understanding of the Bible, but one French bishop sighed that all the best minds seemed to be on the other side. Some scholarly ideas, such as the criticism of Original Sin, did win over many people. The Enlightenment historian Peter Gay observes, "Priests less and less emphasized the rigorous Christian teaching of sin; the old grim story of Adam's fall had become less persuasive, and even those who attended Mass without fail were no longer inclined to feel guilty simply because they were human" (354).

Not since Constantine had critics so openly denied what the churches were teaching and even whether or not churches had the right to impose their teachings on the entire populace. The nascent United States fascinated educated Europeans, who looked to see how a country that separated church and state would fare. In the late eighteenth and much of the nineteenth century, various European liberals strove to limit church power in civic life while monarchists and conservatives strove to preserve it in some form or other. Church leaders understandably worked to validate their authority and not just to keep power for themselves because most sincerely believed that moral harm would come to the citizens of countries that weakened or eliminated church influence. Many simply could not accept that the practices of a millennium and a half could be abandoned.

But several historical factors worked against the churches. The Industrial Revolution had changed the face of Europe and the US. People left farms and moved to cities. Power shifted to urban politicians and business leaders and away from the rural nobility that had traditionally provided support for the churches. As the nobles lost their political power, representative governments became more common, albeit usually with a limited franchise, for example, only men. Ominously for the popes, Protestant, democratic, free-speech-supporting England became the dominant Western power, while aggressively Catholic Spain could not even preserve its American colonies. By approximately 1880 the size of England's economy had been surpassed by a country on the wrong side of the Atlantic, one that separated church and state, legalized freedom of religion, and prized freedom of speech. American influence would do nothing but grow.

Another historical factor was the rise of modern geology and evolutionary biology. Churches fought strongly, and many still do, but again they lost with educated people. The world went back millions of years (now, of course, billions), making the traditional biblical chronology of six thousand or so years impossible. God had not created plants, animals, and humans in a few days. They had emerged over several geological epochs. Worst of all, human beings, "a little less than angels" according to the psalmist (8:6), had evolved from lower forms of life. The Scientific Revolution had pushed us out of the center of the cosmos; now we were just another species of animal.

More than ego was at stake here. The theology of Original Sin depended heavily upon an actual primeval couple to commit it. Furthermore, Christians believe that God endowed humans with immortal souls, and since all of us descended from Adam, it made sense that all humans had souls. But as the notion that we evolved caught on, how could one say when and which humanoid beings became close enough to us to warrant infusion of souls? Churches liked to point out that Charles Darwin was an atheist, but personal attacks did not weaken evolutionary biology.

A third historical factor and one directly related to Catholic modernism was the rise of modern biblical criticism. Since the late second century Christian scholars had known about the many discrepancies between biblical books and often within a single book. Assuming that the books could contain no actual error, they worked to reconcile problematic passages and often succeeded, although they frequently had to resort to allegories and spiritual meanings for the texts. When the Dutch Jewish philosopher Benedict de Spinoza (1632–77) suggested that scholars should study the Bible as they would any other work of ancient literature, Jews and Christians were shocked. But by the mid-nineteenth century many scholars, almost all Protestant and mostly German, did focus upon literary motifs and the historical background of the Bible to understand the text. This approach, radical in its day, is now standard exegetical procedure.

Here is one example of the change such work wrought.

Most Christians believed that Jesus had a three-year public career. Why? Because John's gospel, written by one of the twelve apostles, mentions three Passovers (2:13; 6:4; 11:55), and since that feast occurs annually, the public career must have been three years. But the other evangelists mention only one Passover (Mark 14:1; Matt 26:2; Luke 22:1), so how can this be reconciled? There is no need for reconciliation. John was right because he was the disciple "whom Jesus loved" (13:23), and so he would be a far more reliable source for Jesus' career than the other three evangelists.

But if this is so, a few problems arise. First of all, nowhere does John's gospel identify the Beloved Disciple with John of the Twelve. For that matter, this gospel does not mention any disciple named John, although it mentions John the Baptist several times and three times refers to Simon Peter as "son of John" (21:15, 16, 17).

Another major point argues against John of the Twelve as the Beloved Disciple. When the disciple first appears in the gospel, Jesus is already in Jerusalem for the last week of his life, which means that this disciple goes *completely unmentioned* for this supposed three-year ministry for which he was the sole source. There certainly was a Beloved Disciple, and his name could have been John, but no modern scholar thinks this gospel was written by one of the twelve apostles.

There was yet more. "John" was a brilliant theologian who wrote good Greek, another argument against a Galilean fisherman as the author. Furthermore, his advanced, "high" Christology (Jesus the divine Word) points to some sophisticated development that occurred since Mark had written. It also explains some puzzling elements, such as Jesus' encounter with John the Baptist at the Jordan *without* an actual baptism (John 1:29-34), contrary to what the other evangelists had written. John preached "a baptism of repentance for the forgiveness of sins" (Mark 1:4), a baptism the sinless Jesus (Heb 4:15) obviously did not need. The first three evangelists tried to explain why he accepted baptism; John simply left it out since this did not meet his christological needs.

The foregoing are not the only arguments against apostolic authorship of this gospel. Modern scholars further demonstrated that John of the Twelve could not have written the book of Revelation or the three epistles traditionally attributed to him.

Consider what this meant for New Testament scholarship. John's gospel was not an eyewitness account; the chronology of Jesus' career was now uncertain; the literary elements so evident in this gospel, such as the theme of light and dark, could now be identified as literary elements instead of defended as actual events. All the theories built upon apostolic authorship had to be rethought, and the preference routinely given to John over the other evangelists in doing theology had to be redone. On matters of historicity, scholars use this gospel very carefully.

This new scholarly approach had tremendous impact upon nineteenth-century churchmen, who had to accept that the Bible and even the gospels were not what they had thought them to be. Some church leaders simply refused to accept the evidence and condemned those who practiced it. The current struggle over the Genesis creation narratives is one part, albeit the largest, of a struggle that has been going on for a century and a half. And all of this new scholarship stood behind the papal condemnation of modernism.

Besides the new exegesis, the nineteenth century provided a host of other challenges to the popes, absolute monarchs of the Papal States of Italy, in an era when monarchies were fading or struggling to hold on against new ideas and trends. Even the notoriously retrograde Austrian chancellor Klemens von Metternich, who quashed every new idea and movement that he could, accepted that some few changes had to be made, advice he gave to Pope Gregory XVI (1831–46), who ignored it and so paid an enormous price.

Gregory simply loathed the modern world. He thought separating church and state would lead to "indifferentism," that people would think there was no difference among religions. He called freedom of religion "madness" (*delirium* in Latin), and he condemned freedom of speech and of the press. In the Papal States, he refused to allow railroads, which prevented the States from developing economically as the other areas of Italy were. Gregory believed in repression, even in minor matters such as forbidding Roman taverns to serve alcohol and warning Roman women about wearing tight dresses, but, far more seriously, he refused to let people elect their mayors, allowed his police to accept anonymous denunciations of people, and forced the Roman Jews back into a ghetto. The Italians would not put up with this and rebelled. The pope called in Austrian troops to prop up his rule, thus using foreign troops to suppress his own people. When the Austrian forces left, the rebellion became a full-scale revolution that made it dangerous for papal officials even to travel in the States, much less to try to govern them. But Gregory died before the States were completely lost.

His successor, Pius IX (1846–78), bore the brunt of the modern world's intrusion into papal affairs. Barely two years into his pontificate, the Italian Revolution reached Rome, and Pius had to flee ignominiously in disguise. Hoping to check Austrian power in Italy, the emperor Louis Napoleon offered French help in restoring Pius to Rome. Pius accepted the offer, the French troops prevailed, the pope returned to Rome, and all of Italy saw another Italian pope using foreign troops against his own citizens. When in 1870 the Franco-Prussian War required the French army to return home, Pius lost Rome and the Papal States as Italy became a united country, which the popes refused to recognize for more than half a century. No longer secular rulers, the popes would have to rethink their place in the modern world. Pius now turned his energies toward ruling the church.

This pope never understood the modern world, but he did realize that many modern attitudes, especially in democracies, could impact his church. He saw religious freedom as promoting indifferentism. He saw democracy as an implied challenge to the church's monarchical structure. Freedom of speech meant no way to stop or suppress heresy. Freedom of the press made the Index of Forbidden Books useless and exposed Catholics to books that would challenge or corrupt their faith. He would use his position to fight these threats. As Rev. Marvin O'Connell puts it, "Pius IX's inability to differentiate among the diverse currents of thought that swirled around the nineteenth century was his greatest weakness. He never grasped . . . the profound changes European society underwent . . . when the old agricultural economy gave way to an industrialized system dominated by an aggressive middle class and a vast urban prole-tariat, and when monarchies had to surrender to . . . more or less . . . representative regimes" (24).

In 1864 Pius published an encyclical to which he added a list of eighty errors to be condemned. This list quickly became known as the Syllabus of Errors. It was an indictment of modern civilization, condemn-ing freedom of religion, of speech, and of the press; public schools (the church controlled education in several European states); civil marriage; and the separation of church and state. He finished by condemning the notion that the papacy should adapt to the modern world. The document would present problems for Catholics living in democracies, but Pius would not back down.

If he could not stop modernity, he could keep it out of the church. In 1869–70 he presided over the First Vatican Council, considered ecu-menical by Catholics. It dealt with a number of issues, the most famous being the definition of papal infallibility, for Pius a sign that one man could speak the truth even if the entire modern world fell into error. Infallibility made people wonder how often popes might use it, but in the almost century and a half since Vatican I, that has only happened once, when in 1950 Pius XII (1939–58) defined as infallible the bodily assumption of Jesus' mother Mary into heaven.

On a practical level and far more important, the council gave the pope the power to intervene in any diocese at any time on any matter, power not even dreamed of a half century before. This meant, for example, that a pope could intervene in a diocese to transfer a priest from one parish to another, and the local bishop could do nothing about it. To be sure, the popes have not often used this power in so petty a way, but Vatican I made it clear that the popes have universal, immediate authority in the church, regardless of what the world at large and/or Catholics might think. As for Catholic scholars who disagreed and raised questions, Pius simply had no use for them. "The seeds of [the modernist] tragedy . . . were sown by the clumsy manner in which Pius IX's Vatican dealt with Catholic scholars. . . . Skeptical and wary of any learned initiative, . . . [its] style of response was all too often heedless administrative fiat" (O'Connell, 28).

After Pius's death in 1878, the cardinals chose an Italian aristocrat to be pope. Like Pius, Leo XIII (1878–1903) loathed the Italian state and refused to recognize it. He repeatedly tried to convince the Catholic powers to restore if not the Papal States then at least Rome to the popes. But no government either wanted to do it or would dare offending popular wrath by invading a sovereign European state to restore an absolute monarch. In a more realistic mode, Leo lifted some restrictions on Catholic participation in the Italian state, and, in his best and most famous encyclical, *Rerum Novarum* (Of New Things), he addressed the immorality of the deplorable situation of modern industrial workers. Leo's own sympathy ran toward medieval guilds under clerical guidance, but he put the weight of the church behind social reform.

Leo disliked modern thought, but unlike Pius, he did not condemn it but rather tried to reform it. A strong devotee of Thomas Aquinas (1225–74), he believed that Thomistic philosophy would be a good antidote to the modern philosophies that he considered to be at odds with Catholic teaching. Thomas was a member of the Dominican order and a scholastic, a term referring to the philosophical and theological thinking done in medieval European universities, especially the University of Paris, where Thomas and other significant scholastics had taught. Recognized as a great man in his own era, Thomas later became a major source for Catholic theology. His approach to theology became widely known as Thomism. Although the word "scholasticism" can apply to the teachings of literally hundreds of academic theologians from the twelfth century onward, for many Catholics Thomism and scholasticism became synonymous.

In his encyclical *Aeterni Patris* (Of the Eternal Father), Leo XIII made Thomism the official basis for Roman Catholic theology. No empty words here. Leo insisted that the bishops reform seminary curricula to accommodate this overall approach, and he planned for the teaching of Thomism in Catholic educational institutions. Using the power Vatican

I had given the pope, he brooked no opposition. The Franciscan Order had traditionally venerated another great scholastic theologian, Bonaventure (1221–74), the second general of their order, but now they had to adopt Thomism. The Jesuits had already been using Thomism but as it had been reworked and articulated by Francisco Suarez (1548–1617), a Spanish Jesuit. But now the Jesuits had to use Thomas himself and not their order's Spanish Thomist.

"The revival of . . . Thomas Aquinas was a tacit admission that the church's house of intellect stood in need of grave repair" (O'Connell, 34). Leo's solution initially worked well. Thomas was a monumental intellect whose brilliance provoked much thought, and Thomism did indeed revivify Catholic intellectual life. What Leo and many others liked about Thomas was his insistence on the primacy of reason and his belief that rational people could objectively accept and understand truths clearly presented to them. Leo rejected thinkers who argued that the knowing subject plays a major role in the apprehension of truth. "Philosophy, if rightly made use by the wise, . . . tends to smooth and fortify the road to true faith" (*Aeterni Patris* 4). A solid philosophical base would enable theology to receive "the nature, form, and genius of a true science" (6). "It is the glory of philosophy to be . . . the bulwark of faith and the strong defense of religion" (7). The pope went on to include the *Summa Theologica* of Aquinas along with "*sacred Scripture* and the decrees of the Supreme Pontiffs" as the places "whence to seek counsel, reason, and inspiration" (22; emphasis added). Thomism would be a "great and invincible force to overturn those principles of the new order" (29). The Catholic philosophers and theologians who followed the pope's lead were called neo-Thomists.

Thomistic philosophy was believed to both support Catholic theology and challenge modern intellectual trends. It never achieved the second goal. The voluminous Catholic studies of Thomas made others aware of him, and all philosophers now recognize and honor his historical significance, but modern philosophers go their own way. As for supporting theology, that happened initially, but too quickly "Thomas" became a series of classroom manuals that provided hasty reviews of unacceptable philosophers and then proof of Thomism's superiority to their erroneous ideas. (This author's freshman philosophy class at Boston College used such a book.)

For all its strengths, Thomism had considerable weaknesses as a modern philosophy. The historical Thomas had little scientific knowledge that had any value in the modern world. He accepted a geocentric cosmos only a few thousand years old and knew little of the physics, chemistry, and biology behind its functioning. A bright, modern adolescent knows more mathematics than he did. Thomism per se could not address intellectual questions raised by modern science. Furthermore, theology must deal with human nature. Thomas's common guide, Aristotle, considered women to have resulted from an error in the generative process, a view Thomas accepted. How could a theologian deal with human nature when he thought half of humanity was the result of a mistake? Thomas's theories of government were monarchical. And so on.

Studied in his historical context, Thomas proves to be a supreme genius, but this genius became distorted when twisted into a sourcebook of responses to questions raised by the supposedly hostile modern world.

Like Pius IX, Leo just did not trust that world. "He proved himself an extraordinarily subtle, sophisticated, and well-informed man, but he discerned behind . . . the biblical scholar who questioned the Mosaic authorship of the Pentateuch, an anticlerical politician anxious to close Catholic schools [and] suppress religious orders" (O'Connell, 34). Others shared Leo's concerns. "Precipitated by a fear of modern political and intellectual freedom, the neo-Thomists advocated suppression rather than open discussion in theological matters" (Kurtz, 39).

O'Connell chose a good example here because far more threatening to Catholic thinking than new philosophies was the development of modern biblical criticism. Aquinas, a product of his age, accepted the Mosaic authorship of the Pentateuch, Johannine authorship of the fourth gospel, and the like, so while modern Catholics exegetes respected him, they still planned to go their own way. But not for long.

In 1893 Leo published *Providentissimus Deus* (Most Provident God), an encyclical on biblical studies. The pope took a very traditional line, warning about "fallacious and imprudent novelties" (2). He urged scholars to pay attention to biblical literary devices and even sentence structure (8) but quickly rejected the results of modern exegesis. "Rationalists . . . [claim that] the Apostolic Gospels and writings are not the work of the Apostles at all," (10) a warning to Catholic scholars who had reached similar conclusions. Catholic scholars must "defend the sacred writings" (13) and rely upon "'the true sense of Holy Scripture which has been held and is held by our Holy Mother the Church. . . . It is permitted to no one to interpret the Holy Scriptures against such sense or also against the unanimous agreement of the Fathers.' By this most wise decree the Church by no means prevents or restrains the pursuit of Biblical science but rather protects it from error" (14, quoting the Council of Trent). Exegetes must do that because "in these times . . . the thirst for novelty and unrestrained freedom of thought make the danger of error most real and proximate" (15). "The best preparation [for biblical studies] will be a conscientious application to philosophy and theology under the guidance of St. Thomas Aquinas" (16). Leo does acknowledge that sometimes "the sacred writers . . . described and dealt with things in a more or less figurative language or in terms commonly used at the time . . . and sometimes expressed the ideas of their own times and thus made statements which in these days have been abandoned as incorrect" (18–19). This sounds promising for exegesis, but Leo then justifies this view as "according to the saying of St. Thomas" (19), proof that any good exegesis cannot be a novelty.

The pope did not want the church defending literal or scientific statements proven to be untrue, but he still insisted that scholars were to follow the exegesis of the Fathers who lived fourteen hundred years earlier, most of whom cold not read Hebrew and many of whom could not read Greek. He also demanded that exegetes and scholars rely upon Thomas Aquinas, who could not read either of the biblical languages, a minimum prerequisite for getting a degree in biblical studies today

Biblical exegesis would play a great role in the modernist controversy.

Leo produced another encyclical that played a role in that controversy, the 1899 *Testem Benevolentiae* (Expression of Good Will) on the phantom heresy of Americanism.

Although technically a mission country until 1907, the United States was a wealthy, powerful, aggressive country, a young democracy with little liking for the old monarchies and values of Europe but with a constitution that enshrined and protected freedom of religion, freedom of speech, freedom of the press, and other freedoms rejected by many monarchies, including the Vatican. American Catholics valued their freedoms and did not back down from them. At Vatican I, the bishop of Pittsburgh, having heard one criticism too many of the US, stood up on the floor of the council and pointed out that the church flourished in the US and that Americans made good Catholics who went to church, unlike the Romans, who did not. The European monarchist bishops promptly shouted him down.

But American values did present a problem for the church. Although American Catholics never pushed for democracy in the church, they were building a new church, not preserving an old one. They emphasized activity, an appropriate goal since the millions of Catholic immigrants from Europe needed parishes and schools, and the bishops lived in a country of over three million square miles, geographically larger than all the predominantly Catholic countries of Europe combined.

The US church had produced a new order of priests, the Paulists, founded in 1857 by a convert named Isaac Hecker (1819–88) who wanted a dedicated group of men who would use modern American means to evangelize. Hecker always remained simultaneously loyal to the papacy and to American values. After his death, another Paulist, Walter Elliott, wrote a biography of Hecker, which was translated into French and published in 1898 with a strongly liberal introduction by the French Abbé Félix Klein. French conservatives reacted very strongly against Klein and demonized political liberalism as a capitulation to the godless, secular state. The charge of "godless, secular state" had often been lodged against the religiously neutral United States, then on the outs with the Vatican because of the Spanish-American War, which saw Spain's overwhelming Catholic-populated colonies (Cuba, the Philippines) come under American secular rule. French conservatives accused several progressive American bishops and clerics of holding the views espoused by Klein. European Catholics now spoke of "Americanism" as a new heresy. They held American bishops responsible for the views of a Frenchman.

Leo addressed the encyclical *Testem Benevolentiae* to the primate of the American church, James Cardinal Gibbons, archbishop of Baltimore (1877–1921). The pope generously praised the faith of American Catholics and made it clear that he did not consider heresy to be rampant among them. Perhaps with tongue in cheek, he said that Gibbons presumably knew "that the biography of Isaac Hecker . . . has excited not a little controversy." The pope condemned "lovers of novelty" as well as those who thought the church should adapt to the times and accept freedom of religion and of the press. He stressed that Catholics should stay on familiar paths. His central concern was the "exaltation" of active virtues over passive ones, something "extolled by innovators . . . who are fond of novelty." By this he meant that activist American bishops might prefer religious orders who taught and nursed and evangelized to those who lived in cloisters and "charmed with solitude, give themselves to prayer and mortification." No American bishop ever publicly expressed dissatisfaction with contemplative orders, although people building dioceses from scratch needed active, not passive, clergy and religious, and some bishops may have injudiciously indicated such a preference.

The pope closed the letter to Gibbons by using the word "Americanism" to refer to the attitudes expressed by Klein, but then he quickly noted that if such an attitude did exist in the US, "there can be no doubt that our venerable brethren, the bishops of America, would be the first to condemn it as being most injurious to themselves and to their country."

Americanism as an *-ism* never existed, but this phantom heresy gave Leo a chance to condemn the notion that the church should adapt to modern society, an echo of the closing line of the Syllabus of Errors. "The condemnation, mild as it was, was somewhat contrived. The doctrines summarized were not from American writings but from their opponents' characterizations of them" (Kurtz, 47). This same approach would be used for the condemnation of modernism.

When the aristocratic Leo died in 1903, the cardinals chose Giuesppe Sarto, patriarch of Venice, who took the name Pius X (1903–14) to let the world and especially the Italian government know that he admired his much maligned predecessor of that name.

Unlike centuries of previous popes, Pius X had spent most of his life in dioceses rather than in papal officialdom. He came from modest circumstances, and he never forgot where he came from. He cared much for the simple believers, and most Catholics know this now canonized man as the pope who allowed young children to receive the sacrament of the Eucharist. But he lacked Leo's education and cultivation. That pope wanted to counter what he considered the hostile trends of modern society by advocating the study of Thomistic philosophy, but Pius dealt with his perceived enemies with threats, restrictions, and condemnations. He considered Leo too political and hoped instead to be a religious pontiff, but troubles with France, the familiar problems with the Italian state, and the relentless spread of democratic ideals in heavily Catholic countries forced him into a role for which he was ill fitted. "Pius X was horrified by most aspects of the modern world and operated from an acute sense of crisis" (Kurtz, 50).

As C. J. T. Talar points out, the popes carried a specific burden in dealing with the modern world. They took the concept of the church as the *Body* of Christ very seriously, almost literally. The church continued the incarnation, and "this lent a more than human character to its authority" (198), which is why the popes believed they could intervene in almost any area but especially in theology. Some like Leo could understand disagreement, even if he did not accept it, but Pius X simply could not fathom it. He dealt with what he would call modernism in the only way he knew how.

Philosophy would also be an issue for this pope, but ultimately, the real struggle, decades old and still unsettled, would focus on the Bible and how to understand it, especially those segments traditionally accepted as literal but severely challenged as such by modern exegesis. To these can be added questions about extrabiblical traditions with similar traditional authority, such as Matthew the apostle as the author of the first gospel.

For many religious people, literalism means truth and vice versa. To deny that Adam and Eve existed historically leads inexorably to denying that Jesus existed historically. No modern exegete has ever said that, but the fear still exists. To say that a miracle cannot be proven historically is to deny that any miracle took place. This too is not true. Historians can only deal with what can be historically verified. A miracle means that God intervened to overcome some natural problem, such as a crippling disease. One can say historically that someone recovered from a disability in a way that currently defies a natural explanation, but one cannot say historically that God intervened to do so. Yet just because one cannot prove something historically does not mean that it did not actually happen. Unfortunately, most people do not make that distinction. (Ironically, the gospels say that Jesus did miracles not to get people to believe in him but rather the opposite. Time and again he asked people if they had faith in him *before* he performed the miracle, just the reverse of what most Christians believe [cf. Matt 9:2; Mark 10:52; Luke 8:50]).

The biblical scholars who would fall under suspicion or be condemned as modernists were like many "heretics," people who considered themselves loyal to their church and fearful that if their church did not employ up-to-date methods to understand the Scriptures, it would lose credibility with modern, educated people, especially if the church defended something that was simply nonsense.

Consider the Bible's most spectacular episode, God via Moses parting the Red Sea so that it stood in two walls for the Hebrews to escape the Egyptians (Exod 13:17–15:31). Pharaoh arrives at the sea with his army, and this man, smart enough to rule much of the Near East, blithely assumes that his enemy Moses and his deity will conveniently keep the walls of water standing so that Pharaoh's army could cross through in order to kill or enslave the Hebrews. Can anyone seriously believe that any general, no matter how incompetent or even genuinely moronic, would do such a thing? Along the same lines, does anyone really believe that one man, Samson, killed one thousand Philistines (Judg 15:15)? And think of the one thousandth Philistine soldier. Seeing 999 other soldiers dead, he thought that he could kill Samson by himself?

What concerned modern exegetes was that if churches asked people to accept the historicity of such obvious legends, believers would simply not do so and might even extend that skepticism to other parts of the Bible. What concerned traditionalists was that questioning the literal truth of these parts of the Bible would extend to denying the literal truth of any part. For example, the infancy narratives of Matthew and Luke do not agree in all parts. Luke says Joseph and Mary lived in Nazareth of Galilee at the time of the annunciation, while Matthew says they moved to Nazareth because they could not safely return to Judea upon their return from Egypt—a clear contradiction. But the infancy narratives are the only places in the entire New Testament that mention Mary's virginal conception of Jesus. Given the immense role that the Virgin plays in Catholic spirituality and practice and given the immense devotion that many Catholics, including the popes, have had for Mary, challenging the historicity of the infancy narratives had and still does have grave consequences in Catholic circles.

Why did such challenging questions arise at the beginning of the twentieth century? Modern communications and the freedom of the press guaranteed that Catholic scholars would come to know the work that progressive Protestants were doing, especially in Germany, where Catholics and Protestants encountered one another in daily life. A Catholic exegete might learn that a Protestant had questioned the traditional authorship of John's gospel, check out the evidence for himself, and conclude that the Protestant scholar was correct in saying, for example, that John of the Twelve could not have written the gospel attributed to him. But what was the Catholic exegete to do with that knowledge? This was not just a scholarly decision but also a moral one. Could the exegete continue to teach what he knew was untrue? But what would happen if he did not? His only realistic option was to present the evidence in such a way as to convince Vatican authorities that it did not threaten the faith.

Before turning to two prominent exegetes, we must note one of the oddities of this situation. Catholics who want to find the basis for all their teaching directly in the Bible sound like conservative Protestants. In 1546 the ecumenical Council of Trent had decreed that revelation was passed along in Scripture and in unwritten traditions, so Catholics do not have to find everything they teach directly in Scripture. Biblical literalism is simply not essential to Catholic doctrine. As we saw above, the word Trinity does not appear in the New Testament, but no word can be more central to Catholic belief. Yet in this era many Catholics seemed entranced by biblical literalism.

Two French exegetes, both priests, wished to raise new questions and to update exegesis. They were Alfred Firmin Loisy (1857–1940) and Marie-Joseph Lagrange (1855–1938).

When they were in seminary, the neoscholastic curriculum was not conducive to new thinking. Talar describes it thus: "Theology derived its first principles from revelation. . . . 'The Catholic theologian can proceed from his revealed first principles . . . to his theologically certain conclusions.' [Theology's] status as a genuine science was secured with the aid of philosophy. The latter provided the structure through which the various parts of theology were organized into a single, interrelated body of knowledge" (196). The higher certitude of theology established the subordination of philosophy to theology (196–97).

What about biblical exegesis? "This same doctrinal emphasis reappears in this theology's conception of the proper role of exegesis. The proof-texting role [taking a biblical verse out of context to support a doctrinal point] assigned to exegesis recapitulates the 'essentialist' character of neo-scholasticism in general and neo-Thomism more particularly. The comparatively marginal status assigned to biblical studies in the seminary curriculum for most of the nineteenth century reflects its marginality in neo-scholasticism" (ibid., 97).

Biblical scholars thus had two barriers to surmount: their own deficient education in exegesis and the prevailing ecclesiastical attitude that what they were doing was important not on its own but only as a support for scholasticism. When exegetes wanted to do their studies independently of scholasticism, that is, the way non-Catholic exegetes were able to work, they challenged the theological establishment backed by the pope.

Marie-Joseph Lagrange (1855–1938)

Lagrange entered the Dominicans, the order of Saint Thomas, and he learned a great deal of Thomistic philosophy, which he appreciated. A superb linguist, he could read not just the biblical languages but other Near Eastern ones as well. In 1889 he moved to Jerusalem to his order's Priory of Saint Stephen to found what became the École Biblique, a leading center for biblical study. At the school's opening, Lagrange gave a speech that mentioned "progress" four times and expressed his belief that the more one understood the Bible in its historical setting, the better one could appreciate it as the Word of God.

He specialized in Old Testament studies and soon concluded that the Pentateuch, traditionally the work of Moses, was a combination of several documents produced by a number of writers over some centuries. When he began to hear criticisms of his views, he responded that criticisms, especially biting ones, do not overcome the problems. He used the classic defense: "I am too passionately attached to the Roman Church not to hope that we emerge from the situation of intellectual inferiority [compared to Protestant exegetes] where we now are on certain points. The obvious value of the new methods . . . and an ardent desire to contribute to our getting out of our dishonorable stagnation are also contributing factors" (Montagnes, 41). His Roman superiors quickly responded by telling him to limit his presentations at biblical conferences because "the hearers are not all benevolent and some interpret badly the most inoffensive words" (ibid., 42). Note the approach: the critics are unnamed, and although Lagrange's words may be "inoffensive," these unnamed critics interpret them badly. Note too that his Roman superiors do not offer to tell the critics to be fair or to correct their misinterpretation.

By 1897 Lagrange had finished a large commentary on Genesis, which he submitted to censors in Rome. "The Roman censor deemed the publication of the manuscript inopportune. One of his censors explained: 'The work does not contain anything that could be reproved. But theologians are not well informed about Orientalism [the new method]. That is why modern criticism frightens them more than it benefits them. . . .' Father Lagrange, putting aside Genesis, for better days he hoped, set to work on [the book of] Judges" (ibid., 48–49). The "better days" never arrived for the Genesis commentary. In mid-1906 Lagrange learned "that [the teaching that] Moses was the author of the first five books [of the Bible] had been ordained as normative teaching in a four-part decree dated June 27, 1906, of the [Pontifical] Biblical Commission" (Gannon, 349). In 1907 Pius X forbade publication of Lagrange's Genesis commentary. As for his intended work on the book of Judges, his Dominican superior concluded that any work he did on the Old Testament "would be little appreciated or would be judged badly. And my advice is that you abstain from such a work" (ibid.). Once again concern for the ignorant trumped scholarship.

Lagrange wrote at the wrong time. One of the greatest church historians, Louis Duchesne (1843–1922), whom Lagrange knew, had, in a small but caustic essay, proved that, contrary to hoary tradition, the French diocese of Sens had not been founded by one of the seventy-two disciples sent out by Jesus (Luke 10:1-24). This infuriated the archbishop of that city, who duly complained about Duchesne to the appropriate authorities. Other historical scholars questioned "the authenticity of venerable relics [such as] the Holy Shroud of Turin and the Holy House of Loreto" (Montagnes, 60). The Holy House is supposedly Mary's home in Nazareth. When the Muslims recaptured the town from the Crusaders in 1291, angels carried the house to Tersato Fiume, near the Balkans. When the locals did not venerate it sufficiently, the angels then transferred it to Recanti in

Italy. Again the reverence was insufficient, so in 1295 the angels moved the house to a local hill. The situation did not improve there either, and so the angels moved it for the fourth and last time to Loreto at a location close to a major road. It says much about the tenor of the time that the critics of geniuses like Lagrange and Duchesne would strenuously defend the authenticity of superstitious drivel like this.

Lagrange persisted and attended ecumenical religious conferences. He "perceived how much the search for new solutions to the biblical crisis demanded a climate of freedom" (ibid., 63), which he would never get. "None of Father Lagrange's articles were to be published without the endorsement of designated censors" who were instructed to "set aside any article that might not comply with the traditional interpretation and that *might be considered* an innovation" (ibid., 65–66; emphasis added).

Bad as things were, they got worse. The always-cynical Duchesne wrote to Lagrange that the Vatican secretary of state, Monsignor Merry del Val, "would rather believe that Jonah swallowed the whale rather than to let anyone to doubt the contrary" (ibid., 81). By 1904 traditionalist critics had mounted a large-scale assault on any form of criticism rather than literalism, and the secretary general of the Jesuits, a Spaniard named Luis Martin, actually organized attacks on Lagrange. When a Jesuit named Delatte assailed Lagrange, his superiors did not permit him to reply, even though Delatte's major contribution to biblical studies was defending the historicity of Lot's wife being turned into a pillar of salt (ibid., 84–85).

When Pius X forbade publication of Lagrange's work on Genesis in 1907, the Roman reprimand noted that the book "was inspired by criteria opposed to those upheld by the [Pontifical] Biblical Commission." The obedient Lagrange replied, "Most Holy Father, prostrate at the feet of Your Holiness, I accept, with the most filial obedience, your decision . . ." (ibid., 92).

Lagrange had made his decision. To stay in the church and to remain a Dominican meant that he had to be obedient, even to a decree that he thought was not just wrong but harmful to the church since it meant that biblical exegesis could never achieve the intellectual status that it warranted. Lagrange produced work on the New Testament that proved both scholarly and acceptable to the authorities, and he worked as best he could to promote modern biblical studies and to defend the École Biblique against critics who thought its program of studies smacked of modernism. As late as 1934 he observed, "It is very difficult nowadays, to publish anything on the Old Testament. The exegetes still have as little liberty [as in 1907]" (ibid., 171). Only late in his life did he get the public accolades that his decades of work deserved.

Bernard Montagnes, OP, his biographer and fellow Dominican, blasts the ignorance prevailing in Rome but says that "the worst was that the Roman Congregations were roused to action by anonymous informers. Those denounced were powerless to defend themselves against their accusers" (95). Shades of the Cathars. In a preface to Montagnes's biography, another Dominican, scholar and former superior general of the order Timothy Radcliffe, says, "Driven by a passion for truth and a great love of the Bible and of the church, Father Lagrange wanted to open the book of scriptures to Catholics. . . . He had to pay the price for it, that of suffering and renunciation until the end of his life" (xiii). Radcliffe accepts what Lagrange had always insisted, that he did his work not to attack the church but because he loved it.

But Lagrange was never denounced as a modernist, an epithet routinely bestowed on Loisy.

Alfred Loisy (1857–1940)

Alfred Loisy was a contemporary of Lagrange and, like him, a priest. He did not learn much in seminary; O'Connell puts it bluntly: "The seminaries allowed and indeed fostered an intellectual program that was little short of scandalous. . . . The sciences, mathematical and physical, were simply ignored" (13). Astonishingly, Loisy did not even learn about Thomas Aquinas there, but he did once hear a sermon by a famous scholar who claimed that in the Apocalypse, its author, Saint John the apostle, predicted the First Vatican Council of 1869–70. For further education, Loisy studied in Paris at the Institut Catholique and became an instructor there. In 1884 he met Louis Duchesne, who identified himself as a "critical" historian, "applying the techniques of modern scholarship to the data of Christian origins," such as asking, "Had [a document] in fact been written by the authors to whom it was attributed, and did it in fact issue from the era it purported to represent? Such procedures, . . . commonplace now, were relatively new in 1875" (ibid., 59) and, as Duchesne learned, often unwelcome. That scholar marched his way through early church history but did not work on the New Testament. Duchesne's critics suspected that he knew the Vatican would move against him if he applied his devastating historical methods to the New Testament.

Loisy adopted Duchesne's method, and he did apply it to the New Testament. He knew about the advances in biblical studies being made by

German Protestant scholars, some of whom outraged their coreligionists as well as Catholics, but Loisy valued much of the work being done by the greatest of these scholars, Adolf von Harnack (1851–1930), whose personal bibliography would eventually exceed 1,300 items, a virtual library. Loisy feared that by standing still in biblical studies and reading the Bible through neoscholastic lenses, the Catholic Church would fall behind intellectually and might well lose educated believers. He set out to change things, apparently not realizing how few Catholic believers and leaders wanted things to change. (Recall that Lagrange was warned not to write anything that might be *considered* an innovation.) The censors did not consider Loisy's work innovative; they *knew* it was, and he never denied it.

Loisy's commitment to scholarship made him willing to use non-Catholic scholarship, particularly that of German Protestants, starting with a critical edition of the New Testament done by Alexander von Tischendorff (1814–74), whose Greek text made Loisy aware of the contradictions in the gospels (such as the two versions of the Lord's Prayer in Matthew and Luke), leading him to the ominous conclusion that "one cannot treat as rigorously historical texts that are not historical" (O'Connell, 63). He began to realize that although the gospels contain much historical material, they were not primarily biographical in nature. He drew the inevitable conclusion that things such as Christ's miracles were not historical events in the sense that they could be verified historically. He did not deny that they had occurred; he only asserted that they could not be proven to have occurred. He realized the troublesome nature of this insight, and, when appointed to the Institut Catholique in 1890, he even professed that he would interpret the Scriptures only as the church Fathers had. "He proceeded with great circumspection. He never made a statement . . . without protesting his unswerving loyalty to the teaching authority of the church" (ibid., 126).

But he could not maintain this fiction forever. In 1892 he gave a lecture that included this sentence: "The church can of course promulgate a definitive statement about the origins of the Pentateuch; but at the present time one cannot find *a single Catholic theologian genuinely informed about this subject*" (ibid., 128; emphasis added). Loisy did not consider many of the bishops to be "genuinely informed" either, and by 1893 he had to give up his teaching position at the Institut.

In November of the same year Leo XIII published *Providentissimus Deus*, which "permitted . . . no one to interpret Holy Scripture against . . . the unanimous consent of the Fathers" and which warned against "the thirst for novelty and unrestrained freedom of thought" (14, 15).

Loisy was not the only target; as O'Connell nicely puts it, "Lagrange and his associates in Jerusalem determined to keep their heads firmly down" (135). Less than a month later, the cardinal archbishop of Paris closed down a journal that Loisy had been editing.

Yet he did not despair. He truly believed that if the Vatican and even the neoscholastics could see the benefits of the new exegesis, they would appreciate it, not just for its intellectual content but also as a way of responding to that powerful new movement in theology, liberal Protestant scriptural interpretation. One wonders if he realized that his opponents simply did not consider this new movement a threat because they presumed that anything coming from Protestant intellectual circles could have no consequence for Catholics.

Loisy valued Catholic theology. He "insisted [that] Catholic doctrine had once been an adequate expression of religious truth and could change in order to be so again" (Hill, "The Politics of Loisy's Modernist Theology," 171). But first the theologians had to understand that doctrines developed historically, as John Henry Newman had argued. Loisy set out to prove his point by taking on the great Harnack, who had just written a book claiming that Christianity had been "Hellenized" with the importation of Greek thought and that Hellenized dogmas corrupted the primitive faith. This contrasted with the traditional Catholic attitude that the New Testament contained the basics of dogmas formulated later—for example, the seven sacraments, even though the word "sacrament" does not appear in the Bible. "For Loisy the church and its doctrines are the means whereby the gospel perpetuates itself and speaks to every age. He also saw doctrines as relative to every age and replaceable by later formulations" (Daly, "Theology and Philosophical Modernism," 106). Loisy proved the necessity of an organized church for the preservation of Christianity and attacked the notion of the Bible versus the church. He believed he could refute Harnack, but only by using modern exegetical methods.

He indeed used those methods, and the result was *The Gospel and the Church*, published in 1902. It proved an effective response to Harnack, who sent Loisy a congratulatory note (even though he always claimed that he did not understand why Loisy had attacked him). Writing against Harnack required Loisy to use the best modern arguments, and he did. Here are some of them:

- "It must be admitted that it is often difficult to distinguish between the personal religion of Jesus and the way in which His disciples have understood it, between the thought of the Master and the interpretations of apostolic tradition" (*Gospel and Church*, 14). Jesus did not enunciate current Catholic beliefs; furthermore, what he taught and how his disciples interpreted his teaching could have differed. This could be understood as development, but for his critics the notion that Jesus himself did not teach the basic dogmas put Loisy in the same camp with the Protestant Harnack.

- "The historian will find that the essence of Christianity has been more or less preserved in the different Christian communions" (ibid., 18). Note the respectful reference to other "communions."

- "The gospels are not strictly historical documents" (ibid., 23). This challenged traditional Catholic teaching.

- "Viewed as history, the point of view of the Gospel of John is incompatible with that of the other Gospels" (ibid., 31). But how could John be incompatible with Matthew if they were both members of the Twelve Apostles?

- "It seems inconceivable that Jesus should have preached at Jerusalem, declaring Himself the Messiah, on several occasions, during several years, without being arrested" (ibid., 32). That is, a gospel cannot be historically true if it does not make sense historically.

Loisy succeeded brilliantly in responding to Harnack, and a number of Catholic scholars thanked him for that. But Catholic authorities loathed the book because of its emphasis upon historical change, especially the assertion that Jesus did not personally teach everything the contemporary church believed and that his disciples may have interpreted his teachings rather than passing them along intact. The devaluation of the historical value of John's gospel went against the traditional belief that its author was one of the Twelve, and the blunt use of historical method (why was Jesus not arrested sooner?) showed that Loisy preferred modern exegetical methods over patristic and scholastic exegesis. Following the lead of the cardinal of Paris, several French bishops banned the book in their dioceses and warned both clergy and laity not to read it. Loisy tried to defend himself, but on December 16, 1903, the Holy Office placed that and four of his other works on the Index of Forbidden Books, where he joined Luther, Calvin, and a host of other threats to the faith.

By that time Pius X had become pope. While patriarch of Venice, he had commented that Loisy was one of the few theologians whose books never bored him. But the view is always different from the top. Pius now had to concern himself with the church at large. Added to this, he had a deep-seated fear of almost anything modern, and Loisy soon realized that the Vatican would not be receptive to his efforts to get his books off the Index or to update Catholic exegesis. But he had a strong commitment to his goals and to the discipline of history. Still a priest, he continued with his work, and his publications came pouring forth.

We will encounter him again when the day of reckoning for him and other prominent modernists arrived.

Before moving on to Maurice Blondel and George Tyrrell, it is worth comparing Lagrange, who accepted papal authority and did not publish his great work on Genesis, with Loisy, who published his works and was eventually excommunicated for doing so. Moderns almost instinctively side with the latter, who stood up for free speech. But we must remember the thought world in which Lagrange lived. He belonged to a religious order of priests for whom obedience to superiors was almost absolute. Ignatius Loyola, founder of the very order that attacked Lagrange so vehemently, had told his fellow Jesuits, "We should always be disposed to believe that that which appears white is really black, if the hierarchy of the Church so decides." Lagrange made the choice that seemed natural— and difficult—for him, and his scholarly work paid the price. In a study of the two exegetes, Nadia Lahutsky observes, "By today's standards Loisy's critical work sounds eerily contemporary and Lagrange's quaint and traditional" (cited by Talar, 193). One could say that Loisy was the better scholar and Lagrange the better Catholic, but Loisy's campaign for modern scholarship, gradually adopted by the church after his death, did result in better Catholic exegesis and a firmer grounding of theology in Scripture, the very goals for which he strove. It is best to respect both men for the individuals they were. (Note: they met only twice and never after 1895, and each had respect for the other's scholarship, if not for his ecclesiastical stance.)

Maurice Blondel (1861–1949)

Maurice Blondel was a French philosopher who grew up in a strongly Catholic family and had a childhood desire to be a priest. When deciding upon a career as a philosopher, "Although he feared its possible dangers to his faith, Blondel was drawn to this modern expansive world and wanted to understand it on its own" (Kaminski, 119). Somewhat like Loisy, Blondel had "a deep desire to bring the truth to unbelievers, to dispel their errors by speaking their own language, [and] 'to prove that

Catholic thought is not sterile'" (ibid., 135). Like Loisy, he would fail because Rome did not wish to engage the modern world.

Like most philosophers, Blondel wrote difficult, highly technical prose, and this is not the place to discuss his philosophical theories in general. Instead, since we are focusing on Catholic modernism, we will examine how his thought related to that phenomenon.

For Blondel, the problem was neoscholasticism's being the form that Catholic doctrine took. The neoscholastics believed that their doctrinal formulations were ahistorical and literally beyond time. A common phrase for this view was Thomism's designation as the *philosphia perennis*, or "perennial philosophy," which transcended the ages because of its correctness and usefulness for Catholic doctrine. Although moderns would point out that scholasticism had emerged only in the twelfth century, that authors such as Augustine had never used it, and that its medieval milieu impacted it, no neoscholastic of the modernist era seems to have been troubled by that. What made it perennial was that it could be grasped rationally by anyone, so that any thinking person, open to the truth, would recognize the truth of Catholic teachings, regardless of the era in which that person lived.

But neoscholasticism also played a defensive role. Nineteenth-century philosophy and historiography and the newly rising social sciences like sociology and especially psychology stressed that the process of learning involves more than rational apprehension of an idea, syllogism, or dogmatic statement. It also involves the one who is learning, and that person's individuality plays a great role in what she or he learns. This, of course, implied a degree, no matter how small, of subjectivity, and this was anathema to the neoscholastics and their hierarchical supporters. Catholic doctrine was formulated rationally and could be apprehended by any rational person. Period.

Blondel found himself in a difficult position. A good Catholic, he truly believed that his church was going in the wrong direction by denying the importance of any new learning. He optimistically believed that he could convince Catholic scholars and authorities of the validity of another approach.

Although Blondel used his terminology carefully, his Catholic critics accused him of immanentism, which they understood to mean that humans have psychological needs that include religious experiences. They claimed that Blondel taught that from those experiences doctrines eventually emerge, whereas for the neoscholastics doctrines can be apprehended from divine revelation, freely given by God. In this view, immanentism is heretical because it effectively denies divine revelation because that revelation emerges from human needs rather than from a supernatural being. Blondel did not mean that, but his neoscholastic critics interpreted his work that way.

Unlike his critics, Blondel did shy away from bringing personal faith into understanding doctrines. "Neo-scholastic reliance on miracle and fulfilled prophecy as proofs of divine presence" could not actually be considered proofs; for him miracles are such "only for those who are already prepared to recognize the divine action in the most unusual events" (Kaminsky, 103). Miracles do not give us faith; we recognize them because we have faith. As Gabriel Daly observes, "Rarely can a theological war have been declared so casually." For the traditionalist, miracles provided "the principal cognitive method for diagnosing presence of the transcendent in history" (*Transcendence*, 37).

Blondel's view was actually more biblical than that of his critics. He recognized that neoscholasticism presented a static God unrelated to history, which changes, but Blondel, perhaps unknowingly, focused on the biblical deity, particularly that of the Old Testament, who always involved himself in this very changeable world. Blondel did not accept the cruder biblical accounts of divine activity, but he did stress God's involvement with fallible humans and their environment rather than portray a biblical deity preparing dogmatic statements for rational believers to accept.

Blondel wrote that humans have an intrinsic need for the divine. Contra Friedrich Nietzsche and other contemporaries who thought humans must eschew God to be truly human, Blondel argued that the human cannot be fulfilled without interaction with the divine. As Kaminsky puts it, "Only in the action of the finite subject does 'a principle of transcendent truth become immanent'" (117, quoting Blondel), a principle that informed Blondel's own spiritual life. He argued that in the choices we make and the desires we have, "we discover an incompleteness, a natural inachievability that cannot be fulfilled without going beyond ourselves" (ibid., 120). For Blondel, "nothing can enter into a man which does not emerge from him and correspond in some way to a developmental need" (Daly, *Transcendence*, 38). Revelation involves human seeking and not just the presentation of truths to our minds. Somehow we sense the absence of God and thus long for it with our total being. "Blondel's method shows that we arrive at questions of faith and salvation within human existence *in all its concrete, social, political, and cultural reality*" (ibid., 124; emphasis added).

This immanence is transcendent but not supernatural, an important distinction. Immanence can be open to the natural as well as to the supernatural, "which is inaccessible to man until made the subject of God's free gift" (ibid., 39). This is how and why we can understand doctrinal propositions about the divine, an understanding that involves far more than simple rational apprehension and acceptance. Humans have an intrinsic need for the transcendent and the supernatural, even if they do not recognize it as such—something Blondel knew his neoscholastic critics would never do.

This devout Catholic philosopher argued that revelation is far more complex than the neoscholastics taught. Faith involves movement and even mystery. It cannot be reduced to propositions, a method that too often resulted in a defensive attitude and the denunciation of those who did not accept those propositions.

Blondel rejected radical immanence, the notion that all knowledge is subjective and that doctrines are responses to the human psychological need for some more-than-human element. With the neoscholastics, he accepted the need for doctrinal formulations and the ability of the human intellect to understand them, but he could not do so in an absolutist manner. Some people, including lifelong Catholics who were illiterate or lived in mission countries, never heard of doctrinal formulations or of Thomas Aquinas, but, as humans, they still had a sense of incompleteness and a need for the divine. As a Catholic, Blondel believed that his "method of immanence showed the meeting point of philosophy and theology in the condition and activity of the concrete human person" (Kaminski, 138).

He rejected not neoscholasticism but rather the view that it was the only way to knowledge of the divine. Like Lagrange and Loisy, he believed that if the church refused to accept modern progress in the various disciplines, it would fall behind intellectually. He never really gauged how threatening Rome saw almost anything modern or how any rejection of scholasticism would call his orthodoxy into question.

George Tyrrell (1861–1909)

George Tyrrell was born to a once socially prominent but then impoverished Anglo-Irish Protestant family in Dublin. A fine student, he "learned quickly, was bored easily, and chronic idleness was the natural consequence. Formal study and memorization were dead bones to him. He despised routine" (O'Connell, 106). At age eighteen he left Ireland and the Church of Ireland forever. Arriving in London, he went to a Jesuit church for information about Roman Catholicism and was baptized a Catholic a month later. He soon entered the Jesuits. He eventually studied scholasticism, going directly to Thomas Aquinas. Like Blondel, he appreciated scholasticism but realized that it could not be transferred wholesale into the modern world.

His contacts with Baron Friedrich von Hügel (see below) caused him to rethink some of his attitudes toward philosophy. By 1897 he could write, "When [the church] condemns certain formulae and verbal expressions, she takes them only in the sense they bear in the philosophy which she has adopted and takes no account of the sense other philosophies may attach to them" (ibid., 174). Blondel would have agreed. As long as ecclesiastical authorities viewed every philosophical statement only through scholastic eyes, how could they ever appreciate other approaches to doctrinal formulations? Like most Anglophone Catholics, Tyrrell admired Newman and saw his notion of doctrinal development as a possible way to open up Catholic thinking to new approaches by demonstrating that teaching had developed over the centuries.

But Tyrrell soon got into difficulties. He published an article entitled "A Perverted Devotion" that criticized neoscholastic teaching on damnation as "pert rationalism" that lacked an awareness that "we are in the region of faith and mystery" (ibid., 188). Like the late medieval mystics, he criticized the scholastics for taking the mystery out of the divine mysteries. But he had hit an English nerve.

English Catholics lived in a predominantly Protestant democracy, unlike the Jesuit superior general Luis Martin, who came from 99 percent Catholic Spain, or the Roman Jesuits, who lived in 99 percent Catholic Italy. The English Jesuits were ipso facto open to non-Catholic influences, and they quickly recognized that, like Newman, many English Catholics had reservations about "Italianate" devotions and, as democrats, did not feel comfortable with the increasing absolutism of Rome. Tyrrell soon found himself welcome in prominent English Catholic circles because educated aristocratic believers appreciated his openness, intelligence, and, no small point, the quality of his writing. Like him, they did not feel comfortable with Rome's constant fears of scientific developments. Tyrrell feared that "institutional Catholicism . . . had become irrelevant to men and women of the twentieth century, because it refused to come to terms with findings of modern science. . . . [By insisting on neoscholasticism,] the church committed itself to an anachronistic intellectualism which put it at odds [with science since Copernicus]" (ibid., 277).

For Tyrrell change is a constant, and thus doctrinal formulations that worked for one generation may not necessarily work for another; that is, he had pastoral as well as intellectual concerns. "The church's obsessive insistence on a static rather than a dynamic view of life, and so of religion itself, had led it into a blind alley where thoughtful persons will no longer follow" (ibid., 278). He feared for his church. One could easily reply that the church consisted of many poorly educated and even illiterate people who did not share the concerns of educated Englishmen, but, as Tyrrell and so many other "heretics" pointed out, educated people move societies. In the Middle Ages church officials routinely worked with monarchs and nobles, knowing that to reach the leaders was to reach the people. Tyrrell realized that the new leaders of society were educated people who knew that science had discovered and described a world that the medieval scholastics could never have imagined. Such people simply would not look backward and would not follow those who did. Tyrell found acceptance among learned believers, and even the primate of England, Herbert Cardinal Vaughan (1892–1903), saw nothing amiss with Tyrrell's writings.

Significantly, the English Jesuits supported Tyrrell. As a group, they did not agree with all that he said, and many urged caution, yet they did not want him sacrificed to appease Rome. But they belonged to a religious order with a strict line of obedience, and their Spanish superior general removed the English provincial who supported Tyrrell. One prominent English Jesuit, Herbert Thurston, complained to Martin that the Roman censors did not read English well enough to appreciate "Tyrrell's ironical and humorous style" and further argued that "[although] I do not wish to condemn the old Hell Fire sermons . . . [which] are good even now for the crowds who flock to [parish] missions . . . my experience here is that in England they do far more harm than good" (Schultenover, 94–96). The English Jesuits also stressed that Tyrrell's popularity with the educated classes boded well for the future of Catholicism in England. But none of that mattered to Luis Martin. In a letter about Tyrrell's article on hell, Martin actually used the phrase "offensive to pious ears" as if it were the Middle Ages.

In 1905, as his writings headed toward the Index, Tyrrell decided to leave the Society of Jesus. He liked being in the English province, but he knew that the superior general would get his own way and that good Englishmen in the Society would pay a price for trying to protect him.

Tyrrell recognized that the crucial issue in his disagreements with the official orthodoxy was revelation. Although he did not define revelation as the person of Christ rather than dogmatic statements (such an understanding would not emerge until the Second Vatican Council), he was moving toward the personal in revelation. For him faith could not be just the neoscholastic intellectual assent to provable dogmatic statements, because those were always encased in theological formulation. As Daly puts it, "Tyrrell dug [a ditch] between revelation and theology" (*Transcendence*, 143). Like Blondel he linked transcendence with immanence but was never able to reconcile the two. He feared absolute immanence, the notion that religion emerges from human psychological needs, but he finally accepted that "a transcendent being is known, or experienced, only to the extent that that being operates immanently in the human spirit" (ibid., 157).

Of one thing he was certain: the neoscholastics simply misunderstood the process of revelation. For Tyrrell, "prophetic language falls flat unless it encounters in the hearer 'a spirit to answer the Spirit,'" a far cry from the neoscholastic emphasis on Jesus' fulfillment of prophecies as factual proof of his divinity. Tyrell contemptuously defined this as "the cold repetition of inspired utterance by uninspired lips" (ibid., 158–59). He accepted the historical approach to the Bible as a necessary way of understanding in context what the ancients meant when they prophesied and how other ancient people, first Jews and then Christians, responded when they read or heard those words.

Tyrrell always considered himself a good Catholic. He loathed liberal Protestantism and believed that the Catholic Church descended faithfully from the primitive church of the New Testament. For him the problem was not the church but what the papacy had made of it since Vatican I, when the popes "seized power," a view he hid less and less. A man that intelligent surely knew what his attitudes and writings would just as surely bring down on him.

Circa 1905, in the midst of all this turmoil, he showed the first symptoms of Bright's disease (as nephritis was called then), a kidney disease that caused, inter alia, severe back pain, frequent vomiting, and elevated blood pressure. This disease would take his life in 1909.

* * *

So far we have discussed scholars accused by the papacy of being modernists, but was there a modernist movement? Our next subject tried to create one.

Baron Friedrich von Hügel (1852–1925)

"From Rome to Paris to London-town: the multilingual and peripatetic Friedrich von Hügel would provide, whether by land or by sea, whatever fragmentary unity or coherence possessed by the movement to be labeled Catholic Modernism" (O'Connell, 42).

Von Hügel (1852–1925) is something of a controversial figure for historians. He had an Austrian father and a Scottish mother. He lived mostly in England but traveled a great deal on the continent. "He became the 'nerve' center of the fledgling Modernist movement. He read widely, traveled extensively, and corresponded with a large number of persons, relaying to them what he had learned on his travels, discussing with them the latest books, encouraging their intellectual pursuits, and introducing them to each other" (Jodock, 22). He could also use his noble rank to get access to Vatican officials, who would not think of talking with Loisy.

Like the other figures under discussion, Von Hügel considered himself to be a loyal Catholic who wanted his church to face up to the challenges of the modern world and to utilize current scholarship. He could read several languages and was remarkably well informed about what writers as diverse as Loisy and Blondel were doing. When he read something he deemed important, he would alert prominent scholars and friends; often he would get copies of new books to give to others. O'Connell characterizes him this way: "Von Hügel was, in short, a well-fixed private layman, free to indulge his interests in a private manner and also free to encourage, cajole, and admonish others less advantageously positioned than himself." He also has a strong observation about the baron's status after the Vatican crackdown of 1907: "He had risked nothing professionally in the scholarly wars, because he had no profession to risk" (51).

O'Connell makes a good point. Although Von Hügel wrote some favorable reviews of works by suspect authors along with an occasional article, his only major work at the time was his 1906 two-volume *The Mystical Element of Religion as Studied in Saint Catharine of Genoa and Her Friends*, hardly the type of work to exercise the Roman censors. On the other hand, he alone kept many supposed modernists in touch. As a wealthy, titled layman, he could go where he wished without needing the permission of a bishop or a religious superior, and he used that freedom to spread new ideas and to introduce authors to one another. Also, he was often there when authors found themselves in difficulty.

The baron faced problems. "Von Hügel tried to create cohesion within a group that resisted organization, and he was unable to avoid some of the difficulties of mobilizing a movement of intellectuals" (ibid.). (Modern deans refer to this as "herding cats.") It may well be that Von Hügel's travels and contacts helped to convince Rome that there actually was a movement.

Although these were the most important figures, there were a number of other European modernists, including some in Italy and Germany, and several of the titles in the bibliography, especially O'Connell's, treat them well. We must now go on to the Vatican's response.

Pascendi

One of the most important books on Catholic modernism is *The Politics of Heresy: The Modernist Crisis in Roman Catholicism* (1986) by Lester Kurtz, a sociologist who delineated clearly how the Vatican organized its defense against the perceived enemy. Kurtz's approach also explains a perennial problem for those who have not deeply studied Catholic modernism. "What is puzzling at first glance is why so much concern arose on the part of a powerful institution over the work of a few somewhat isolated scholars and their sympathizers" (10). Here is his answer: "Group solidarity is seldom strengthened by anything so much as the existence of a common enemy, and the heretic, as a 'deviant insider,' is close at hand. The identification of heretics shores up the ranks, enables institutional elites to make demands of their subordinates, and reinforces systems of dominance. . . . Moreover, the labeling and suppression of heresy and heretics serve as rituals for institutional elites, facilitating their dominance within the institution" (ibid., 1, 3). And that is exactly what happened. By creating "modernism" as a threat, the Vatican could extend its authority over the church at large, an authority that would survive after the heresy had been eliminated. "Furthermore, ecclesiastical elites recognized and capitalized on the possibility of fortifying their own position by *constructing a caricature* of the modernists' position through weaving their opponents' views into a coherent whole and condemning modernism as a heresy" (ibid., 55; emphasis added).

Many of those who opposed modernism called themselves "integralists"; that is, for them Catholic teaching is a grand whole, and no one teaching can be separated from that whole. "In the minds of such 'integralist' Catholics as Monsignor Umberto Benigni [see below], the church's enemies merge into a unified whole that ran the gamut from anticlericalism to liberalism, antipapism, radicalism, feminism, republicanism, immanentism, interconfessionalism [ecumenism], and intellectual modernism" (ibid., 9). The "heresy" would provide Pius X and his associates with an excuse to repudiate much of the modern Western world.

Those attacking the modernists had personal goals as well as theological and institutional ones. "The [Roman] Jesuits were opposed to modernist ideas not only from an intellectual and religious point of view but also because their privileged position in the ecclesiastical hierarchy was threatened by any group with rising popularity and an ability to operate in the sphere of doctrinal interpretation" (ibid., 16). For Kurtz, people in places of power will strike out at those who threaten that power but will never admit that, even—or perhaps especially—to themselves.

Pius fired his first shot across the modernists' bow with his syllabus *Lamentabili* of July 3, 1907. Its opening sentence makes it clear what the pope really found to be lamentable: "Our age, casting aside all restraint in its search for the ultimate causes of things, frequently pursues novelties. . ." His first concern is with "our age," not the specific teachings of those who "go beyond the limits determined by the Fathers and the Church herself" and do so "in the name of higher knowledge and historical research." The pope then lists errors to be condemned, some of which went well beyond Catholic theology. Error 5 reads: "Since the deposit of Faith contains only revealed truths, the Church has no right to pass judgment of the assertions of human sciences." Were modern scientists to submit their findings to church approval?

The document is skillfully written, including as errors things that no Catholic scholar had ever said as well as others hazily defined and even some proposed by scholars who were not Catholic.

Error 13 manifests a deliberate vagueness: "The Evangelists themselves, as well as the Christians of the second and third centuries, artificially arranged the evangelical parables." The "error" is presented as a combination of two clear statements that its authors knew could not be reconciled by modern scholars. Why not? Because the first-century evangelists did arrange the parables, but second- and third-century Christians did not do so but rather accepted the gospel arrangements as handed down from the first century. If a scholar agreed that this statement was erroneous, he was saying that the evangelists did not arrange the parables; if not, he was saying that second- and third-century Christians did arrange the parables. There was no way to agree or disagree fully with error 13.

Error 11, by contrast, is straightforward in its rejection of a major tenet of modern exegesis: "Divine inspiration does not extend to all of Sacred Scripture so that it renders its parts, each and every one, free from every error." The phrase "every error" could include literal or historical ones, thus protecting the historical reality of the six-day creation, the Garden of Eden, the crossing of the Red Sea, and the travails of Jonah.

No scholar ever actually said what is in error 15: "Until the time of the canon was defined and constituted, the Gospels were increased by additions and corrections." The canon was not defined for the Greek fathers until the mid-fourth century and for the Latins until the early fifth century. No scholar in Pius X's day thought additions were made to the gospel texts so late.

Error 35 allowed for no intellectual development in Jesus: "Christ did not always possess the consciousness of His Messianic dignity." So he possessed divine consciousness even as an infant in the manger at Bethlehem? For those who believe in Jesus' humanity and divinity, the development of Christ's consciousness of his divine nature presents a perennial theological problem, and apodictic statements cannot solve it.

Lamentabili rejects modern historical scholarship, condemning as error 36 that "the Resurrection of the Savior is not properly a fact of the historical order." That means that the resurrection is of the historical order even though it cannot be proven historically.

This syllabus basically listed errors, but the encyclical *Pascendi*, dated September 8, 1907, would provide a far-ranging condemnation not just of errors but of the heresy behind it, modernism. Written to the world's bishops, the encyclical would also provide a strategy to eliminate this contagion and prevent it from ever arising again. It begins with the same themes as *Lamentabili*, novelty and "the increase in the number of the enemies of the Cross of Christ" in the modern era (1). Pius wanted nothing modern and nothing new.

Section 4 identifies the heretics as "'Modernists, as they are commonly and rightly called'. . . when in fact the term was new" (O'Connell, 342). As many Catholic scholars have pointed out, Pius gave this name to them at the same time he chose "to bring their teachings together here in one group, and to point out their interconnection" (*Pascendi* 4); that is, he would give the various scholars and their teachings a unity they did not previously have.

He started with philosophy and strongly criticized immanence. He then moved to the question of doctrinal formulae, which he considered immutable in their scholastic form. The modernists thought that if the belief remained the same, the formula could change—and indeed had done so—over the years. Pius rejected this as novelty, the second of nine times he would use that criticism. Borrowing a medieval scholastic idea, that philosophy is the "handmaiden" (*ancilla*) of theology, Pius reminded philosophers of their discipline's duty "not to command but to serve," thus denying philosophy status as an independent discipline. But the modernists strove "by profane novelties to cross the boundaries fixed by the Fathers" in philosophy (17).

The modernist treatment of the biblical books reflected the looseness of the modern world. "For we are living in an age when the sense of liberty has reached its highest development. In the civil order the public conscience has introduced popular government" (23). "Formerly it was possible to subordinate the temporal to the spiritual," but now "the state must be separated from the church" (24). Note that Pius's views on the state match those of the medieval scholastics. Also, one can wonder what Catholics in Britain and America thought of hearing their revered form of government being denounced. But Pius did not stop there. For him, even in the modern world it was not wrong for the church "to condemn and proscribe a work without the knowledge of the author, without hearing his explanations, without discussion" (25). Like the Cathars, theologians would be condemned without even knowing who accused them or what the accusation was.

Almost as bad, the modernists had introduced "that *most pernicious doctrine* which would make of the laity a factor in the progress of the Church" (27; italics added), effectively saying, "Who cares what more than 99 percent of Catholics think?"

Almost certainly with Loisy—whose works Pius knew—in mind, he turned to scriptural studies, attacking modern historical methods and "that branch of criticism which they call textual," when they should be imitating the "Doctors [of the church], far superior to them in genius, in erudition, in sanctity" (34). It did not matter that few of the Doctors could read the Bible in the original languages and were thus incapable of doing textual criticism; they were the sanctified traditional teachers. Pius went on to give some more biblical examples, but then, by understanding their theories in a scholastic way that thus allowed them to be put into a system, the pope showed "that their [the modernists'] system does not consist in scattered and unconnected theories." As we noted above, Tyrell pointed out that the neo-Thomists evaluated all philosophy and theology by scholastic standards and categories. Scholastically, so to speak, modernist theories could be gathered together into "the synthesis of all heresies" (39).

Why did the modernists do this? "Curiosity and pride," the former leading to novelty and the latter to a "demand [for] a compromise between authority and liberty" (40). "The passion for novelty is always united in them with a hatred of scholasticism, and there is no surer sign that a man is tending toward modernism than when he begins to show his dislike for the scholastic method" (42). Criticizing scholasticism had become a sign of incipient heresy. As for liberty in discussing theology and doctrine, there are many who "have been so infected by breathing a poisoned atmosphere as to think, speak, and write with a degree of liberty ill becoming a Catholic" (43). Readers must have wondered what degree of liberty did not ill become a Catholic.

Pius had outlined the virus; now came the antidote. "We strictly ordain that scholastic philosophy be made the basis of the sacred sciences," and the other arts and sciences will wait upon it after the manner of handmaidens (46). This meant, for example, that textual critics must step back and let scholastic theologians, who may not have had any formal training in this discipline, decide what the biblical text actually says. An erroneous text would inevitably lead to erroneous exegesis, but that concern never surfaced.

Scholarly disciplines, even safe ones like scholastic theology, depend upon those who teach them, and so Pius set out to make sure no Catholic teacher ever slipped in any modernist ideas. "Anyone who in any way is found to be tainted with Modernism is to be excluded without compunction from [ecclesiastical] offices." Bishops should watch out for "those who show a love of novelty in history, archaeology, and biblical exegesis" (*Pascendi* 48). Gannon calls this simply "a witch hunt" (345).

But wrong ideas can also be spread by books, so "it is also the duty of the bishops to prevent writings of Modernists, or whatever savors of Modernism or promotes it, from being read when they have been published and to hinder publication when they have not" (50). Since any new idea could be labeled as "savoring" of modernism, the range of dangerous books was endless. But if it were too late to prevent or hinder publication, "we order that you do everything in your power to drive out of your dioceses . . . any pernicious books that may be in circulation there" (51). All dioceses should have censors, and the bishops should also monitor Catholic booksellers. But individual censors may not be enough, so "we decree . . . that in every diocese [there will be what] We are pleased to name the 'Council of Vigilance,' . . . [which] shall watch most carefully for every trace and sign of Modernism." Furthermore, the vigilantes "shall be bound to secrecy as to their deliberations and decisions" (55). Every diocese would have its own heresy-hunting committee.

Yet even these rigorous measures proved insufficient, and so in 1910 Pius X published an Oath against Modernism that all priests had to take until that requirement was abolished by Pope Paul VI in 1967. The Oath required priests to acknowledge that "miracles and prophecies are the surest signs of the divine origin of the Christian religion" and that the doctrines of the faith were "handed down to us from the apostles through the orthodox Fathers in exactly the same meaning"—that is, doctrine did not really develop. The priest also had to "submit and adhere with [his] whole heart to the condemnations, declarations, and prescripts contained in the encyclical *Pascendi* and in the decree *Lamentabili.*"

All the basics for repression were now in place: scholasticism meant orthodoxy and questioning it indicated incipient modernism; scholars did not have the authority to pursue their researches where they led them but had to make sure that their research did not contradict what had been taught by the Fathers and Doctors; episcopal supervision and diocesan vigilance councils were put in place; and all the ills of modernism were laid at the feet of the real enemy—the modern world, which promoted individual liberty, separation of church and state, freedom of religion, of the press, and of speech, and anything else that called into question papal authority and totalitarian methods of dealing with dissidents.

The Impact

"In Jerusalem, Marie-Joseph Lagrange, already under a cloud, maintained a prudent silence" (O'Connell, 350). He escaped condemnation. So did von Hügel. He agreed generally with the modernist writers, but he had not written much himself, and he had his noble status. He conducted himself carefully after 1907.

Blondel likewise avoided condemnation in spite of *Pascendi*'s condemnation of immanentism. He had disagreed, sometimes strongly, with Loisy, and his views did not echo those of the worst offenders. But he did not get off scot-free. In 1913 a journal he owned and sometimes edited, *Annales de philosphie chrétienne,* was forced by a French bishop to cease publication.

The Vatican told Loisy's local bishop to give him ten days to submit or face excommunication. Loisy had long before decided he owed more allegiance to scholarship than to the Catholic Church, and so he declined to submit and was formally excommunicated by the Holy Office on March 18, 1908. But by 1909 he had secured a position as professor of the history of religions "at the prestigious Collège de France . . .[and] became a colleague of giants like [Émile] Durkheim and [Henri] Bergson" (ibid., 370). He had a fruitful scholarly career until his death in 1940.

The increasingly ill Tyrrell went down fighting, writing two articles for the London *Times* that denounced *Pascendi*. His local bishop excommunicated him on October 22, 1907.

Modernism in any sense of a movement had ended. But Pius still remained worried and so took further steps.

Uncertain of even his own bishops, the pope entrusted Monsignor Umberto Benigni to be his personal watchdog of orthodoxy. Benigni worked initially from the Vatican secretariat of state, but his crude methods and extensive reach offended many Catholics outside of Rome. In Rome even the local Jesuits came to fear and resent him. Thus in 1909 Pius and Benigni created the Sodality of Pius V (pope from 1566 to 1572 and an inquisitor), "an organization designed to expose crypto-Modernists and to denounce them and their activities to the Roman authorities. . . . Grown out of the network of stringers Benigni had established to supply material for his [antimodernist] journalistic ventures, the society provided for all those who cared to label as modernists their bishops, parish priests, professors, local editors, or indeed anyone with whom they disagreed." One need hardly add that all the Sodality's activities were carried out in total secrecy. O'Connell sums it up simply: "No one was safe" (363).

The Sodality accused the cardinals of Vienna and Paris along with a Belgian cardinal and both Jesuit and Dominican theologians on charges ranging from laxity in ferreting out heresy to holding questionable views. If such men could be suspect, who would be safe? Eamon Duffy calls the purge "nothing less than a reign of terror," which he traced back to *Pascendi* and the "undiscriminating character of the condemnation [of the modernists], its unfocused severity and paranoia" (250). The character of the Sodality's work can best be seen when we consider who two of its victims were.

An obscure church historian at the seminary in Bergamo, northern Italy, was "duly frightened out of his wits" (ibid.) by a Vatican cardinal because he had assigned a "suspect" book to his students, something the Vatican had learned from an informer who had checked the records of a local bookstore. The book was a history of the early church by Duchesne, and the seminary professor was Angelo Giuseppe Roncalli. When he became Pope John XXIII (1958–63) and opened up the church to the modern world, he no doubt recalled what Pius's fear of the modern world had done to him.

Pius X died in 1914 and was succeeded by Benedict XV (1914–22), who, while going through his predecessor's papers, found his own name on a list of suspects. Benedict, knowing he was not a heretic, quickly realized how many other supposed heretics would also have been innocent. He soon abolished the Sodality. How amazing it is today to think of two future popes having been reported to the Vatican as suspected heretics.

The Sodality of Pius V had only about fifty members to conduct its witch hunt, and sometimes the results were almost ludicrous. For example, at this time there were about fifteen million American Catholics, yet the local vigilance committees could uncover only three modernists (all priests), that is, one modernist for every five million Catholics. To be sure, there had to be others who had modernist sympathies, but a one to five million ratio of heretic to general Catholic population indicates an absurd overreaction.

Many scholars have delineated the harm that *Pascendi* did to Catholic intellectual life, especially for theologians. But an American secular monsignor, Michael Gannon, has demonstrated the harm it did to the American priesthood. In a long essay, "Before and After Modernism: The Intellectual Isolation of the American Priest," he showed that after modernism, seminarians "were asked to memorize, in Latin, answers to questions and problems that had not been posed for hundreds of years. A combative atmosphere prevailed. Adversaries were seldom considered in their context; instead straw men were set up for swift kicking down. Students developed the weakest of all attitudes toward adversaries, that of contempt" (351–52). In 1938 a famous Jesuit scholar wrote about research, "You cannot be a possessor of truth [a Catholic] and a pursuer of truth [a researcher] at one and the same time" (ibid., 358); that is, who needs new knowledge when you already have the truth? Gannon sums up the attitude toward scholarship: "Original research became original sin" (350).

At the bottom of all this repression was a base motive: fear. Pius, his advisors, the dogmatic neoscholastics (as distinct from the many, many scholars who admired Thomas but did not think him the only theologian), the Roman censors, and those who thought like them realized that they could not control the modern world with its free speech, democratic societies, and scientific advancement. In impotent fury Pius and his associates struck out at those within their power, hoping to forestall the future within the church. They won the battle but lost the war.

In 1943 a very learned pope, Pius XII (1939–58), halted the antimodernist attack on modern exegesis with his encyclical *Divinae Afflante Spiritu* (The Divine Spirit Inspiring), a Magna Carta for Catholic biblical studies. He urged exegetes to recognize the various types of literature and literary forms in the Bible as well as to acknowledge that much of the Bible should not necessarily be taken as factual when doing so would present serious historical problems. The pope encouraged the use of textual criticism and urged scholars to work with the Hebrew and Greek texts. He naturally referred back to Leo XIII's encyclical on Scripture and urged exegetes to look at what the Fathers and Doctors had taught, but Pius XII made it clear that exegetes should use the new methods. He did, however, use mostly Old Testament examples to make his points;

many Catholics and other Christians still want the New Testament to be more historical than exegetes often think it is. But the highest office in the church had now opened the doors to the research Catholics had been fearful or forbidden to pursue. Exegetes jumped at the chance; within twenty years, Catholic biblical scholarship ranked with the best that Protestants and Jews could do.

To the modern believers, the most amazing element of the anti-modernist crusade is its utter, complete failure. In Western democracies, most Catholic scholars now teach in universities that guarantee them freedom of speech as part of the university's accreditation requirements, even in Catholic institutions. The faculty's relationship to the university is determined by legally binding documents, such as the institution's constitution, bylaws, and faculty contracts. Unless such documents give the local bishop or another church official a role in the university and specifically in the evaluation of faculty, church officials cannot discipline a faculty member for perceived heresy. A Catholic faculty member can convert to another church or tradition or have no religion at all without jeopardizing her or his status at the university. The university would, of course, have its own freedom to separate itself from the professor's views and even to repudiate them, but it would still have to support her or his right to express them. Furthermore, many Catholic scholars teach in public or non-Catholic private institutions where the Vatican's view of a professor's orthodoxy carries no weight at all.

Another significant factor is that the vast majority of professors at Catholic institutions, including theologians, are now lay people who are beyond ecclesiastical discipline. For example, if a priest belonging to a religious order wrote something that disturbed the Vatican, the university would stand up for his right to free academic expression, but his superior could remove him from the school. The local bishop could likewise discipline a priest in his diocese. But lay people can pursue their research as they wish without such concerns. Additionally, half of lay theologians are women, thus bringing in voices that had literally never been heard in theological matters before the late twentieth century. *Pascendi*, of course, had vilified modernism for daring to make the laity "a factor in the progress of the church" (27). Now, with incredible irony, most of the people interpreting modernism and the career of Pius X and teaching about them to students are those despised lay people.

But did this vast transition cause the harm that Pius feared? Not really.

As a lay Catholic faculty member at a Catholic institution, let me emphasize that the university and the faculty want to work with the local diocese, as both my university and I do. We do not see a clerical-lay conflict; on the contrary, we are colleagues and Catholics committed to the good of the church. There are sometimes differences in outlook—how could there not be?—but what unites us always overrides whatever issue may separate us.

But does not the immunity from hierarchical governance that lay faculty enjoy make them less respectful of ecclesiastical authority? Once again, not really.

Lay faculty must remember that they are members of the church and should act that way. They should move circumspectly when questioning or challenging church teachings, and any challenge should include a thorough, clear, and respectful presentation of the church's official position along with very clear and strong reasons why the scholar takes issue with it. But Catholic scholars must have academic freedom, and today most bishops respect that. They realize that Catholic colleges and universities have produced the best-educated generation of Catholics in history, and, appreciating that, they have no desire to interfere with Catholic higher education. Indeed, both hierarchy and university usually envision and work for a fruitful collaboration, based not upon fear of reprisal but upon mutual amity, trust, and a desire to further the work of the church.

* * *

Was Catholic modernism a heresy? Pius X provided a name, a definition, a set of beliefs, a philosophical method (immanentism), a method of exegesis, and a passion for novelty, all of which he said characterized the movement. Since he created it, Catholic modernism is what he said it was, a heresy, even if it existed only in his mind, in his encyclical, and among his supporters. Did it exist in reality? Scholars claim that it could have existed as an attitude but not as a movement, since Von Hügel's travels provided the only "movement" that may have existed among disparate scholars, some of whom never even met. There was no unified front, much less uniformity of teaching or method. But the name has stuck.

Protestant Modernism and Fundamentalism

Unlike Catholic modernism, Protestant modernism, a largely American phenomenon, was indeed a movement and was labeled as such by its practitioners, who identified themselves as modernists and who maintained contact with one another.

A leading figure in the movement, Shailer Mathews of the University of Chicago Divinity School, wrote in 1924, "In brief, the use of scientific, historical, and social methods in understanding and applying evangelical Christianity to the needs of living persons, is Modernism" (Larson, 34). Note the explicit value given to scientific, historical, and social methods; that is, Mathews favored learning from new disciplines, not just the physical sciences but also new methods in history and the social sciences. He wanted these methods applied to evangelical Christianity so that the faith would have relevance to "living persons," an oblique way of saying "those living in the modern world." And, of course, he proudly used the word "Modernism," with the capital *M*.

Why did Protestant modernism come into being? Like Catholic modernism, it had its roots in the Scientific Revolution and the Enlightenment, the twin challenges to the notion that human reason had been corrupted by Original Sin, could not function well on its own, and should rely upon religious authority. For Protestants, this would usually mean *Sola Scriptura*, or "Scripture Alone."

Sola Scriptura had served the Protestants well in their Reformation conflicts with Roman Catholics, whose emphasis on papal authority was always met with the question, "Can this particular teaching or doctrine be found clearly in Scripture?" But, as we have seen already, Scripture requires interpretation. For example, rigorist Calvinists strongly believed in Original Sin, a phrase not found in the Bible but part of Augustine of Hippo's interpretation of Genesis. They also believed in predestination, another notion not found explicitly in the Bible. But most Protestants understood the need for interpretation and concurred with the Reformers' approaches to the Scriptures.

As with the Catholics, the trouble arose with the advent of modern biblical scholarship, pioneered by German, mostly Lutheran, Protestants, and with the spreading acceptance of Darwinian evolution, both in the nineteenth century. These new movements challenged many aspects of the traditional understanding of the Bible, but the conflicts—and there were many—would revolve around the opening chapters of the book of Genesis.

The first book in the current order of biblical books, Genesis focuses primarily upon the three Hebrew patriarchs—Abraham, his son Isaac, and Isaac's son Jacob—and Jacob's twelve sons. But Genesis also includes eleven prefatory chapters that deal with the creation of the world and the progress of society down to Abraham. Chapter 1 recounts the six-day creation; chapter 2, the creation of Adam and Eve and God's placing of them in the Garden of Eden; chapter 3 deals with the Fall (eating the forbidden fruit) and the expulsion of the primal parents from the Garden; chapter 4, Cain and Abel; chapter 5, the patriarchs before the Flood (Methuselah et al.); chapters 6–9, Noah and the Great Flood; chapter 10, the descendants of Noah; and chapter 11, the tower of Babel and the ancestors of Abraham (here called "Abram"—God changes his name to Abraham at 17:5).

The ancient Israelites did not take these opening chapters very seriously. Adam is mentioned at only one other place in the entire Old Testament (1 Chr 1:1), while Eve appears literally nowhere else in the Old Testament. They do play a role in some Jewish apocryphal literature, that is, books that claimed to be by or about biblical figures but were not accepted into the canon of Scripture. (There are also Christian apocrypha, for example, the second-century *Protogospel of James*, which claims that Mary's parents were named Joachim and Anna.) The Jewish apocrypha changed the Eden story in a significant way by identifying the serpent in Eden as Satan, an interpretation wholly accepted by the Christians.

In the First Epistle to the Corinthians and in the Epistle to the Romans, the apostle Paul presented Jesus as the New Adam, come to redeem humanity from the sin of the first one. The pseudonymous author of 1 Timothy made a point of blaming Eve for the sin by saying that she listened to the serpent first because she was a lesser person, having been formed after Adam. The book of Revelation (Apocalypse) constantly uses Genesis imagery, referring to "the ancient Serpent, who is called the Devil and Satan" (12:9), and speaking of a "new heaven and a new earth" (21:1). By the mid-second century the Christian writer Justin the Martyr compared Mary to Eve, while the late second-century author Irenaeus of Lyons called Mary the New Eve.

But the person who put Genesis 1–11 in the center of Christian thought was Augustine of Hippo in the late fourth and early fifth centuries. He created the term Original Sin and gave it a powerful interpretation. When Adam and Eve sinned, they corrupted human nature and stained it with their guilt. All human beings are born with the guilt of Original Sin, a guilt that would send us all to damnation, were it not for Christian baptism. Those who receive it are freed from the guilt; those who do not receive it merit damnation unless God in his infinite mercy chooses to save a few of them.

Augustine went on: although the guilt may be gone, we have inherited a tendency to sin. We suffer from concupiscence, a burning desire for money, sex, and power. This desire is a consequence of Original Sin. Because of our weakened human nature, we cannot do anything good on our own, but only with the help of divine grace, which we can do nothing to earn. God freely gives or withholds the grace we need. We cannot fault him for withholding grace from some because God is by nature good and cannot do evil, so this withholding cannot be evil. The fact that God chooses in his infinite mercy to save anyone is a sign of his unfathomable goodness.

To whom will God give this grace? Before he created the world, he chose whom he would save. The Latin word for "choose" is *eligo*, and thus those whom God chose to save were the Elect. God predestined them from all eternity for salvation, and he equally determined whom he would not save. Even though churches taught that no one could be sure of salvation, over the centuries most people thought they were among the Elect. After all, why would anyone who did not expect to be saved accept a doctrine like predestination?

This appallingly brilliant theory, well worked out by Augustine in a number of books, was received by Western Christians and became Latin orthodoxy. Yet theory stands or falls on the historicity of Genesis 1–11. If there were no Adam or Eve or the serpent or the Garden, then there was no Original Sin as Augustine understood it.

We should bear this in mind when considering modern fundamentalists who insist upon the historicity of Eden. The issue for them is not just biblical accuracy but also where they will stand at the Last Judgment, with the sheep or with the goats (Matt 25:32). This attitude always applied to

Original Sin, but until the mid-nineteenth century no Christian challenged the historicity of Eden. Modern theories that do challenge it endanger the Elect status of many believers.

Much of the problem with Adam and Eve's historicity is that their story is part of Genesis 1–11, which treats of much more than the Garden of Eden. For example, if one were to accept the historicity of the dates and work backward from the birth of Jesus through all the biblical genealogies right back to the descendants of Noah (Gen 10) and the patriarchs before the Flood (Gen 5), it would be possible to determine or at least approximate the date of creation. The Anglican archbishop James Ussher (1581–1656) did just that and came up with a date of 4004 BC during the evening of October 23. This was a remarkable achievement for his day, and although the exact day did not catch on, the year did. Many nineteenth-century Protestant editions of the Bible listed 4004 BC in the margin next to Genesis 1:1. Later scholars, also accepting the biblical history, came up with some different dates but still maintained a brief existence for the world.

A literal reading of Genesis also meant that animal and plant species could not evolve because God created all of them, and he could obviously not have created them other than perfectly. For animals, there was also the point of special creation since in Genesis 2 God created them so that Adam would not be lonely. Like perfect creation, special creation made evolution impossible because evolution taught the gradual emergence of species rather than an immediate special creation.

Expanding upon Genesis 2 (Eden before the Fall), Christians believed that the lion lay down with the lamb. (This comes from a misreading of Isaiah 11:6, which says that a wolf would lie down with the lamb.) Following Augustine, Christians believed that animals did not devour one another until after Original Sin, which not only corrupted human nature but also destroyed the harmony of the natural world. For more than a millennium Christian exegetes agonized over how now-carnivorous animals could have eaten plants before Original Sin.

Acceptance of the historicity of Genesis 1–11 meant acceptance of all of these: short period of time for the earth's history, fixity of species, special creation, and harmony among animals. To this can be added accepting the existence of people who lived more than nine hundred years (Gen 5) as well as a worldwide flood that covered the whole world "until the highest mountains *everywhere* were submerged" (Gen 7:19; emphasis added). Since Mount Everest is more than twenty-nine thousand feet, that means that the Flood rose to five and a half miles above sea level.

If Genesis 1–11 is to be taken literally, then all of these individual elements must be factually true. Nineteenth-century science would attack that notion, but inadvertently; that is, scientists set out to do science and could not have foreknown what their researches into the age of the world and the evolution of life would do to a literal understanding of Genesis 1–11.

Before the nineteenth century, people believed that the large physical changes in the earth's surface were caused by catastrophes such as volcanic eruptions, earthquakes, and, historically, the biblical flood. By the early part of the century, scientists concluded the true explanation was uniformitarianism, that is, that the earth was constantly changed by forces such as the sun, water (both running water and rain), temperature changes, wind, and other ongoing natural factors. If one could measure the rate at which these changes occurred, it would be possible to determine, for example, how long it took for a river to carve out a canyon. Charles Lyell (1797–1875), the father of modern geology, used uniformitarianism, and soon geologists were pushing back the age of the earth into millions of years (now, of course, billions), that is, far beyond the six thousand allowed by a creation date of 4004 BC. Lyell was a devout Anglican who did not see any harm to the faith in his researches, but a lynchpin of Genesis historicity had been destroyed.

Geological research also challenged the literalness of a worldwide flood since no geological proof survives for it. Given water rising five and a half miles above sea level, the currents and pressure should have left evidence everywhere, but there is none. If a modern fundamentalist were to argue that forty days and forty nights is a very short time to leave a record, she or he should recall that the 2011 Japanese earthquake lasted only three minutes and left abundant evidence that will be visible to geologists for millennia.

Avid digging done by geologists and paleontologists uncovered hoards of fossils of animals and plants. The scientists quickly noticed that different types of animals, such as reptiles or mammals, made their appearance at different places in the fossil record, demonstrating that some species had lived before the others came into being. But how could that be if all were created by God in just four days, as it says in Genesis 1:9-30? And why were human fossils always in the most recent strata when they had been created on the same day as the land animals? Even more, Genesis 2:18-20 says that Adam was created *before* any animals, so human remains should have been found at every level, not the just top one.

Lyell gave a copy of his text *Principles of Geology* to the young naturalist Charles Darwin (1809–82) to bring with him on his famous voyage onboard the *Beagle* (1831–36). As Darwin moved toward his theory of evolution by natural selection, he utilized the now-increased age of the world to argue that there had been the time for the slow evolution of biological species. Darwin's work and that of his followers would demonstrate, at least to scientists, that species had evolved over enormous periods of time and were not all created in a few days. Furthermore, evolution meant that there was no immediate special creation to console the lonely Adam, and it also meant that animals had indeed changed and were not the fixed species required by a divine creation that was perfect. Evolution also abolished a central point of Augustine's Genesis theology—that is, that before Original Sin, animals lived in harmony. Darwin demonstrated that plants and animals had always struggled to survive and reproduce. The lion had never lain down with the lamb but instead had always eaten it.

These scientific advances dealt a crushing blow to biblical literalists. Before the nineteenth century, much science had supported biblical literalism. For example, the great Swedish taxonomist Carl Linnaeus (1707–78) had classified plants and animals by genus and species so that each one fit in its place, just as Genesis had taught and well before evolutionary biology had suggested that species could change. Now, however, the fundamentalists saw biblical literalism attacked by scientific discoveries.

Contemporary with scientific developments challenging the historicity of Genesis came the rise of modern biblical exegesis, which we discussed briefly in the previous chapter.

From the first century, Christians had recognized the difficulties inherent in biblical literalism. They knew that not all passages were to be taken literally, especially the poetic images used in the Psalms, as well as many prophetic passages. Yet they had few if any problems with the miraculous or the demonic, elements that make literalism difficult for modern believers. If the Bible said that the Red Sea parted and stood up in two walls of water, then that is exactly what happened.

When critics raised questions about so many biblical miracles, the fundamentalist rationale was simple and direct: to question one miracle would be to question them all. But that approach has a flaw. To question is not to deny, and denying one miracle does not necessarily deny them all. Christians pray to God because they believe that he can act in the world and sometimes in ways that modern knowledge cannot explain—that is, God performs miracles. Without faith in the possibility of miracles, one could not be a Christian.

Yet miracles are in the eye of the beholder. If a Christian prays for someone suffering an almost incurable illness and that person recovers, the Christian would believe her or his prayers proved effective and God worked a medical miracle. But an atheist could correctly point out that all we can prove is that someone unexpectedly and unexplainably recovered from a deadly illness. We cannot prove that God intervened. If the illness were 99 percent fatal, then this person belongs to the fortunate 1 percent. Or if one wishes to bring in unprovable supernatural beings to explain the cure, why not invisible beings from outer space who have medical knowledge far more advanced than ours? But the believer would have no difficulty with this reasoning because the believer acknowledges her or his faith in God and knows that the atheist does not share it.

As we saw in our look at Roman Catholic modernism, many very conservative Catholics considered miracles to be historical facts and as such capable of being apprehended by any rational person, even an atheist, and conservative Protestants joined them in a wholesale acceptance of biblical miracles as actual historical events. Modern biblical scholars, however, often attribute many miracles to the credulity of ancient peoples, to the growth of legends about what had been a historical act or person, and to the outright creation of a miracle by a biblical writer who used the miraculous to prove the sanctity and power of the person about whom he was writing.

For modern exegetes, the existence of demons fell into the same category as many miracles, that is, ancient credulity. Ancient peoples blamed many evils upon demons, who, significantly, are never once described in the Bible. Modernists explained demonic possession psychologically. Jesus' temptation by Satan, which differs in the gospel accounts, symbolized the various temptations he overcame and was not an actual contest between good and evil.

What made this struggle so much more difficult for conservative Protestants than the one facing Pius X was Protestant respect for one another's churches. Pius could tell any Catholic bishop what to do, and the bishop had to follow the pope's command. Protestantism has no central disciplinary authority, and a scholar who feels unwanted or even threatened in his or her church can leave it and go to another and remain a Protestant. Also, Reformation leaders had argued for *Sola Scriptura*, and so who had the right to tell another Protestant what to believe? To be sure, there are points upon which all Protestants agree, such as the inspiration of Scripture and the redemptive work of Jesus, but there points upon which the churches do not share agreement. Overall, Protestant conservatives simply did not have the weapons available to popes.

The threat to a literal understanding of the Bible and especially of Genesis continued to grow. In 1882 a German Protestant biblical scholar, Julius Wellhausen (1844–1918), published his *Prolegomena to the History of Israel,* in which he advanced what became known as the "documentary hypothesis" to explain the Torah (Genesis, Exodus, Leviticus, Numbers, Deuteronomy), traditionally the work of Moses alone. Wellhausen demonstrated the Torah's creation via a redaction of four originally independent texts, all dating from several centuries after Moses' lifetime. Wellhausen's view won over almost all modern biblical scholars and remained the dominant approach to the Torah until the late twentieth century when scholars began to modify it, but no one today believes that Moses composed the entire Torah or that one person wrote Genesis 1–11.

Other German scholars belonged to the history of religions school, which advocated the use of comparative religions. Hermann Gunkel (1862–1932) argued that many passages in the Old Testament derived from Semitic myths, such as those of ancient Babylon, and also from Egyptian myths. In 1901 Gunkel wrote *The Legends of Genesis*; the title reflects the contents.

Although the focus of conservative Protestant wrath would focus on the understanding of Genesis, German scholars also produced some radical new interpretations of the New Testament. In 1835 David Friedrich Strauss published his *Life of Jesus,* in which he rejected all the miraculous material in the gospels as unhistorical. He believed that Jesus' disciples, in the period after his death, created the miraculous elements and wrote them into the gospels.

Albert Schweitzer (1875–1965), famous as a medical missionary, interpreter of Bach, and Nobel Prize recipient in 1952, was also a New Testament scholar who insisted that Jesus expected an imminent end of the world and that only when he realized this was not going to happen did he conclude that he must suffer and die—that is, the Suffering Messiah was not part of a divine plan. In his famous *The Quest for the Historical Jesus* (1906), he contended that the historical Jesus, so wrapped in miracle and legend, cannot be recovered by scholars.

Ferdinand Christian Baur (1792–1860) made a case that early Christianity arose out of conflict among various groups such as Judaizers and universalists, thus rejecting the traditional view that orthodoxy started with the twelve apostles and marched through history, fending off heretics. In effect, he revised the history of doctrine. Baur also proved that Paul could not have written the Pastoral Epistles (1–2 Timothy, Titus).

Yet the focus for conservative Protestants, at least in the United States, would be the interpretation of Genesis. They could not understand the so-called benefits that the new scholarship brought to the study of that biblical book. By contrast, for many mainstream scholars and Protestant believers, the benefits were many and tangible.

Now scholars could explain some serious difficulties in a literal account. For example, in Genesis 1 God creates all the animals and then humanity as the summit of earthly creation. But in Genesis 2 Adam exists before the animals, a contradiction of Genesis 1, a problem that could now be explained by an ancient editorial merging of two different traditions.

In the Flood story, Noah brings on two of every kind of animal into the ark in chapter 6, but in chapter 7 he brings on one pair of every unclean animal and seven pairs of clean animals, not just a contradiction of chapter 6 but plain nonsense because the ancient Israelites judged animal cleanliness mostly on laws supposedly given by Moses, who, of course, had not yet been born. Again, diverse traditions preserved by the authors of Genesis would provide an answer.

After the Flood, all humankind descends from Noah's three sons, but a check of their descendants shows that the races arising from them are the Semites, the Indo-Europeans, and the Africans—that is, the three races known to the ancient Israelites. By 1900, European Christians were well aware of many other peoples, such as those of the Americas and the Pacific Islands, who were not included in the Genesis catalog of peoples. The obvious answer, of course, is that the ancient Israelites did not know of these people and thus saw no reason to give Noah more than three sons. Had the ancient Israelites known about the natives of the Americas or the Pacific Islands, Noah simply would have had more sons to explain the origins of those peoples.

Many moderate and liberal Christians, especially educated ones, gladly accepted the idea that Genesis 1–11 includes a collection of tales intended to teach a religious message (for example, there is just one God) instead of providing an early history of the earth. These Christians did not have to reject the theory of evolution or pretend that the problems in Genesis 1–11 could just be ignored. To be sure, many of these Christians flinched a bit when exegetes turned their new approaches to the New Testament and had little difficulty proving that some gospel miracles had not occurred and that the evangelists, especially Luke and John, routinely put their own words in the mouth of Jesus, but, in general, modern Christians wanted a modern approach to the world. To them modernism was not a dirty word.

* * *

Unlike their Roman Catholic counterparts who were labeled modernists by their chief enemy, Protestant modernists embraced the term. As Protestants, they were not subject to the censure that befell the Catholic intellectuals, and so they proclaimed their views openly.

Shailer Mathews (1863–1941), a lifelong, devout Baptist, served as dean of the Divinity School of the University of Chicago. In 1924 he published *The Faith of Modernism* to explain his views. Here are some excerpts:

> What then is modernism? A heresy? An infidelity? A denial of truth? A new religion? So its ecclesiastical opponents have called it. But it is none of these. . . . It is not a denomination of a theology. *It is the use of the methods of modern science to find, state, and use the permanent and central values of inherited orthodoxy in meeting the needs of the modern world.* . . . [Modernists] do not vote in conventions and do not enforce beliefs by discipline. Modernism has no confession. Its theological affirmations are the formulations of results of investigation both of human needs and the Christian religion. . . .
>
> An examination of the modernist movement will disclose those distinct aspects of these characteristics.
> 1. The modernist movement is a phase of the scientific struggle for freedom in thought and belief.
> The habits of medieval Catholicism and national churches, the appeal to some supernatural authoritative church or Bible, arguments based neither upon a study of the nature and history of either Bible or church, but upon ecclesiastical action does not satisfy free minds. . . . The freedom [the modernist] asks for himself he would grant to his opponents. If he had the power to enforce his beliefs on the church, he would not use it. Truth can be trusted to find its own defense in efficiency. (text in Gatewood, 55–56; emphasis in original)

Mathews makes it clear that modernists will use the results of science but will not attempt to impose them on anyone else. Note the two references to freedom of thought. Knowing that Pius X had used the word "modernism" to criticize dissident Catholic intellectuals who rejected medieval scholasticism, Mathews takes a quick shot at "medieval Catholicism."

He goes on to his second characteristic:

> 2. Modernists are Christians who accept the results of scientific research as data with which to think religiously.

When, therefore, he [the modernist] finds experts in all fields of scientific investigation accepting the general principle of evolution, he makes it a part of his intellectual apparatus. He does this not because he has a theology to be supported, but because he accepts modern science. . . .

He is not content simply to accept a doctrine. He seeks to understand its real purpose and service. He therefore seeks to understand why it arose. He searches for its origin and its efficiency in the light of its conformity with social forces. . . . The beliefs of Christians are less extensive than the loyalty of Christians. A religion is a way of living, and the modernist refuses to think of it as an accumulation of decrees. (ibid., 56–57)

Mathews pointedly refuses to accept a Christianity with "an accumulation of decrees" and so favors a historical approach in examining doctrines—the modernist "searches for [Christianity's] origin" (ibid., 57). He keeps to these themes in point 3. Note another implicit reference to Catholic modernism—the modernist does not have a theology to support, that is, Protestants do not have to conform exegesis to scholastic norms.

3. Modernists are Christians who adopt the methods of historical and literary science in the study of the Bible and religion. . . .

The modernist is a critic and an historian before he is a theologian. His interest in method precedes his interest in results.

Modernists believe themselves true to the spirit and purpose of Jesus Christ when they emphasize his teachings and inner faith of a century-long movement rather than the formulas in which aspects of this faith were authoritatively expressed. (ibid., 57)

He makes three more points that deal with social questions and then returns to the issue of correct interpretation of biblical texts by using modern methods rather than just rehashing older formulas, but he smartly points out that the received formulas were themselves products of history, as are modernists:

As the early church fathers were Christians who utilized their Hellenistic training to expound the Christianity brought to them by Jews; as the Schoolmen [scholastics] were Christians who followed Aristotle; so the modernists are Christians who use the scientific method to estimate and apply the values of that evangelical inheritance which they share. . . .

In brief then, *the use of scientific, historical, social method in understanding and applying evangelical Christianity to the needs of living*

> *person, is modernism.* . . . Modernists are thus evangelical Christians
> who use modern methods to meet modern needs. (ibid., 59–60;
> emphasis in original)

Mathews was an effective writer, a good scholar, and had the influence of the University of Chicago behind him, and so his book enjoyed significant influence among modernizing Protestants. One suspects that like-minded Catholics could see in Mathews's work a challenge to the views espoused by Catholic antimodernists.

Harry Emerson Fosdick (1878–1969) was a clergyman, a Baptist who served as a guest minister to the First Presbyterian Church in New York City and as a professor at Union Theological Seminary. In 1922 he preached a famous/notorious sermon entitled "Shall the Fundamentalists Win?" The general assembly of the Presbyterian Church charged the local presbytery to look into his views; a prominent Presbyterian layman, John Foster Dulles, defended him, but Fosdick resigned from his post. John D. Rockefeller, a major financial supporter of the University of Chicago, arranged for Fosdick to move to a Baptist church and then in 1930 to Riverside Church, which Rockefeller had funded. Fosdick's sermon gave a concise view of Protestant modernism.

> Even within the New Testament, therefore, there is no static creed.
> For, like a flowing river, the church's thought of her Lord shaped
> itself to the intellectual banks of the generation through which it
> moved, even while, by its construction and erosion, it transfigured
> them.
>   From the day the first disciples saw its [Christianity's] truth until
> now, the intellectual formulations in which it has been set and the
> mental categories by which it has been interpreted have changed
> with the changes of each age's thought. (ibid., 60–61)

This is a direct assertion of the development of doctrine and the historical setting of creeds along with a rejection of the notion that any formulation can transcend time.

And what happens to church authority if this is so? "Obviously, the point where this progressive conception of Christianity comes into conflict with many widely accepted ideas is the abandonment which it involves of an external and inerrant authority in matters of religion. The marvel is that the idea of authority, which is one of the historic curses of religion, should be regarded by so many as one of the vital necessities of the faith" (ibid., 62).

The rejection of "an external and inerrant authority" was a direct shot across the conservative bow—not even the Bible is inerrant because, like all things, it was a product of its age and place. Fosdick does provide a role for ecclesiastical authority: "It can lead us up to the threshold of a great experience where we must enter, each man for himself" (ibid., 64).

Fear of change in religion is not just foolish but deadly. "Stagnation in thought or enterprise means death for Christianity as it does for any other vital movement. Stagnation, not change, is Christianity's most deadly enemy, for this is a progressive world, and in a progressive world no doom is more certain than that which awaits whatever is belated, obscurantist, and reactionary" (ibid., 65).

Fosdick vigorously defends modern biblical exegesis. It enables believers to understand what the authors really meant, frees them from having to defend or explain crudities or nonsense, and makes the Bible relevant to educated modern believers. "This, then, is the result which follows from all these disciplines of modern scholarship converging on one point: the world in which the Bible was first written lives again in our thoughts. We can enter into its mind, understand its problems, catch the native connotation of its words." And such an approach is absolutely crucial for the church. Why? "We live in a new world, we picture with increasing clearness the contemporary meanings of an old world, and we feel the incompatibility between them—that is the difficulty which multitudes of modern folk are having with the Bible" (ibid., 72–73).

* * *

From this point on, we will not deal much with modernist thinkers because they became the majority in colleges, universities, and seminaries. Modern exegesis, more commonly called Higher Criticism, has constantly changed since the 1920s, but the basic presuppositions, as laid out by Shailer Mathews, have not: acceptance of modern scientific findings, the need to relate the Bible to contemporary believers, and, most importantly, trying to understand the Scriptures in terms of the eras and places in which they were written, even if that means challenging long-accepted beliefs, such as the creation, the virginal conception, the physical ascent of Jesus from the earth, and his impending physical return from the heavens for the Last Judgment.

The most significant changes occurred not among the modernists but among their opponents, and so we will concentrate less on the "heretics" and more on those who set out to refute them.

* * *

By the early twentieth century, liberal theologians who favored the newer exegesis occupied the most prestigious academic chairs in theology and biblical studies in universities and seminaries as well as some of the most prominent pastorates in several Protestant churches. Put on the defensive, the conservatives did not know what to do. As Protestants, they had to acknowledge the freedom of individual churches, and if those churches chose to go with Higher Criticism, Protestants should respect that. But how could they respect churches which, they believed, were betraying the Bible? And how could those churches really be Protestant if they betrayed the Bible?

A moral element also entered the debate. Evolution, the conservatives believed, endorsed "the survival of the fittest," a provocative phrase created not by Darwin but by the British philosopher Herbert Spencer (1820–1903). In this view, a human could become "the fittest" by engaging in any kind of behavior that guaranteed survival, including behavior that was sinful and even criminal. Evolution made moral decisions, such as helping the physically ill or the poor, seem foolish. Why help someone when such helping would not benefit you? For conservative Protestants, such an attitude mocked Christ's self-sacrifice for all of humanity.

Yet the conservatives lacked focus. In a word, they needed a leader. They soon got one, not from the ecclesiastical world but from the business one.

Lyman Stewart (1840–1923) was a cofounder of Union Oil, which eventually became Unocal. A devout and conservative Christian, he had also cofounded the Bible Institute of Los Angeles, now Biola University. He attended a sermon by A. C. Dixon, a prominent preacher from North Carolina who had held pastorships in several cities. In 1909 he was affiliated with the Moody Bible Institute in Chicago but was visiting Los Angeles. Dixon hammered away the notion that something must be done to bring the authentic message of the Bible to the hordes of true believers who were both offended and frightened at the exegetical methods employed by Higher Criticism. This new approach meant applying literary and historical analysis to the biblical books but without bringing the researcher's faith to such work—if the researcher even had any faith!

Hearing Dixon's sermon, "Stewart realized that he was being called to carry out that mission. Within days, aided by his brother and business partner Milton, he had laid out plans to publish a series of inexpensive paperback books containing the best teaching of the best [meaning the most conservative] teachers. The volumes would be distributed free of charge to church people across the country. They would be called *The Fundamentals*" (Lienesch, 8).

It was a brilliant idea, and Stewart got Dixon to agree to be editor. He was soon called to a pastorate in London, and two other editors finished the job. Between 1910 and 1915, twelve volumes containing ninety essays appeared. The editors did a superb job of finding the foremost conservative scholars to contribute. This was important because they needed scholars to offset the prestige of the academic positions held by Higher Critics. For preachers to oppose the modernists unaided would yield little. Conservative believers needed to know that their views had support from learned men (and all were men).

The Fundamentals achieved unanticipated success. Churches wrote to the editors for more and more copies. Many uneducated people owned some of the volumes. Lienesch stresses the sociological importance of the volumes. They provided a common source to which conservative believers could turn. People read them and discussed them. Traditionalists had more self-confidence now, knowing that their views, so patronized by modernists, actually had scriptural and even scientific support, since the contributors to *The Fundamentals* stressed that "true" science, as opposed to Darwinian evolution, did not challenge the biblical truth and often actually upheld it. *The Fundamentals* also helped conservatives "to create boundaries that were both broadly inclusive and selectively exclusive, admitting as many moderate-to-conservative evangelicals [Christians whose faith centered around the Bible] into the conservative camp while as the same time identifying and isolating the liberals and modernists among them" (Lienesch, 17). Some Baptists became so enraptured by this approach to the Bible that in 1920 Curtis Lee Jackson, a conservative editor, invented the word "fundamentalists" to describe this particular Baptist group. It soon became a name for all those who held a certain attitude, always conservative and often uncompromising, toward Scripture and the church.

How exactly did the contributors to *The Fundamentals* hope to defend the truth and slay the modernist dragon?

Sensibly, the contributors started out by directly attacking modern exegesis and exegetes. The initial essay by a Canadian, Canon Dyson Hague, tells the reader, "For hypothesis-weaving and speculation, the German theological professor is unsurpassed. . . . The most learned German thinkers are men who lack in a singular degree the faculty of common sense" (*The Fundamentals* i.1.12). This personal attack, albeit without citing names, suggests to the readers that they need not take much of this German exegesis seriously since it was done by dreamers whose fantasies bear no relation to true belief.

Hague stayed with this theme. "We must now investigate . . . the religious views of the men most influential in this movement." Unsurprisingly, they are not at all religious, but "avowed unbelievers in the supernatural" (ibid., 19). And again, "Their theory of revelation must be, then, a very different one from that held by the average Christian" (ibid., 29). In a mocking tone, "Are we not bound to receive these views when they are advanced, not by rationalists [that is, atheists], but by Christians, and not by ordinary Christians, but by men of superior and unchallengeable scholarship?" (ibid., 38).

In sum, a group of overeducated professors of little faith have concocted a collection of theories that bear no relation to the Christianity that the solid, faithful believer has. This type of attack has been used by fundamentalists ever since.

Another author, Franklin Johnson, attacked Higher Criticism for its denial of miracles, especially when exegetes use the method of comparative religion to demonstrate that such wonders as a virginal conception were common in ancient religions.

A German professor, listed only as F. Bettex, provided proof for the Bible's divine inspiration: "First, by the fact that, as does no other sacred work in the world, it condemns man and all his works." In spite of the Bible's condemnation of human works, "millions of men, troubled in conscience," believed in it, so it "must contain more than mere ordinary truth" (ibid., 80).

Bettex also argued that "the Bible sets the seal of its divine origin upon itself by means of the prophecies" (ibid., 81), an argument used by the neoscholastics against Catholic liberal exegetes. Of course, since the Bible not only provides the prophecies but also claims that they were fulfilled, only those who believed in the Bible beforehand can be convinced. But Bettex went on, again using a moral argument. "The Bible shows itself every day to be a divinely given book by its beneficent influence among all kinds of people" (ibid., 82). Of course, so does the Holy Qur'an, but Bettex did not bring that up.

Another Canadian, G. Osborne Troop, defended the apostle John's authorship of the Fourth Gospel: "The whole wondrous story of the betrayal, the denial, the trial, the condemnation and crucifixion of the Lord Jesus, as given through St. John, breathes with the living sympathy of an eye-witness" (ibid., 198). The inconsistencies with the passion narratives in the other three gospels simply went unmentioned.

Since nineteenth- and twentieth-century science had raised so many questions about the Bible's historicity, Reverend James Orr went after not the science but the scientists because of their skeptical attitude. "This was not just the attitude of the older investigators of science. Most of these were devout Christian men" (ibid., 335). This notion of "true science" would become a centerpiece of fundamentalist argumentation, starting with this approach and morphing into creation science. Yet Orr went lightly with Genesis literalism, instead suggesting that ways of interpretation exist that avoid conflicts with science. "The 'six days' may remain as a difficulty to some. . . . One may well ask . . . what kind of 'days' these were. . . . There is no violence done to the narrative in substituting in thought 'aeonic' days—vast cosmic periods—for 'days' on our narrower, sun-measure scale" (ibid., 344).

This theory would come to be called the "day-age" theory—that is, that each of six days symbolized some geological epoch; it still has many adherents. But it has two enormous drawbacks. First, why does the Hebrew word for "day" mean "twenty-four hours" every other place in the Bible but not in Genesis 1? Second, if one admits symbolism into the Genesis 1–11 narrative, why must it stop with the six-day creation and not include the Garden of Eden or the Great Flood?

In 1912 the editors reprinted a sermon by a deceased Anglican bishop, J. C. Ryle, that offered a fundamentalist version of *nulla salus extra ecclesiam*. In language that would have won the approval of Pope Pius X, Ryle defined what he considered to be the true church, which he called the Church of the Elect, and went on to warn that "if you do not [belong to that church], it will be better for you if you had not been born" (ibid., ii.i.319), recalling the words of Jesus about Judas (Mark 14:21), which his readers would have recognized.

With the publication of *The Fundamental*'s first volumes discussion groups sprung up, and conservative believers now had the weapons to respond to those who leaned toward the new understanding of Scripture. This success may have gone to the heads of the writers because Lienesch points out that "turning from religion to society, the essayists found even more enemies, portraying Christianity as threatened by secular philosophy and at odds with contemporary culture. Unlike the earlier essays, which had shown at least some respect for secular scholarship, the later ones were consistently critical and frequently dismissive of it. A few authors were conspicuously anti-intellectual, proudly boasting that they spoke for 'less learned folks'" (26). This latter approach, standing up for the humble, would have and still has a long future.

Several of the later essays specifically targeted evolution.

The Reverend Henry Beach of Colorado proclaimed "the decadence of Darwinism." He offered a number of scientific, as he understood them, refutations of Darwinism, most augmented by a mocking tone. He also found moral as well as scientific shortcomings. "In the struggle for existence the stronger gloat over the slain while poverty of spirit, meekness, mercy, and peace [recalling the Beatitudes of Matthew's gospel] die unhonored and unsung. By these means every kind of organic being will eventually gain the summit of finitude. It is immoral" (*The Fundamentals* ii.ii.67).

Beach sounded an important theme here. Although the initial conservative Protestant reservations about evolution focused on what it did to the Garden of Eden and thus to Original Sin and the notion of being the Elect, more and more preachers focused on the notion of the survival of the fittest, interpreting it to mean that evolution validated any means, moral or immoral, to get ahead, which effectively meant that evolution promoted immorality. Thus, the survival of the fittest opened the door to heinous sins of all kind. [To use a current reference, visitors to the Creation Museum in Petersburg, Kentucky, will learn how evolution has promoted abortion and drug use.]

In a hopefully titled essay, "The Passing of Evolution," the American geologist George Frederick Wright attacked various aspects of Darwinian evolution. He took issue with Darwin's contention that variations in specific animals might provide them with the advantages they needed to survive and procreate. He used deer as an example, discussing how the deer had the advantage of antlers that required the additional advantage of a neck to support them. "It is impossible to conceive of this *combination* of advantageous variations without bringing in the hand of the designing mind of the Original Creator" (ibid., ii.ii.76).

An anonymous author found an even deadlier threat to the faith, "evolutionism in the pulpit." The author's use of language suggests he was a preacher. "Still more remarkable [than scientists' acceptance of evolution] was the fact that so many theologians and Christian ministers adopted the new philosophy and were so ready to give up large portions of Holy Scripture because they could not be reconciled with it; inventing as a salve to conscience the doctrine that 'the Bible was not intended to teach science'" (ibid., ii.ii.88–89).

Warming to the topic, the anonymous author went on: "The evolutionary theory was conceived in agnosticism, and born and nurtured in infidelity; *[proving] that it is the backbone of the destructive criticism which has so viciously assailed both the integrity and authority of the Scriptures, . . .*

that it denies the personality of God and man . . . and regards man as being simply a passing form of universal Energy, and thus without free will, moral responsibility, and immortality, it becomes evident to every intelligent layman that such a system can have no possible points of contact with Christianity" (ibid., ii.ii.92; emphasis added).

As for the ministers who accept evolution, "the pulpit efforts of some ministers at reconciling them would be laughable from a logical stand-point were the issues involved not so serious and the effects upon their unthinking hearers not so deplorable. . . . In the interest of common honesty, these men ought to either drop their materialism or leave the Christian pulpit" (ibid., ii.ii.94).

A corner had been turned. Conservative Protestants now had the intellectual forces to fight the corrosive effects of modernity. Further-more, they had discovered where the attacks on the Bible had truly origi-nated—not just from the theological meanderings of German professors but also from evolution, which robbed all life of meaning and morality. The author of "Evolutionism in the Pulpit" actually had linked evolution and Higher Criticism. Yet, the authors told their readers, all was not lost. True ministers and simple believers would stand up for the Bible.

The series had proved the value of publication. It had also highlighted the danger of having false teachers in Protestant pulpits, teachers who should be removed. Now conservative leaders had to put the funda-mentals of *The Fundamentals* into practice. But in a large country with so many churches, seminaries, and schools, this would be no easy task. The faithful needed organization. Stepping up to meet this need was William Bell Riley.

Riley (1861–1947) was a Baptist minister from Minneapolis who believed in biblical inerrancy. Lienesch describes him as "a gifted preacher, a skilled administrator, and a successful fund-raiser" (40). Riley arranged for a prophecy conference at Carnegie Hall in New York in 1918 and was stunned at the numbers in attendance, more people than the hall could seat. Riley next planned another conference for Philadelphia in April of 1919. Some of the most famous preachers not just in the United States but in the Anglophone world participated, a testimony to the immense reserves of conservative and even fundamentalist Protestants.

Not wanting to lose momentum, Riley founded the World's Christian Fundamentals Association (WFCA) to continue the work. He networked among conservative seminaries, colleges, and Bible societies, and several state WFCA groups arose. He worked with publishers of religious jour-nals. He and his associates promoted meetings of local Bible groups. In

1923 Riley founded the Minnesota Anti-Evolution League; by 1924 there was a national Anti-Evolution League, headed by John Porter of Kentucky and T. T. Martin of Mississippi, a foreshadowing of the future Southern leadership of the fundamentalist movement. Inevitably in large groups disputes broke out about tactics and goals, and an organization heavy on preachers guaranteed that strong-willed people would disagree with other strong-willed people. Other organizations soon appeared. But they mostly had the same goal—to stop or refute these modernist attacks on biblical inerrancy.

The groups' interests covered many areas but soon came to focus on education. High schools never and colleges rarely taught the new exegesis of the Bible, but they all taught evolution. This was especially threatening to traditionalists because the students experiencing such teaching were not positioned to question it and thus assumed that what they heard must be true. The fundamentalists (as we shall call them from here on) launched attacks against colleges and universities. They quickly found out that professors were protected by tenure as well as by the schools' desire to get or maintain academic stature, which could be jeopardized by changing the science curricula to suit religious conservatives. Furthermore, the professors were quite willing to fight back. If a preacher condemned evolution, a professor could ask him, "How then would you explain the knee-joint in the Pleistocene Smilodon?" The preachers quickly learned not to debate with professors about science.

Some colleges were church-supported institutions. One such was Baylor University in Waco, Texas, founded by Baptists. In 1921 a Fort Worth preacher, J. Frank Norris, led a campaign to engineer the removal of "evolutionists" on the Baylor faculty and succeeded in forcing one to resign. Yet such successes were rare. High schools, however, were different.

The Catholic Church in the United States had established a school system that educated many, although never a majority, of Catholic students. Protestants, by contrast, depended almost completely upon public schools that depended almost completely upon tax money, a point repeatedly emphasized by a Presbyterian layman named William Jennings Bryan.

Bryan (1860–1925) was a three-time (1896, 1900, 1908) Democratic candidate for president and later secretary of state in the Woodrow Wilson administration (1913–15). A very conservative Protestant, he was not a full-blown fundamentalist. He was a superb orator and knew how to use words; he realized that many passages in the Bible employed literary devices. He also thought that the six days of Genesis 1 could mean eons rather than twenty-four-hour days, that is, the day-age theory. This background might have made Bryan sympathetic to fundamentalism but not a campaigner for it.

What motivated him to join the cause was his deep concern for the common people. His nickname was "the Great Commoner," and he had earned it and liked it. He supported the vote for women. He supported a progressive income tax that helped poor people. He supported the popular vote for US senators against the previous practice of having state legislators choose them. His concern for the common people also made him a majoritarian—that is, the government should do what the majority wished.

People trusted him and wrote to him for advice. With great concern, Bryan noticed that more and more of the letters to him came from parents whose children had come to doubt their faith or had even lost it when they went to high school and learned about evolution. These sometimes heart-wrenching letters disturbed Bryan deeply, and he decided to do something about them.

Bryan began a speaking campaign that drew enormous audiences and encouraged local opponents of evolution. His central points were clear and powerful: Why do the schools in a democracy not follow the wishes of the majority of its citizens? Why should good Christian people have to pay taxes to support schools that were corrupting their children's faith? He read from letters sent to him by concerned parents, and he brought onto the stage with him students who would testify to how "atheistic" teachers had mocked the Bible in the classroom. Going after individual schools or school districts would be a waste of time and energy, so Bryan and his ever-increasing allies decided upon pressuring state legislatures because the states provided certification for teachers. In the 1920s the South was the Solid South, which voted Democrat almost automatically. His three campaigns and long service to the party had made Bryan well-known in the region, and many legislators, themselves conservative Protestants if not outright fundamentalists, welcomed him.

Bryan and his allies eventually got twenty-one states to introduce bills outlawing the teaching of evolution in public schools. The opposition to these bills turned out to be surprisingly strong, often led by educators but also by businessmen concerned that their state would look backward and would encourage the negative view much of the country held of the South. In the end only five states actually outlawed the teaching: Arkansas, Florida, Mississippi, Oklahoma, and, fatefully, Tennessee.

The newly formed American Civil Liberties Union opposed such laws, convinced that they were unconstitutional by limiting what teachers could teach, but the ACLU needed citizens in those states to challenge the laws. As it happened, local businessmen in the small town of Dayton, Tennessee, knew that a challenge to the law would bring national publicity to the place where it occurred, and they thought Dayton would benefit from such publicity. They quickly found someone to challenge it, a first-year high school teacher named John Scopes (1900–1970), whose name has forever been associated with Genesis and evolution.

There is a remarkable irony about all this: Scopes had never formally taught evolution. He taught mathematics and physics and coached football part-time but did not teach biology. But at the end of each semester the biology teachers would do a review of the course work to prepare the students for the final exam. In 1925 one of the teachers was the school principal, who, having a busy administrative schedule, asked Scopes to conduct the review for him. Scopes did so and thus, however briefly, did cover evolution in a classroom. He opposed the Tennessee law and agreed to acknowledge his violation of it.

Local authorities promptly accused Scopes, and the ACLU promptly agreed to defend him, getting for the defense Clarence Darrow (1857–1938), one of the most famous trial lawyers in America. Bryan, who had not practiced law for thirty-one years, volunteered to assist the defense.

The 1925 "Monkey Trial" has entered American lore and been the subject of dramas and movies, but its real importance lies in what it did to fundamentalism. Led by H. L. Mencken (1880–1956), nationally and internationally known reporters descended upon Dayton. Almost all sympathized with Scopes and opposed the Tennessee law as oppressive of free speech. The visiting reporters quickly came to loathe the locals, whom they frequently portrayed as gap-toothed, gun-toting illiterates who believed anything their uneducated preachers told them, an image that would stick with fundamentalism for decades. In the most famous part of the trial, Bryan agreed to be a witness on the literal truth of the Bible, and in a two-hour grilling in the oppressive heat (the trial had been moved outdoors to accommodate the crowd), Darrow showed that Bryan knew nothing about science or evolution and that even he would back off from accepting as literal several narratives parts of the Bible. "Did Jonah live inside the whale for three days? How could Joshua lengthen the day by making the sun (rather than the earth) stand still? Where did Cain get his wife? . . . As Darrow pushed various lines of questioning, increasingly Bryan came to admit that he simply did not know. He had no idea what would happen if the earth stopped moving [scientists had repeatedly pointed out the cosmic chaos it would have caused], or about the antiquity of human civilization, or even about the age of the earth" (Larson, 187–89). When Bryan insisted he was defending the Bible against skepticism and atheism, the crowd cheered, but Darrow had achieved his goal: "I made up my mind to show the country what an ignoramus he was, and I succeeded" (ibid., 190).

There was no doubt that Scopes had violated an existing law, and the jury found for the prosecution. The judge imposed a fine of one hundred dollars upon Scopes, which Bryan promptly offered to pay. The ACLU would not accept the verdict and decided to appeal with the intent of questioning the constitutionality of the state law against the teaching of evolution in public schools. Much of the state and most of the country had considered the trial to be a circus, which had not brought Tennessee the positive publicity the Dayton businessmen had wanted. Possibly wishing to end the matter, the state supreme justices who heard the appeal upheld the statute but pointed out that the trial judge had set the penalty (the one-hundred-dollar fine), which should have been done by the jury, and so they overturned the verdict. Prosecution and defense attorneys both recognized this misstep by the judge at the time of the trial, but neither objected or brought it up on appeal. This decision by the Supreme Court effectively brought an end to the case/circus because the prosecutor accepted the decision, which in turn meant that there was no longer a conviction to appeal, and the defense thus had no grounds to challenge the state statute.

Some ACLU lawyers cried foul, but Darrow accepted the decision and observed "It will probably require another case to clear up the matter." But there would be no second case. No other Tennessee teacher wanted to be involved in proceedings like the Monkey Trial, as the Scopes trial was widely known. When the ACLU turned to the Mississippi law, they could find no local teacher willing to challenge it. No one wanted a repeat of Dayton.

The Tennessee statue remained on the books until 1967 when someone decided to bring a suit against it. The state legislature promptly repealed the law, thus avoiding another trial. In 1968 the United States Supreme Court struck down the Arkansas antievolution law as a violation of the First Amendment separation of church and state.

Bryan died less than a week after the Scopes trial, venerated as a martyr by many people who believed his death had been caused by the strain of the trial. No other fundamentalist leader had national credentials, and the negative publicity and outright mockery the trial had engendered in the national press had made many fundamentalist leaders wary of publicity.

As it happened, the Great Depression slowed down the national fundamentalist cause since so many of its adherents belonged to the lower socioeconomic groups so devastated by the Depression, and they could not provide much support for the movement.

But fundamentalism did not disappear. The Scopes trial helped to make it a largely Southern movement, as the rest of the country had been led by the media to see it as the product of backward, barely literate yokels who rejected the ongoing and impressive findings of modern science. This was a significant change: Lyman Stewart came from California, Bryan from Nebraska, W. C. Riley from Minnesota, and several contributors to *The Fundamentals* from Canada and Great Britain as well as from many different parts of the United States, such as Ohio and New York. The earliest national meetings were in New York and Philadelphia. Many northerners continued to support fundamentalism, but the movement's leaders would be mostly southerners.

Yet to an extent this national rejection aided fundamentalism. Many southerners, including mainstream Protestants, resented the offensive and largely untrue picture painted of them, and fundamentalist preachers could draw upon a well of local support. Eschewing the national stage, they turned to work among churches and in small towns. The antievolution laws remained on the books in several states, and much of the population still opposed the teaching of evolution. In order to avoid more national exposure, many Southern prosecutors simply declined to enforce the antievolution teaching laws, and, as just noted, no other teacher wanted to make it an issue.

Fundamentalists or at least antievolutionists won election to local school boards and sometimes to higher political posts. In 1926 North Carolina eliminated from schools textbooks that mentioned evolution. Teachers who disagreed were not reappointed or were even fired outright. Antievolution candidates won elections in cities as big as Atlanta and Charlotte.

The fundamentalist gains in the schools produced another victory. Since textbooks covering evolution would guarantee trouble, school board members and educators

> often felt that the best way to insulate their schools from this controversy was to have *neither* evolution nor creation in their classrooms. The publishers of scientific textbooks [often located in liberal New York City] altered their products to conform to this attitude, so that evolutionary topics received only superficial treatment in

textbooks. Explicit mention of evolution disappeared from science textbooks. . . .

Several influences stoked publishers' fear of evolutionary topics. The southern and western states, where anti-evolutionary sentiment was most intense, had a disproportionately strong influence on the purchase of biology textbooks because their agricultural economies required widespread education in plant and animal life. Furthermore, these states made centralized decisions about which textbooks to subsidize. . . . Finally, the authors of these textbooks were high school teachers responding to their publishers' marketing requirements, not scientists presenting their colleagues' consensus." (Toumey, 26)

Throughout the 1930s and 1940s Southern fundamentalists had fewer and fewer issues to deal with in the schools. Furthermore, some of these bowdlerized texts would inevitably have been used outside the South.

The battle continued to be fought by the churches. "Evolution eventually overshadowed all the other issues raised by the conservative evangelical revolt against liberal Christianity" (Szasz, 131). Conservative churches ran more than two hundred summer Bible camps in the 1930s, sponsored folk music concerts, and organized relentlessly on the local level. Fundamentalist-themed publications also arose, such as the tabloid *Sword of the Lord*. Presaging the contemporary fundamentalist television programs, "by the mid-1940s the Reverend Charles E. Fuller's 'Old Fashioned Revival Hour,' carried by over 450 stations nationwide, would be the most popular program on the air" (Lienesch, 201). Since colleges and seminaries could not be trusted, fundamentalists founded their own, including Bryan College in Dayton, Tennessee, chartered in 1930. All this went on largely unnoticed by the national media, which, of course, focused on the Depression, then on World War II, and then on the Cold War.

Fundamentalists had been doing more than organizing; they had been thinking hard about achieving a greater legitimacy and thus improving their chances of winning America back to the true faith.

The inerrantist approach to Genesis 1–11 ran afoul of the widely triumphant new exegetes, but the exegetes in their turn ran afoul of almost everyone else. Not only did they question the historicity of Genesis 1–11, they also challenged the historicity of many other Old Testament passages and then went on to do the same to parts of the gospels, something that offended and frightened enormous numbers of Christians. The denial of the facticity of Jesus' virginal conception outraged many Roman Catholics with their deep devotion to Mary, making Catholics and fundamentalists allies on some issues, in spite of some strong anti-Catholic articles in *The Fundamentals*.

The deepest fundamentalist hope was to win back American society at large, which, from the revolution until 1900, had been conservatively Protestant in character. This task would have to go beyond religion and into the realm of science, so unquestioningly accepted by so many citizens. The fundamentalists would have to prove that evolution was scientifically wrong and that a biblically based explanation of the world's origin and development was correct or at least more *scientifically* accurate.

But the very idea of having to prove the scientific validity of the Bible was a new one. Toumey explains it well. "Early in the nineteenth century . . . Protestant philosophy of science was the idea of 'two revelations.' God had revealed himself to us twice, in scripture and in nature, so that curiosity about nature was a good Christian virtue, provided *it was guided by the same kind of piety* that steered one's interest in scripture. Although the methods of studying nature were different from those for scripture, the end result was expected to be the same: a person was morally enriched by seeing the evidence of God's character in his creation. The adaptation of a creature to its environment . . . was a sign of God's careful design" (14; emphasis added), a challenge to the Enlightenment-spurred secular approach that looked at nature without any religious basis or goal.

The Protestant view depended heavily upon the natural philosophy of Francis Bacon (1561–1626), which "implied that truth was a single, uncomplicated whole. . . . Science, then, was the simple business of observing, collecting, and classifying the facts of nature. . . . The result was that, for the first half of the nineteenth century, evangelical Protestant thinking about scripture was practically identical to American scientific thinking about nature" (ibid., 16–17).

Toumey continues: "During the middle third of the nineteenth century, many U.S. scientists turned toward the secular model of science. Their change of heart was not a conscious rebellion against the Protestant model. Rather, it was a consequence of the specialization and professionalism of higher education" (ibid., 18). As we have seen in previous chapters, some nonreligious historical forces inevitably impact religion.

Szasz makes the same point. "Like most men of their moral nineteenth-century background, conservative opponents of evolution were very unclear about scientific terminology. [W. C.] Riley, for example, defined science as 'knowledge gained and verified by exact observation and correct thinking.' . . . Not one [of these men] understood the difference between the idea of a positivistic fact and a theory for which evidence is gathered, arranged into a pattern, and perhaps discarded as more research develops" (130). The conservatives' frustration grew until "evolution eventually overshadowed all the other issues raised by the conservative evangelical revolt against liberal Christianity" (ibid., 131).

Szasz goes on to another major point: "The fight in the 1920s over the issue of evolution brought with it something that . . . in the long run may have more importance than any other aspect of the controversy—the role of experts in a democracy. . . . Opposition to an 'educational elite' was a major part of Fundamentalism. . . . Many [fundamentalists] felt the rise of higher criticism had virtually the same effect on the Bible" (132–33), that is, that experts might come to dominate its interpretation.

Szasz writes, "Ordinary citizens might be content to leave some fields to the experts, but others remained in the public realm, including social mores, public education, and the interpretation of the Bible." Bryan mercilessly exploited this point, claiming that scientists wanted "to set up an oligarchy in free America," and, Szasz suggests, "the Fundamentalists' complete confidence in ordinary people . . . carried with it a distrust of the exceptional. . . . [The dominance of experts] presented a direct threat to the conservatives' understanding of American democracy" (134). The prominent evangelist Billy Sunday (1862–1935) luridly summed up the conservatives' attitude: "When the word of God says one thing and scholarship says another, scholarship can go to hell" (quoted in Toumey, 22).

In the face of expert testimony that went contrary to their beliefs, what could the fundamentalists do? They had two choices: first, ignore what the experts had to say, which many did but which simultaneously guaranteed that fundamentalism would remain a minority, regional movement with no intellectual credentials and no chance of impacting the larger American democracy. The second choice proved more appealing: prove that the experts were wrong.

The fundamentalists believed that Genesis 1–11 provided a factual account of how the earth and its inhabitants came into being. This is *biblical creationism* and is ultimately a matter of faith, an acceptance of Genesis as God's inerrant Word. But such a view would never win over educational institutions or many judges. On the other hand, *scientific creationism*, the attitude "that the events mentioned in Genesis can be substantiated with technical evidence, without direct mention of scripture" (Toumey, 13), could do so.

This new scientific enterprise grew up around the country, largely unnoticed by mainstream scientists. Its most prominent advocate was

George McCready Price (1870–1963), a Canadian Seventh-day Adventist whose scientific credentials bordered on zero but whose published works, relying heavily on the Genesis Flood to explain most geological questions, won him a fundamentalist audience. He did "field work" in the western United States, claiming to find proof for his theories in the sedimentary rock formations in mountains. He even found the occasional accredited scientist willing to debate him. In 1906 he published *Illogical Geology* and received a "most thoughtful and candid" response from the president of Stanford University, who was an authority on fossil fishes. "Price [was] titillated by the risk of sparring with a superior opponent and grateful to be taken seriously" (Numbers, 106).

But more perceptive fundamentalist scientists realized that people like Price could never really advance the cause. In 1941 a group of five scientists, urged by a faculty member of Chicago's Moody Bible Institute, met to discuss how to "[disseminate] 'accurate' information on the relationship between religion and science" (ibid., 181). The five founded the American Scientific Affiliation. Of the five scientists, four taught at accredited institutions, including two public ones, Oregon State College (now University) and Pasadena City College, while the fifth was a commercial chemist in Boston.

These scholars' acceptance of creationism cost them the respect of colleagues at mainstream institutions, but they did bring some academic credentials and organization to the scientific creationist movement. Also akin to mainstream institutions, they soon engaged in debates about what scientific creationism was, whether to focus on Genesis 1 or on the Flood, and the like.

It is worthwhile to note that mainstream scholars and believers often think of creationist thinkers as a solid, unified group, but, as Ronald Numbers demonstrates so well, they too have schools of thought, fierce debates, and bitter personal rivalries—none of which is well-known because mainstream scholars just do not take them seriously as scientists.

The status of creation science changed significantly in 1961 with the publication of *The Genesis Flood* by Henry Morris and James Whitcomb.

Whitcomb (b. 1924) was a young theology student with a rudimentary knowledge of science, but he had graduated with honors from Princeton University in 1948. While still at Princeton, he had converted to evangelical Christianity. After graduation, he matriculated at Grace Theological Seminary, earning a bachelor of divinity in 1951. During his later doctoral work in theology, Whitcomb got to know some creationist scientists but found himself leaning toward Price's argument for a catastrophic flood. He wanted to write a book that combined theological and scientific arguments to support his views but could find no creationist scientist who agreed with him enough to be a coauthor. Then he thought of Morris, whom he had met in 1953.

Morris (1918–2006) had been born in Texas and grew up a southern Baptist. He attended Rice University in Houston and graduated Phi Bea Kappa with a bachelor's degree in engineering in 1939. He first worked for a government water commission, which sent him to El Paso. Lonely for his fiancée back in Houston, Morris read the Bible fervently, and "after an intense period of soul-searching, he concluded that creation had taken place in six literal days because the Bible clearly said so and 'God doesn't lie'" (Numbers, 217). He taught for a while at Rice and became involved with student Christian organizations. In 1946 he began his doctoral studies at the University of Minnesota, specializing in hydraulics because of his growing interest in the biblical Flood. "In 1950 Morris received his Ph.D. from the University of Minnesota. Despite having made his creationist views widely known, he had earned excellent grades and had encountered no overt prejudice" (ibid., 221).

He had a solid academic career, teaching first at the University of Louisiana at Lafayette, then at Southern Illinois University, and, starting in 1957, at Virginia Polytechnic Institute (Virginia Tech) as professor of hydraulic engineering and chairperson of the department in 1963. In sum, he had the scholarly and academic credentials that other creationist scientists usually lacked. He also had professional and academic experience. Morris's credentials and abilities were such that his chairmanship of his department at Virginia Tech occurred after the publication of his creationist classic *The Genesis Flood*, and he left that institution in 1969 of his own choosing.

The book appeared in February of 1961. In the next twenty-five years it went through twenty-nine printings and sold more than two hundred thousand copies, unheard-of numbers for a "science" book. Although "outside conservative religious circles, *The Genesis Flood* caused hardly a ripple of recognition" (ibid., 235), fundamentalists relished it, finally seeing what they accepted as scientific validation for their views.

Numbers sums up its contents:

> According to Morris, three events—"the Creation, the Fall, and the Flood"—dominated early world history. In six literal days, using methods unknown and unknowable, God had created the entire universe and populated the earth with "full-grown" plants, animals, and human beings. . . . The Fall introduced a period of "decay and deterioration." . . . Because there had been no death before this

> time, Morris felt "compelled to date all of the rock strata which contain fossils of once-living creatures as subsequent to Adam's fall." Most of these formations he attributed to the flood, which he and Whitcomb placed at between five thousand and seven thousand years before the present. (228)

So anxious was Morris to give the work scientific legitimacy that he "addressed such issues as the capacity of Noah's ark (equal to eight freight trains with sixty-five stockcars each)" (ibid., 226). But he did not back down when his evidence pushed him in a difficult direction; for example, he asserted that humans and dinosaurs inhabited the earth at the same time.

Not all fundamentalists were pleased with the book, especially those who had favored the day-age theory, the belief that the "days" of Genesis 1 represented geological epochs, a way of reconciling the truth of Genesis with common scientific dating. Others resented that the focus for scientific evidence had turned from the days of creation to the Great Flood. Yet all fundamentalists rejoiced that an accredited scientist had made a case for scientific creationism. In fact, Morris was far from being the only creationist with degrees from mainstream and occasionally prestigious institutions, but he was the one who had written the book. In short order came other books by other authors.

So did other means of promoting creationism. The Creation Science Institute was established in San Diego in 1970. In 1972 Morris founded the Institute for Creation Research, partly after a disagreement with the leaders of the Creation Science Institute. More modern institutions are the Northwest Creation Network, which has had twenty-eight million hits on its website since 2004, and the Creation Museum in Petersburg, Kentucky, which opened in 2007.

With "evidence" provided by Morris and others, fundamentalist leaders could now make their case against evolution, sort of. They did not try to stop the teaching of evolution, but they did insist that "creation science" also deserved a place in the high school and even the college science curriculum. When the United States Supreme Court overturned the Arkansas law against the teaching of evolution, the wisdom of this new approach became evident.

The creationists had a powerful weapon—public support. As in the 1920s, they focused on local and state school boards, requesting that in fairness the schools should present creationism as a reasonable, scientific alternative to evolution. Between 1971 and 1980 "the creationist movement enjoyed victories in textbook selections or curriculum guidelines in

Texas, Georgia, and Alabama, plus local successes in Columbus, Ohio; Dallas, Texas; Kanahwa County, West Virginia; Pulaski County, Arkansas; Tampa, Florida; and Melville School District, Missouri" (Toumey, 38). 1981 was a banner year when "the Arkansas legislature passed the first of the modern laws mandating equal time for creation science (as distinguished from biblical creationism) whenever evolution is taught" (ibid., 40). The movement enjoyed a similar success in Louisiana.

The opponents of creationism, from parents to schoolteachers to the National Science Foundation, soon began to challenge it in the courts, especially the federal courts. "By 1980 a pattern had become clear. Creationists could persuade many school boards to include creationism in their science curricula and text books, but their enemies could persuade the courts that those decisions violated the Establishment Clause of the U.S. Constitution" (ibid., 41–42). The US Supreme Court eventually struck down the Arkansas and Louisiana statutes along with a number of smaller ones. Many school boards and legislators could see the writing on the walls and dropped creationism before being sued.

Creationism seemed doomed; the modern world had triumphed yet again over the true faith. But the fundamentalists had another powerful arrow in their quiver.

The problem with creationism was just that—*creation*ism. "Creation" was simply not a scientific term. It was a religious term and was widely understood to be one. For its opponents, creationism brought religion into the science classroom where it did not belong, and for two reasons: first, it violated the separation of church and state, and second, religious teachings are not scientifically verifiable. How could anyone teach creationism without at some point using the "G word"?

Those arguments had much merit, but for so many people the well-ordered, functioning cosmos pointed, if not to a Creator, at least to "design," and if there was design, then there had to be a designer. Enter "ID."

ID, as Intelligent Design is often abbreviated, asserts that the complexity and the workings of the physical world point to the existence of an intelligent being who "designed" the world. No ID supporters have ever suggested who such a being might be besides God, but they generally refrain from saying "God" because that implies a religious dimension behind the argument. Critics could say that because ID supporters believe in God, they also believe in Intelligent Design. In fact, ID supporters argue, it is just the reverse. ID is not a form of belief; it is a scientific concept. ID supporters argue that the obvious rationality behind the cosmos as we know it *may* point to a deity, but whether or not someone acknowledges a deity, all *humans* can see that the cosmos could not have just happened.

Such thinking had deep roots in Christianity. Genesis 1 presented God as the Creator, and the book of Job (38–41) has God demonstrate to Job the wonders of his creation. More to the ID point, the apostle Paul said, "For what can be known about God is evident to them [the wicked], because God made it evident to them. Ever since the creation of the world, his invisible attributes of eternal power and divinity have been able to be understood and perceived in what he has made. As a result, they have no excuse; for although they knew God they did not accord him glory as God or give him thanks. Instead, they became vain in their reasoning, and their senseless minds were darkened. While claiming to be wise, they became fools" (Rom 1:19-22). For Paul, only wicked fools denied Intelligent Design.

Such reasoning also echoed throughout the ancient and medieval periods. Thomas Aquinas offered his five proofs for the existence of God, some of which depended upon observations of the physical world and the obvious, for him, design behind its creation.

The best-known design argument in the English-speaking world came from the Anglican bishop William Paley (1743–1805) in his book *Natural Theology.*

> In crossing a heath, suppose I pitched my foot against a stone and were asked how the stone came to be there, I might possibly answer . . . that it had lain there forever, nor would it perhaps be very easy to show the absurdity of this answer. But suppose I had found a watch upon the ground, and it should be inquired how the watch happened to be in that place, I should hardly think of the answer I had given before [that it might always have been there]. . . . We might never be able to explain how the watch came to be on the heath but we would know that the watch must have had a maker: that there must have existed, at some time and at some place or another, an artificer or artificers who formed it for the purpose which we find it actually to answer, who comprehended its construction and designed its use. (Dawkins, 5)

What bothered creationists and ID supporters was the randomness of Darwinism. Was there really no intelligence behind the world?

In 1984 three scientists who were believing Protestants, Charles Thaxton, Walter Bradley, and Roger Olsen, published *The Mystery of Life's Origin.* In 1986 an English geneticist, Michael Denton, published

Evolution: Theory in Crisis, in which he argued for evidence of divine design in the natural world. An ex-Protestant who dismissed scientific creationism, he could not be accused of religious partisanship. The two books "attracted comparatively little public interest, but they both helped to lay the intellectual foundations for the ID movement of the 1990s" (Numbers, 374).

In that same year a British atheist scientist, Richard Dawkins of Oxford, struck back with *The Blind Watchmaker*, an obvious reference to Paley. Religious believers accustomed to deference found the Genesis creation account caricatured as a creation myth "that happened to have been adopted by one particular tribe of Middle East herders. It has no more special status than the belief of a particular west African tribe that the world was created from the excrement of ants" (Dawkins, 317). For Dawkins, "natural selection, the blind, unconscious, automatic process which Darwin discovered, . . . has no purpose in mind. It has no mind. . . . It does not plan for the future. It has no vision, no foresight, no sight at all" (ibid., 5). This book served as a warning to ID supporters that the scientific establishment would fight them and would show no quarter.

In 1989 appeared *Of Pandas and People* by Dean Kenyon and Percival Davis, a best-selling textbook author. This was "the first book explicitly to promote intelligent design" (Numbers, 375). Two years later a prestigious scholar, Phillip Johnson, professor of law at the University of California, Berkeley, applied his skills to evolutionary theory and produced another ID book, *Darwin on Trial.* Possibly to Johnson's surprise, much criticism came from conservative Christians who thought ID sold out the Bible. The critics included Henry Morris, who labeled as "nonsense" any attempt to speak of an Intelligent Designer and not identify him as God.

With or without the "G word," Intelligent Design was making progress in conservative academic circles. In 1992 Southern Methodist University hosted the first academic conference devoted to Intelligent Design. Yet in 1999 when William Dembski, a mathematician, established an ID center at Baylor University in Waco, Texas, his scientific colleagues protested so strongly that the university president closed the center.

History was repeating itself. A movement that would defend the historicity of Genesis 1–11 had failed to gain traction in colleges and universities. Like Bryan and his followers, the leaders of ID groups now turned to high schools, local school boards, and state school boards. They enjoyed early successes, sometimes spectacularly. In 1999 the Kansas state school board voted six to one to remove evolution from the required state standards for science. The national publicity enraged voters, who in

2001 elected a new board that rescinded the 1999 decision. Yet in 2004 "Kansas voters returned a majority of conservative Republicans to the supervisory body. The next year the board, again by a vote of 6-4, radically revised the science standards, calling for teachers to challenge evolution in the classroom and redefining science to allow for the possibility of supernatural explanations" (ibid., 386).

Clearly these chameleon-like changes could not go on indefinitely, and inevitably the matter ended up in a federal court via another Monkey Trial, although this time in the North.

In 2005 the Area School District Board of Dover, Pennsylvania (population 1,943), decided that students should know about the "problems" relating to Darwinian evolution. A message to teachers included this: "Because Darwin's Theory is a theory, it is still being tested as new evidence is discovered. The Theory is not a fact. . . . Intelligent design is an explanation of the origins of life that differs from Darwin's view. The reference book, *Of Pandas and People*, is available for students to see if they would like to explore this view in an effort to gain an understanding of what intelligent design actually involves" (ibid., 393).

A student's mother asked for help from the ACLU, which agreed, while the school board accepted the pro bono service of the conservative Christian Thomas More Law Center. Both sides knew what the issue would be: Did ID violate the First Amendment of the US Constitution by effectively teaching religion? The trial took place in the fall of 2005 at the federal district court in nearby Harrisburg. Judge John E. Jones III, a conservative Republican, an appointee of President George H. W. Bush, and a practicing Lutheran, presided.

The ACLU had learned from the long-ago Scopes trial. For their expert witnesses, they did not bring a cadre of mocking, scientific atheists but rather believing Christian scholars who publicly acknowledged their faith but still testified against the school board ruling.

The school board's expert witness, an Englishman named Steve William Fuller, insisted that ID is a legitimate scientific enterprise but conceded that it appealed to "supernatural causation," a serious blow to the defense, which then suffered another blow when it became public that the president of the school had told the judge that he did not know where the school library got the money to purchase the copies of *Of Panda and People*, when in fact he knew it had been raised by a former board member at the local fundamentalist church. The trial concluded on November 4. Four days later, before Judge Jones had issued his verdict, "the citizens of Dover, irritated at becoming the Dayton of the North, went to the polls and voted out of office all of the old pro-ID school board members" (ibid., 393).

Judge Jones rendered his verdict on December 20, lambasting the school board for its "breathtaking inanity" and then going on to rule that "it is unconstitutional to teach Intelligent Design as an alternative to evolution in a public school classroom" (ibid., 394).

* * *

Fundamentalists had begun struggling against modernist threats to biblical inerrancy in the late nineteenth century. They lost control of major seminaries but took over some others and founded their own. When they failed to keep state and many private colleges and universities from teaching evolution, they founded some of their own. They could not get high schools to teach biblical creationism, but they did succeed in getting many in religiously conservative areas to simply not teach evolution. Their impact on textbook publishers guaranteed that until the 1960s even many students outside religiously conservative areas knew little about evolution because it was not in the textbooks that their teachers usually followed.

During the Scopes trial, the mainstream media had mocked the fundamentalists, but thanks to radio since the 1940s and cable television since the 1970s, the fundamentalists have widely used media outlets of their own.

When they could not get the biblical creation story taught in science classes, they came up with scientific creationism. When the courts blocked that, they turned to Intelligent Design, a cause they have not yet abandoned, hoping for a more receptive judiciary. This is no vain hope, because many conservative politicians, especially Republicans and including President George W. Bush (in 2005), have expressed support for the teaching of both evolution and intelligent design in schools.

Most importantly, the fundamentalists have the support of a sizeable portion of the population in a country where more than 90 percent of citizens believe in God and attend churches at rates that mystify educated Europeans. Even many people who want the most-modern scientific approaches to be taught in schools still think that God is somehow involved in the coming to be of the natural world and its inhabitants.

Only a fool or someone with no knowledge of history would count the fundamentalists out.

On the other hand, they face major challenges. The most prestigious US science programs, especially the ones with Nobel Prize winners on their faculties, oppose ID, as do the National Science Foundation and other mainstream groups, including institutions like the Smithsonian

Institution, the Cleveland Museum of Natural History, and the American Museum of Natural History. To these can be added the major media outlets that are located in New York, Los Angeles, and Washington, DC, and are often dominated by liberal elites with scarce respect or sympathy for fundamentalists.

The most prestigious seminaries and divinity schools do not deal much with evolution as part of their biblical curricula, but they do employ what is traditionally and correctly known as Higher Criticism, now so common that it is just called modern exegesis. None of these institutions teaches the historicity of Genesis 1–11, and they routinely apply modernist methods to the rest of the Bible. Since such institutions set the pattern if not the standard for others, few mainstream universities or seminaries are likely to support fundamentalist notions of exegesis and science.

Yet unlike the other "heresies" we have studied, this story has not yet reached its conclusion.

* * *

Before considering whether Protestant modernism can be considered a heresy, it worth noting the parallels between the two struggles against modernism. Conservative Protestants dominated not only nineteenth-century American religion but also the country's culture. Papally led Roman Catholicism did likewise for much of western Europe.

Both faced challenges from a changing culture that rejected the dominant religious values. Both attempted to stem the rise of the new culture, Leo XIII by prescribing a revived, Thomistic scholasticism as an alternative to new European philosophies, and the fundamentalists by scientific creationism and then by Intelligent Design.

Both resorted to force, Pius X with great success and the fundamentalists with little.

Neither changed their views, the pope resenting the modern world until his death and the fundamentalists still trying to win back the culture. Pius X had the satisfaction of seeing his program of repression succeed in his lifetime; he was long dead before his successors began modifying and then eliminating his program. The fundamentalists have never had the satisfaction of seeing their program succeed.

* * *

Was (is) Protestant modernism a heresy? There is really no way to answer that question because of Protestant diversity. Liberal northern

Episcopalians and conservative southern Baptists are both Protestants and would recognize each other as such. Contrary to the rigid attitudes of some Roman Catholics, Protestants can see unity strengthened by diversity rather than by imposed uniformity.

All Protestant churches prize the centrality of the Bible, which is a natural instrument of unity, but Scripture must be studied and understood and interpreted. Conclusions about the meaning of particular biblical issues, such as Genesis 1–11, reached in the various churches often disagree. Indeed, the fundamentalist movement began with a disagreement over exegesis.

One can only say that for fundamentalists and other conservative and evangelical Protestants, modernist Protestantism with its acceptance of evolution and higher criticism cannot represent the true church and is thus heretical.

Will this always be the case? Mainline Protestants think not. At some point, the fundamentalists must realize that Genesis cannot be taken literally, that the Old Testament contains much mythical material, that the gospel accounts do not present a historical portrait of Jesus' life and career, that miracles must be questioned in a scientific way, and that the Bible must be understood in its historical context and with its literary devices. Thus, when the fundamentalists finally realize that they have been wrong, they will come around to the truth, unity will be achieved, and accusations of heresy will be no more.

And, of course, the fundamentalists think the same thing will happen—but in the reverse.

With this issue, heresy, like beauty, lies in the eye of the beholder.

Dealing with Heresy Today

Heresy remains a problem for churches, and this chapter will offer suggestions on how churches might deal with it. First, however, we should look back at the impact of historical forces and then at how some modern forces might affect doctrines and prompt some deviation from them.

Montanism simply came along too late. Church history had passed by the age of ecstatic prophecy or, for that matter, almost any kind of prophecy as normative and as a means of church leadership. The Christians had moved into a different world not to eliminate or forestall prophecy but simply because the church expanded geographically and demographically, and church leaders had to respond to those changes.

Monophysitism resulted from a serious theological disputation between the see of Alexandria and those of Antioch, Constantinople, and then Rome. After a time the nontheological factors, especially nationalist Egyptian ones, outweighed the theological ones or at least made them impossible to settle without a resolution of the nontheological factors. Time also played a role. As chances at unity failed, the two sides developed on their own until a separate Monophysite church, consciously independent of Constantinople, came into being. This church survives today. Maybe ecumenical dialogue can do what imperial force could not.

Catharism was a dualistic heresy. It came along at a time when the Western church had no tolerance for any kind of doctrinal differentiation and also when the French monarchy had designs on Languedoc. No option except submission existed for the Cathars, and when they refused to submit, they were destroyed.

Roman Catholic modernism existed mostly in the minds of Pope Pius X and his advisors. It resulted directly from the pope's fear of the modern world and his desire to repudiate it or at least to protect the church from it. When the church's historical situation changed in the 1960s with the Second Vatican Council, which engaged the modern world, Catholic opposition to "modernism" disappeared.

Protestant modernism also results from a fear of the modern world, although in this case a fear of exegetical and scientific developments that challenge a literal, inerrantist interpretation of the opening chapters of Genesis and with it the notion of the Elect. Yet scientists did not set out to challenge Genesis but rather to understand the world of the past. The proponents of Higher Criticism did not set out to undermine the literal approach to the Bible but rather to examine the text's historical background and employment of literary devices. As it happened, both of these did impact inerrantist exegesis. Contemporary physical scientists will not stop their work, nor will professional exegetes turn back the clock, and so fundamentalists will continue to live in a historical situation that challenges their beliefs, that is, promotes "heresy."

Historical factors such as these, as well as many the reader could suggest, will impinge on how churches understand what heresy is and then how they deal with it. This does not mean that churches must give in to the world around them, but it does mean that doctrines such as the Trinity were formulated in a specific place at a specific time. The Trinity may be beyond time and space, but how we understand it is not. Recognition of these factors will not harm belief, but it may help us avoid absolutizing a particular formulation and denouncing as heresy some propositions that suggest a different formulation. Believers and their beliefs cannot escape from history, and it is fruitless to try. We must understand the world we live in and how that world impacts acceptance of traditional beliefs. When we do understand what elements in our world prevent understanding or acceptance of basic beliefs in their traditional formulas, we might be able to find ways to make those beliefs relevant to modern Christians and to avoid generating at least some heresies.

What follows is a list of factors that cause modern believers not to take a particular teaching very seriously and thus to be indifferent when someone deviates from that teaching. It also focuses upon methods previously used to combat heresy but which simply turn off modern believers. What benefit accrues to a church when its members resent the church's methods more than the heresy and thus ignore the threat the heresy may pose?

The difficulty of abusive authority, or at least the perception of such, plays a great role in the modern attitude toward heresy. McGrath phrases it well. "Yet perhaps the ultimate appeal of heresy in our time lies in its challenge to authority. Religious orthodoxy is equated with claims to absolute authority, which are to be resisted and subverted in the name of freedom" (8). Why do people have this attitude? "The debate between heresy and orthodoxy is all too easily transposed to the social and political realms. As a result, any discussion of heresy must acknowledge the darker side of this discussion—the enforcement of ideas by force, the suppression of liberty, and violation of rights" (ibid., 13). Thus, the list will deal with current historical factors that make suppression not just practically impossible but harmful to the church's antiheretical stance. Indeed, to illustrate his point about the "darker side," McGrath cites "western Europe during the Middle Ages" (ibid.). The church is still paying for its "victory" over the Cathars with a hesitancy on the part of believers to accept any response to heresy that violates or even appears to violate the heretic's rights.

After the list come some recommendations about how church leaders can deal with heresy in such a way as to convince their congregants that the issue at hand is a genuine heresy that threatens Christian doctrine and that the church is using ethical, evenhanded methods to deal with it. The list also suggests how to part company with recalcitrant heretics.

Neither section is meant to exhaust the topic or to claim finality; both will include points made in the foregoing paragraphs about the church and the modern world.

Factors Challenging Traditional Means of Dealing with Heresy

Repression/Suppression of Heretical Ideas: The Internet

Even today some church leaders think that they can somehow combat heresy by suppressing the offensive doctrines. This is simply nonsense. Once it has surfaced, any idea, any notion, any belief, no matter how absurd, offensive, vulgar, or even heretical, will end up on the internet and be spread worldwide in less than a day. There is just no way to stop it. And, as something goes viral on the net, it will be picked up by news organizations and publicized even more.

Indeed, it would be in heretics' interest to go online and present themselves as martyrs for free speech. Any document that a church leader sends to a heretic would also end up online, so the accused heretic can show how "oppressive" church leaders are. These leaders will find themselves objects of internet searches, which could turn up embarrassing facts or at least material that could be easily distorted. The net allows heretics and their supporters to fight back and to make their case in public, something that had never been possible before. Finally, believers will be among those on the internet, and, like too many people, they might think that what they read online must be true.

Control of ideas is very much a thing of the past.

Repression/Suppression of Heretics: Free Speech / Fair Play

If ideas cannot be suppressed, can church suppress those who teach them? Not any longer. In modern democracies, people believe that everyone has the right to free expression. The only limits they would put on free speech would be things like using known falsehoods or obscenities or deceitfully shouting out "Fire!" in a crowded theater. Otherwise they believe that people can say what they like, albeit with the understanding that they may pay a price for what they say. For example, an economist who openly attacks a mayor's fiscal program will never be appointed to the mayor's economic council, and a heretic may be dismissed from a seminary, but both retain the right to express their ideas.

For a church to claim that a heretic has no right to publicize her or his views does not resonate with modern attitudes. Stunts like trying to keep a book from being published will only hurt the church and its leaders. Disciplining deviant theologians after a fair and just hearing may be an appropriate method to take, but church leaders who act like totalitarians will simply turn away modern, democratic believers. Let the ideas be expressed and then demonstrated as false or contrary to the faith.

The Modern World

Most modern people like living in the modern world. To use the most basic example, we live longer lives. Scientists believe that the first people who will live to be 150 have already been born. In the United State, centenarians make up the fastest-growing demographic. We also live better. It is no longer news when a septuagenarian is healthy enough to run a marathon.

We are also the best-informed people in history. Nineteenth-century people had to wait for the morning newspaper to get information. Early twentieth-century people had to wait for a scheduled radio news program. We can get the news online, from a notebook, from a tablet, or from an iPhone. We can watch sports events in progress, make appointments, and go shopping, all without a wait. The list could go on indefinitely. We travel to places our ancestors never heard of, and young people today can reasonably expect to enjoy tourist trips into outer space. Nothing seems beyond our reach.

Fondness for the modern world has not always been the Christian view. In the first half of the twentieth century, one of the most popular books among American Roman Catholics was *The Thirteenth: Greatest of Centuries* by James Joseph Walsh (1865–1942), published in 1907 at the height of the Catholic modernist controversy. As late as the 1950s it was given as an academic award to graduating seminarians (Gannon, 380, n. 212). Walsh wrote about Gothic architecture, scholastic theology, epic poetry, and many other great achievements of the thirteenth century, but he did not express much concern about anti-Semitism, the Inquisition, the wretched condition of the peasantry, the lack of democracy or the right to a fair trial, or the endless abuse of women. The thirteenth was hardly the greatest of centuries for more than 90 percent of the population.

Just as traditional Catholics consecrated the thirteenth century, conservative Protestants did likewise for the first century, the apostolic age, often the standard by which later, supposedly corrupt ages would be judged. Anyone believing that should read Paul's First Epistle to the Corinthians: bickering, cliques, sexual immorality, drunkenness, gluttony, and dragging fellow believers into court on petty matters. And these are the people Paul addresses as "saints." One shudders to think what the sinners must have been like.

Many modern believers do not understand their leaders' insistence that they must believe something simply because our religious ancestors believed it. Obviously, churches must not compromise the truth to accommodate modern trends, but religious leaders must recognize that simply citing past Christians, even scriptural writers, carries less and less weight today. Church leaders must have reasons for their teachings, and they must be able to justify them to modern believers. Will modern Christians take seriously the views of thinkers who, by comparison, knew very little about the world and its people? Picture the poor church leader telling a group of believers that the church holds a particular view because it was held by some fourth-century theologian, only to have someone ask why the church follows the lead of a sexist slave owner who believed in religious persecution. In fact, modern believers can still learn much from the early theologians, but church leaders must learn to explain why we should follow ancient and medieval teachings and not just fall back on "We've always done it."

Who Created the Doctrines?

The rise of the social sciences in the nineteenth century changed forever the human understanding of human understanding.

Anthropology proved to what extent we are creatures of the culture in which we live and how that culture impacts our values and even our views of the world and morality.

Sociology has demonstrated that we all live in groups and that we routinely acquire the values of the group. If we lived in different groups, our values would at least be somewhat different. In nineteenth-century America, Protestant ministers, Catholic bishops, and Jewish rabbis produced arguments to justify slavery. Not surprisingly, none of the writers who endorsed slavery as a good was a slave but instead belonged to very different social groups. Does anyone really believe that if they were slaves, they would have praised slavery as a good?

Psychology has taught us that there are many forces operating within our psyche that we do not fully recognize or understand. It also teaches us the inestimable importance of our upbringing. Clergy know that the children of parents who go to church are more likely to be churchgoers themselves. In the other direction, two-thirds of abusive husbands and fathers were themselves abused as children and thus grew up believing that violence is the way to deal with problems and disputes.

These social sciences demonstrate how various forces shape our views, including the views of those who have created Christian doctrines. That hardly means that we need to know everything about the creator of every doctrine, but it does mean that no doctrine fell from heaven with totally objective wording. To use a huge and obvious example, Christianity grew up in Europe and still reflects that upbringing even as it grows more and more into a truly worldwide religion. Ancient and medieval European theologians considered their doctrinal formulations to be objective accounts of objective truths, but moderns know that they relied heavily upon Greek thinkers—Platonists in the early church, Aristotle in the medieval church—and upon Greco-Roman culture as a whole. Must Christian truth be dependent upon a historical Eurocentric expression of that truth? As in the two modernist controversies, what happens when the traditional explanation or verbal expression does not or cannot answer the questions posed by the modern world?

Today, when African and Asian Christians object to having a Eurocentric culture imposed upon them, church leaders are sensitive to that. African and Asian Christians can benefit from the positive elements of the European worldview, but church leaders should not force that worldview upon them. Indeed, the leaders should be open to African and Asian ways of expressing Christian belief. Moving from geography to chronology, church leaders should be equally sensitive to imposing the views of ancient and medieval people upon those who live in a vastly different world. While there is still much that modern Christians can learn from ancient and medieval thinkers, older views should not be imposed on people when those views have been proven incorrect or at least questionable.

To use a personal anecdote, I once had an African Roman Catholic priest in a graduate course on patristic theology that covered subordinationism, *homooúsios*, and Christ as one person in two natures. This priest explained to the class that he found all this very fascinating because in his country, where people have a strong belief in evil spirits, Jesus is the Great Exorcist. It was striking how the American students—and their instructor—were glad that this African Christian had now learned about Greco-Roman theologizing, yet none of us seemed particularly interested in learning this African's concept of Christ. Realization of our ethnocentrism prompted us all to do some embarrassed soul searching.

Women

Feminist scholars have proved that in addition to culture, social status, and upbringing, gender plays a significant role in how people view the world. Outside the churches, this has become so widely accepted as to have reached popular culture: "It's a guy thing"; "Men are from Mars and women are from Venus." In almost all churches from their inceptions into the late twentieth century and in some churches even today, the only people creating the doctrinal formulations have been men. For centuries they could justify that position because they "knew" God was male, as every work of Christian art demonstrates, or they "knew" that women were less intelligent, emotionally weak, and the like. With those absurdities now gone, today the argument for excluding women from doctrinal decisions falls on the fact that Jesus and Twelve were all men, and so ultimately only men can make such decisions. Of course, the Twelve were also all Palestinian Jews, yet no one insists that modern clergy all be Palestinian Jews. Feminists have pointed out that no opponent of women's full equality in churches explains why gender is binding until the Second Coming but ethnicity is not.

Fewer and fewer modern women and men can take seriously church teachings that do not include the views of women or their actual participation in doctrinal formation, and this would be particularly true of teachings on women's roles, marriage, sexual activity, and procreation. This is because for the first time in history the always-neglected and often-oppressed half of the human race is making its deserved impact. The role of women in modern life has done nothing but grow. Women have held the highest offices in the United Kingdom, Argentina, Chile, Germany, the Ukraine, India, Liberia, Kyrgyzstan, and Pakistan, inter alia, and in the United States women presidential candidates are now common. In Western society only churches maintain barriers to women's full participation.

No one would deny the immense contributions made by Paul, Athanasius, Cyril, Augustine, Aquinas, Luther, Calvin, Schleiermacher, Barth, Bultmann, and Rahner, but one can legitimately wonder what their theologies might have been like had these male theologians consulted women. To use a pertinent example, would the people who actually had the babies be as quick as Augustinian and Calvinist theologians to send unbaptized infants to hell?

An all-male church establishment may also find it increasingly difficult to get women and many modern men to agree with them on any number of issues. This is not because these dissidents have "heretical views," but because they question the validity of a decision-making body that ignores half the human race.

Science

Too often people assume that science and religion must oppose one another, something easily disproven by the existence of the many scientists who are believers. But the fact is that discoveries in the physical sciences have forced religious groups to change their teachings, but no religious doctrine has ever forced scientists to change a teaching in the physical sciences.

Since astronomers demonstrated that heaven cannot be a physical place above the skies, Christians cannot talk about physical ascensions into heaven, although there may be people who still believe in them. Nor can they talk about the Last Judgment in biblical terms of the heavens opening since science demonstrated there is no physical heaven above to open. Psychology has made people question the facticity of heavenly or demonic apparitions. The ability of physicians to sustain life even after a heart stoppage or brain death have called into question the nature of death and thus spurred discussion of end-of-life moral issues. Evolutionary ethics has demonstrated that genetic forces push people to act in certain ways. Most importantly, as we have seen, evolutionary biology and uniformitarian geology have demonstrated that a literal interpretation of Genesis 1–11 is simply impossible.

Religious authorities should not bow to science on every issue, but they must accept that science will continue impact religious teachings. Religious leaders also have the obligation to know something about the area that science impacts. Many scientists have understandable disdain for fundamentalists who oppose evolution but have no real knowledge of either biology or geology. How many Christians who oppose stem cell research can identify stem cells? Some religious leaders may understandably resent what they consider scientific intrusion into their teachings, but resentment will not solve problems that scientific advancement may present to those teachings. A theologian or exegete who challenges traditional teaching on scientific grounds could be rendering the church a service.

Traditionally, religious leaders have been reluctant to have their teachings judged by other-than-religious criteria, but nowadays science has made such an attitude a luxury.

Specialists

The rise of the specialist probably presents the greatest threat to religious leaders on matters of doctrine because, like incipient heretics, specialists belong to the church. Specialists just do their jobs in theology, exegesis, ethics and moral theology, liturgy, and church history, and in so doing they can unconsciously and usually unwillingly put pressure on church leaders in matters of interpretation and doctrinal formulation.

To cite just one area of specialization, the minimum linguistic requirement to get a doctorate in biblical studies today is learning four languages: Hebrew and Greek to be able to read the biblical text and then usually French and German to read the secondary literature, although more and more scholars must also learn Italian and Spanish. Scholars working on the Old Testament usually learn one or more other ancient Near Eastern languages, such as Akkadian (language of ancient Babylonia), Egyptian, or Sumerian; since the New Testament was coterminous with the Roman Empire, scholars in that area usually learn Latin.

Formidable as that sounds, it is only the beginning. Scholars are expected to keep up in their fields for their entire careers. They must present learned papers at local, regional, national, and international meetings of scholarly societies. They also must write articles and books ("publish or perish"). Although not always required, they should win grants or fellowships from foundations. Within this specialty, even more specialties arise—for example, participating in archaeological digs or learning paleography (study of ancient handwriting) to access the authentic, oldest biblical manuscripts, a precondition for textual criticism.

In most churches, the leaders rarely have these qualifications, yet the faithful expect them to speak authoritatively on those matters. As we saw with Catholic modernism, those in leadership positions tried fruitlessly to stop the new learning by assertions of authority. Modern exegesis also bothered many conservative Protestants who felt the specialists were not helping them to understand the Bible better but were instead putting up academic walls between the Bible and the believer.

The situation has not changed much. By the late twentieth century Pope John Paul II opposed Catholic exegetes who questioned or even denied the historicity of the virginal conception. But he could not come up with scholarly responses to adequately answer them, and the issue remains unsettled. Yet the pope and not the exegetes determines church teaching. As we just saw in chapter 6, many conservative Protestant leaders often ignore scholarly work on Genesis 1–11.

This applies in other fields. There are scholarly societies devoted to the study of Origen, Augustine, Aquinas, Luther, and Calvin, inter alios. A friend and colleague of this author once described himself as "a specialist in the early, philosophical Augustine." There is simply no way that church leaders can keep up with what specialists are doing.

But then how long can leaders continue to teach what the scholars demonstrate cannot be so or is at best questionable? As just noted, the internet guarantees that these new ideas cannot be suppressed, and educated believers often know that their leaders are teaching things contrary to the findings of modern scholarship. Assertions of authority cannot suffice in an era of specialists. Scholars are impressed by knowledge and technical achievement, not by ecclesiastical titles, especially if leaders think that titles and offices give them understanding of biblical and theological issues superior to that of the scholars. On the other hand, does anyone really want to hand orthodoxy over to scholars who debate every point endlessly and whose findings might change over time? Before Galileo, most *scientists* believed that the planets moved around the earth in concentric, crystalline spheres. Should Christians have to put their beliefs on hold until the professors have finally come to agreement on some point?

I wish I had a solution to this problem. It might help if those in authority would accept that their offices alone do not make them authoritative, that they have the obligation to keep abreast of what scholars are doing, and that they need scholarly reasons for ignoring, much less condemning, what the scholars have concluded or suggested. No one expects leaders to be superpersons, and humility is no vice in any leader.

Religious Studies

Most students in democracies attend public colleges and universities, which by statute must be religiously neutral. These institutions offer courses in religious studies but not in theology in the sense of "faith seeking understanding" because the instructors cannot assume faith on the part of the students, nor must the instructor necessarily be a believer. This may disturb some Christians, but a public institution must be equitable. For example, if a scholar who is Christian teaches a course on Buddhist beliefs, there is thus no academic reason why a Buddhist could not teach a course on Christian beliefs. Some Christians might find that unacceptable, but that would not matter because a religious studies course must be neutral in matters of faith. The instructor cannot ignore the students' faith and can often presume that most come from a Christian background to which she or he must be sensitive, but the instructor cannot privilege Christianity over other religions, and Christian students must accept that.

In such an environment, Christian students learn to study religion objectively, and in comparative religions courses they are exposed to a variety of traditions, all of which must be respected, no matter how much they differ from one another and how much they differ from the student's own Christian faith. Religious studies courses on Christianity must also treat all Christians objectively and, for example, must avoid calling someone a heretic. (The professor should, of course, tell the students that the church considers this person a heretic if that is a matter of fact.)

Let us consider an example. In the fifth century a debate about free will arose between Augustine of Hippo and a British monk named Pelagius. Augustine triumphed, and his views persisted until the twentieth century and, as we saw, still have adherents today. When past Christians spoke about the debate, it was usually characterized as between *Saint* Augustine, *bishop, Father of the Church* and *Doctor of the Church*, against Pelagius the *heretic* if not the *heresiarch*, that is, a leader of a heresy. Clearly, there was no doubt about whose views were correct. But in an objective, religious studies setting, Augustine and Pelagius become two theologians whose views need to be discussed and analyzed without any reference to official recognition by the church. Modern scholars, such as Peter Brown, Henry Chadwick, and James O'Donnell, feel free to discuss Augustine in terms of his relentless social climbing, pettiness, sternness, lack of a sense of fair play, and willingness to use political power and even force in religious matters, along with his remarkable theological, spiritual, and literary genius. Augustine remains one of the best Christian theologians who ever lived, but Augustinian scholars look at him objectively and no longer feel obliged to justify or explain away some of his extreme views simply because he is considered a saint.

Heresy represents unacceptable diversity, and church leaders have difficulty treating it objectively since they recognize a threat to the faith. But leaders must accept that many of their faithful were academically trained in religious studies courses to accept diversity and to analyze religious matters objectively. Melodramatic agonizing about the destruction of the faith and citations of revered, deceased authorities do not play well with modern people educated that way. Far better to explain—objectively— why the heretic is wrong and why the church's position is correct.

Lay Professors

It is also worth noting the vast majority of religion professors, including those at religiously affiliated universities, are lay people who are not liable to any professional restrictions or even sanctions that church leaders can place upon clergy (seminary instructors do not fall into this category). As we noted in chapter 5, religious leaders can excommunicate lay people, but they cannot get them dismissed from a university. Since half of lay professors are women, students will see them as authority figures on matters of religion even though a number of churches still do not.

The other problem for church leaders about lay professors is that students become accustomed to seeing them rather than the clergy as the teachers of the faith. To use a personal note, some years ago while explaining to a class about the bishops' *magisterium* (collective teaching authority) in the Roman Catholic Church, I noticed that the students had genuine difficulty with the concept. Then it dawned on me that all their lives they had been taught by laypersons, even if they went to Catholic elementary and/or high schools. One wonders what will happen to clerical authority among Christians who do not encounter clerics.

Churchgoing lay professors will naturally be loyal to their churches and will not use their professorial positions to criticize them, but, as lay people, they will inevitably differ from the clergy on some matters, even if they teach in religiously affiliated schools. To cite a potent example, a woman who spent eight years getting her doctorate and, along the way, had to learn several languages, secure a grant or fellowship, and write articles or even a book, is not likely to tell students that women are inherently unqualified for ministry. Male professors work with female colleagues, and most would share the views of the women professors. This does not mean that the lay teachers will oppose what the clergy teaches, but rather that they cannot give wholehearted support to a teaching with which they disagree. Lay teachers, especially lay women, would be in a very awkward position if a student were to ask, "Do you personally think women are unqualified for ordination?"

Lay professors are here to stay, and church leaders must now acknowledge the faithful's acceptance of lay persons as authorities alongside or, very problematically, in place of the clergy. This situation may impact the acceptance of an accusation of heresy defined solely by clergy.

Nulla Salus Extra Ecclesiam and Heresy

For centuries churches have taught that only those who belong to the true church and have been baptized will get to heaven, unless God makes some kind of exemption for someone on the outside. The capacity of past Christians to send people to hell is appalling.

But this view has gone with the wind. Modern Christians simply do not believe that God is going to damn to eternal punishment one billion Hindus, 1.2 billion Muslims, and half a billion Buddhists simply because they do not belong to the church. Much of this new attitude originated with church teaching because most churches now acknowledge that God may also work through other traditions. But much of the church's change in attitude grew from historical factors, especially the increasingly small world in which we live.

Christian tourists to India see tens of millions of Hindus. Would God really condemn them all? American troops stationed in Japan and Korea meet Buddhists and Shintoists. Would God really condemn them too? Islam is the fastest-growing religion in the Western world, especially in the United States. As we have Muslim coworkers, neighbors, and friends, do we really believe they are all going to hell? And after the genuinely indescribable sufferings the Jews endured during the Holocaust, do Christians really want to add to that by sending them to hell for not belonging to the church? Such an attitude is simply obscene.

But if God looks kindly on all of his children who are not Christian, does he not also look kindly upon heretics? If those who do not even believe in Jesus can get to heaven, why would those who truly believe Jesus to be both human and divine go off to damnation because they believe he is "from" two natures rather than "in" two natures? How can a dispute over terminology be more reprehensible than non-acceptance of Jesus as the Redeemer? It is simply ridiculous to tell people that God cares for animists in the Amazonian forest but not for those who believe in his Son but use the wrong preposition to do so. Church leaders can expel a heretic from the ecclesial community but no longer from the community of the saved.

Teaching Nonsense

Like many Roman Catholics, I was delighted when in 2005 Pope Benedict XVI sent limbo into limbo. He did not deny that it exists, but he emphasized that God does not automatically deny heaven to unbaptized babies; on the contrary, most unbaptized infants would be welcomed in heaven. Naturally, the Catholic Right attacked the pope for deleting a "truth of the faith" (see, for example, http://www.mostholyfamilymonastery.com/BenedictXVI_new_limbo_heresy.php), but most Catholics were delighted or at least relieved that something so nonsensical—a beneficent God refusing heaven to infants for not getting baptized, an act over which they had zero control—had been put in its place. Has any Catholic heard a sermon on limbo since then?

The problem with asking people to believe in something that does not make sense is that they will then be less likely to believe in something serious. Many Christians continue to insist on the literal meaning of hundreds of questionable biblical texts, but how many modern people really believe that Jonah was swallowed by a huge fish and lived for three days in its bowels (Jonah 1:15–2:11) or that Elijah went off to the sky in a fiery chariot (2 Kgs 2:11)?

If being asked to accept nonsense makes people skeptical about church teaching, how will heresy ever be considered dangerous? After all, what is wrong with someone saying that Jesus did not really die and rise but was anesthetized with a drug and later awakened by his disciples (a theory seriously promoted in the 1980s), when a church expects people to believe that a loving God murdered tens of thousands of Egyptian children just to prove a point to Pharaoh (Exod 12:29-30)?

Clearly, churches must concern themselves with everyone, including people who do accept such things, but the leaders should also concern themselves with the growing number of educated believers. And why not try to educate the more credulous of the faithful instead of keeping them in ignorance? Preaching nonsense is an invitation not to take heresy seriously.

The foregoing list was not a pleasant one to draw up, but heresy is real and must be dealt with by the church, yet using discredited, ridiculous, offensive, and even unchristian methods will never succeed.

Some Positive Suggestions

Development of Doctrine and Alternate Formulations

One of the leading Anglican scholars of the last century was Bishop R. P. C. Hanson (1916–88), who composed a very accessible book, *The Continuity of Christian Doctrine* (1981), on the topic of development. He wrote about one of his heroes, John Henry Newman, and about J. B. Mozley (1813–78), an insightful Anglican critic of Newman. Hanson recounts the many effective criticisms Mozley made of Newman's book *An Essay on the Development of Christian Doctrine*,

> but when Mozley comes to deal with the main point, and the main challenge, of Newman's book—the firm assertion that to say, for instance, that the Son is consubstantial with the Father is not precisely equivalent to what any of the gospels and epistles in the New Testament say about him, nor to what all of them say together—then Mozley's argument fails altogether. Newman, no matter how mildly and indirectly he hinted at the fact, did realize that the Christian doctrine of God had changed, that Justin Martyr and Irenaeus [second century] did not teach what Athanasius [fourth century] taught. (24)

Maybe Newman's moment has arrived. The popularity of his work has done nothing but increase since circa 1950, and the days when critics thought "development" was a euphemism for the change that no Christian leader wanted to acknowledge are now gone. Development is recognized not as something that challenges the truths found in Scripture but as something found in Scripture itself.

We have seen some of that in this book. The leaders of the early Jerusalem community, the very first Christians, did not envision a mission to the Gentiles, but Paul and others changed their mind, as seen in Acts and Paul's epistles, all of which are scriptural books. Paul and others expected an imminent Parousia, but Luke played that down in Acts, and 2 Peter admitted that belief in it was fading—again, evidence of development in Scripture itself.

Yes, but these are peripheral, some might say. Biblical exegetes would not call these peripheral, but, for discussion, let us concede that point. But there is no way that Christology, the theology of Christ, can be peripheral to Christianity. To see christological development, all one need do is consider the image of Christ in Paul's epistles, then turn to Mark's gospel, then to the Christology of Matthew and Luke, who used Mark as the basis for their gospels, and finally to the Gospel of John with its high Christology so different from those of the other three, as well as from that of Paul. And these differences are just in the gospels. Other biblical books would present other christologies, such as Christ the High Priest in the Epistle to the Hebrews.

Examples of other doctrines could be cited. For example, Paul's ecclesiology (theology of the church) focuses on the individual community, while in Acts Luke focuses on a growing international church. But the point is clear: development of doctrine cannot oppose Scripture since it is found in Scripture itself.

The *possibility* of development should be applied whenever an apparent heresy arises. Just because someone is teaching something different does not mean it is heresy. It may be so, but it may also be the beginning of a valid new development that immediate condemnation could cut off. No church leader should allow someone teaching something contrary to accepted belief to go unchallenged, but any challenge should be a Christian one. Unless they have good reason to think otherwise, the leaders must accept the "heretic" as a member of the Christian community who thinks that a new approach or a new formulation of a teaching is necessary for today, maybe not as a replacement for a current formulation but as an alternate mode of expression. Faith first, formulation second.

The leaders should appreciate that someone is doing some serious thinking about an issue even if they disagree with this new thinking. Also, it would help to remember that some of the most reviled heretics in Christian history advanced theology by forcing theologians to think more deeply and clearly about a doctrine; for example, Nicene trinitarianism began with Arius, the archetypal heresiarch, who asked how there can be a subordinate deity. To be sure, his approach, that the Son is a created being, was not the faith of the church, but he destroyed subordinationism and certainly forced the Nicenes to sharpen their own views. It is also worth recalling that some heretics had also been theologians who had advanced doctrine; for example, Apollinaris was a champion of Nicene orthodoxy before he became Apollinaris the heretic.

The foregoing paragraph to an extent makes heretics sound like oppressed innocents, which would be a misleading image of them. There always have been some people who truly do not care what the Scripture teaches or what the church has traditionally understood. Such people present a danger to the church and should be recognized as such. But these people are still children of God who deserve to be taken seriously, to be won over, and to be lamented if they cannot be reconciled with the church. Furthermore, church authorities must be sure that they themselves correctly understand the church's teaching, that they have considered what validity the current community gives to that teaching, and that they have clearly explained to the offending believer why her or his views cannot be reconciled with that teaching. The leaders should also be ready to answer challenges and not to dismiss them. For example, if a male leadership group is told by a woman "heretic" that they simply do not know what they are talking about on a woman's issue, they must be ready to justify why they can speak authoritatively about this issue without any experiential knowledge. If struggling with that forces them to think hard about this issue and maybe even to reconsider it, that is all to the good. Even if they conclude that their teaching and approach remain valid, they have still been forced to think about it and possibly to update and strengthen it. Uncomfortable as they may be, dissidents often keep people and institutions on the alert.

It is also extremely important that church leaders not concede innovation to dissidents. Every educated Christian knows that doctrines have developed over the centuries and that it would be absurd to assume that doctrines will cease to develop in the twenty-first century. If a leader concludes that a traditional interpretation is losing relevance, she or he should not need a "heretic" to force the issue. Augustine challenged the traditional interpretation of the Garden of Eden. Paul challenged the view that the Christians should evangelize only the Jews. And, of course, Jesus challenged the accepted view of the Messiah as triumphant and replaced it with the Messiah as a Suffering Servant. Why, in doctrinal matters, should Christian leadership always mean fear of the new?

What if the received teaching is clear and not currently in need of development, and the heretic still rejects it? Then church leaders must move to separate the heretic from the community. They must make sure that the heretic has been given due process, has been informed clearly where her or his teaching departs from church belief, has been given the opportunity to respond freely, has in turn been responded to openly and clearly, has been given a chance to respond to the response, has been informed of the leaders' decision, has been offered the opportunity to change her or his views, and, finally and most importantly, has been informed that the leaders take the step of excommunication with the greatest regret and with the hope that the heretic will one day return to communion.

Sometimes a leader can deal with the problem without effecting total separation. Let me give a successful Roman Catholic example. In a midwestern American diocese, a tenured professor at a local Catholic university repeatedly, strongly, and publicly challenged church teaching on a particular issue. The local bishop took the intelligent, appropriate, and fair step. He declared that this theologian would no longer be welcome at any diocesan function—no parish lectures, no membership on a diocesan task force, and the like—but the bishop did not once suggest that the theologian lose his position at the university or in any way be reprimanded by university officials. The bishop recognized the theologian's right to free expression of his views. Significantly, he did not excommunicate the theologian, thus preserving the possibility and hope of future reconciliation. This is a model way to deal with doctrinal disagreement.

* * *

The new Jerusalem has not yet arrived. The true church awaits a different reality. The current church lives in history, in change, and in challenge. If a doctrinal formulation has lost its relevance or at least its comprehensibility for modern believers, then the church must do something about it. If someone points out this deficiency and suggests an unacceptable alternative, branding or calling her or him a heretic will not solve the problem. When church leaders can be confident that they have done everything possible to give a doctrine a strong foundation in Scripture and church tradition, to provide a firm and comprehensible base for it with contemporary believers, and to ensure that the doctrine can stand up to modern challenges such as scientific advances, then and only then can they speak of heresy. But when they do, people will listen.

Bibliography

Chapters One and Seven

Walter Bauer. *Orthodoxy and Heresy in Earliest Christianity*. Philadelphia: Fortress Press, 1971.

Peter Brown. *Augustine of Hippo*. Berkeley: University of California Press, 2000.

Henry Chadwick. *Augustine of Hippo: A Life*. New York: Oxford University Press, 2009.

Owen Chadwick. *From Bossuet to Newman*. New York: Cambridge University Press, 1985.

G. R. Evans. *A Brief History of Heresy*. Oxford: Blackwell, 2002.

R. P. C. Hanson. *The Continuity of Christian Doctrine*. New York: Seabury Press, 1981.

Nicholas Lash. *Newman on Development*. London: Sheed and Ward, 1975.

Alister McGrath. *Heresy: A History of Defending the Truth*. New York: Harper-One, 2009.

John Henry Newman. *An Essay on the Development of Christian Doctrine*. New York: Doubleday, 1960.

James O'Donnell. *Augustine*. Boston: Twayne Publishers, 1986.

Jonathan Wright. *Heretics: The Creation of Christianity from the Gnostics to the Modern Church*. Boston: Houghton Mifflin, 2011.

Chapter Two

Rex Butler. *The New Prophecy and "New Visions."* Washington, DC: Catholic University of America Press, 2006.

Elizabeth Clark. *Women in the Early Church*. Message of the Fathers of the Church 13. Collegeville, MN: Liturgical Press, 1983.

Susanna Elm. *Virgins of God: The Making of Asceticism in Late Antiquity*. Oxford: Clarendon Press, 1996.

Francis Glimm, ed. *The Apostolic Fathers*. Fathers of the Church 1. New York: CIMA Publishing Company, 1947. (Useful collection of non-Montanist Christian writings of the second century.)

Ronald Heine, ed. *The Montanist Oracles and Testimonies*. Patristic Monograph Series 16. Macon, GA: Mercer University Press, 1989.

Pierre Labriolle. *Les Sources d'Histoire du Montanisme.* New York: AMS Press, 1980.

Johannes Lindbloom. *Prophecy in Ancient Israel.* Philadelphia: Fortress Press, 1967.

Ramsay MacMullen. *Voting about God in Early Church Councils.* New Haven, CT: Yale University Press, 2006.

Eric Osborne. *Tertullian: First Theologian of the West.* New York: Cambridge University Press, 1997.

William Tabbernee. *Montanist Inscriptions and Testimonia.* Patristic Monograph Series 16. Washington, DC: Catholic University of America Press, 1996.

————. *Prophets and Gravestones.* Peabody, MA: Hendrickson Publishers, 2009.

Christine Trevett. *Montanism: Gender, Authority, and the New Prophecy.* New York: Cambridge University Press, 1996.

Chapter Three

Rosemary Arthur. *Pseudo-Dionysius as Polemicist.* Aldershot: Ashgate, 2008.

John Binns. *Ascetics and Ambassadors of Christ: The Monasteries of Palestine 314–631.* Oxford: Clarendon Press, 1994.

S. J. Davis. *The Early Coptic Papacy: The Egyptian Church and Its Leadership in Late Antiquity.* Cairo: American University in Cairo Press, 2004.

W. H. C. Frend. *The Rise of the Monophysite Movement.* Cambridge: Lutterworth Press, 2008 [1972].

C. W. Griggs. *Early Egyptian Christianity: From Its Origins to 451 C.E.* Leiden: Brill, 1990.

Alois Grillmeier. *Christ in Christian Tradition.* 2 vols. Louisville: Westminster John Knox, 1995 [1988].

R.P.C. Hanson. *The Search for the Christian Doctrine of God: The Arian Controversy.* Edinburgh, T & T Clark, 1988.

Cornelia Horn and Robert Phenix, eds. *John Rufus: The Lives of Peter the Iberian, Theodosius of Jerusalem, and the Monk Romanus.* Writings from the Greco-Roman World. Atlanta: Society of Biblical Literature, 2008.

Volker Menze. *Justinian and the Making of the Syrian Orthodox Church.* Oxford Early Christian Studies. New York: Oxford University Press, 2008.

John Meyendorff. *Christ in Eastern Christian Thought.* Washington, DC: Corpus Books, 1975.

Norman Russell. *Cyril of Alexandria.* London: Routledge, 2000.

Chapter Four

Malcolm Barber. *The Cathars: Dualist Heretics in Languedoc in the High Middle Ages.* New York: Longman, 2000.

Caterina Bruschi. *The Wandering Heretics of Languedoc*. New York: Cambridge University Press, 2009.

Michael Costen. *The Cathars and the Albigensian Crusade*. Manchester: Manchester University Press, 1997.

Malcolm Lambert. *The Cathars*. Oxford: Blackwell, 1998.

———. *Medieval Heresy*. Oxford: Blackwell, 2002.

Sean Martin. *The Cathars*. Edison, NJ: Chartwell Books, 2006.

John Moore, ed. *Pope Innocent III and His World*. Aldershot: Ashgate, 1999.

John Mundy. *Society and Government at Toulouse in the Age of the Cathars*. Toronto: Pontifical Institute of Medieval Studies, 1997.

Mark Pegg. *A Most Holy War: The Albigensian Crusade and the Battle for Christendom*. New York: Oxford University Press, 2009.

James Powell, ed. *Innocent III: Vicar of Christ or Lord of the World?* Washington, DC: Catholic University of America Press, 1994.

Andrew Roach. *The Devil's World: Heresy and Society 1100–1300*. London: Longman, 2005.

Jane Sayers. *Innocent III: Leader of Europe 1198–1216*. London: Longman, 1994.

Yuri Stoyanov. *The Other God: Dualist Religions from Antiquity to the Cathar Heresy*. New Haven, CT: Yale University Press, 2000.

Claire Taylor. *Heresy in Medieval France*. Woodbridge, Suffolk: Boydell Press, 2005.

Walter Wakefield and Austin Evans, eds. *Heresies of the High Middle Ages*. Records of Civilization. New York: Columbia University Press, 1991. (Original sources about the Cathars in translation.)

Chapter Five

Maurice Blondel. *Action*. Notre Dame, IN: University of Notre Dame Press, 1984.

Gabriel Daly. "Theology and Philosophical Modernism." In *Catholicism Contending with Modernity*, edited by Darrell Jodock, 88–112 (New York: Cambridge University Press, 2000).

———. *Transcendence and Immanence*. New York: Oxford University Press, 1980.

Eamon Duffy. *Saints and Sinners: A History of the Popes* (New Haven, CT: Yale University Press, 1997).

Michael Gannon. "Before and After Modernism: The Intellectual Isolation of the American Priest." In *The Catholic Priest in the United States: Historical Investigations*, edited by John Tracy Ellis, 293–383. Collegeville, MN: Liturgical Press, 1971.

Peter Gay. *The Enlightenment: An Interpretation*. 2 vols. New York: Knopf, 1966–69.

John Heaney. *The Modernist Crisis: Von Hügel*. Cleveland: Corpus Books, 1968.

Harvey Hill. "The Politics of Loisy's Modernist Theology." In *Catholicism Contending with Modernity*, edited by Darrell Jodock, 169–190 (New York: Cambridge University Press, 2000).

———. *The Politics of Modernism*. Washington, DC: Catholic University of America Press, 2002.

Darrell Jodock, ed. *Catholicism Contending with Modernity*. New York: Cambridge University Press, 2000.

Phyllis Kaminsky. "Seeking Transcendence in the Modern World." In *Catholicism Contending with Modernity*, edited by Darrell Jodock, 115–41 (New York: Cambridge University Press, 2000).

Lester Kurtz. *The Politics of Heresy: The Modernist Crisis in Roman Catholicism*. Berkeley: University of California Press, 1986.

Michael Lacey. "Leo's Church and Our Own." In *The Crisis of Authority in Catholic Modernity*, edited by Michael Lacey and Francis Oakley, 57–92. New York: Oxford University Press, 2011.

J. B. Lemius. *A Catechism of Modernism*. Rockford, IL: Tan Books, 1981.

Alfred Loisy. *The Gospel and the Church*. New York: Scribner, 1912.

Gerald McCool. *Catholic Theology in the Nineteenth Century*. New York: Seabury Press, 1077.

Anthony Mioni, ed. *The Popes against Modern Errors: 16 Papal Documents; Hard-Hitting Condemnations of Today's Most Noxious Errors*. Rockford, IL: Tan Books, 1999.

Paul Misner. "Catholic Anti-Modernism: the Ecclesial Setting." In *Catholicism Contending with Modernity*, edited by Darrell Jodock, 56–87 (New York: Cambridge University Press, 2000).

Bernard Montagnes, OP. *The Story of Father Joseph-Marie Lagrange*. Translated by Benedict Viviano, OP. Mahwah, NJ: Paulist Press, 2006.

Marvin O'Connell. *Critics on Trial: An Introduction to the Catholic Modernist Crisis*. Washington, DC: Catholic University of America Press, 1994.

Oliver Rafferty, ed. *George Tyrrell and Catholic Modernism*. Dublin: Four Courts Press, 2010.

David Schultenover, SJ. *A View from Rome: On the Eve of the Modernist Controversy*. New York: Fordham University Press, 1993.

C. J. T. Talar. "Innovation and Biblical Interpretation." In *Catholicism Contending with Modernity*, edited by Darrell Jodock, 191–212 (New York: Cambridge University Press, 2000).

George Tyrell. *Christianity at the Crossroads*. London: George Unwin & Unwin Ltd., 1963.

Online Sources

Leo XIII. *Aeterni Patris.* http://www.papalencyclicals.net/Leo13/l13cph.htm.

———. *Providentissimus Deus.* http://www.papalencyclicals.net/Leo13/l13provi.htm.

———. *Testem Benevolentiae Nostrae.* http://www.papalencyclicals.net/Leo13/l13teste.htm.

Pius X. *Lamentabili Sane.* http://www.papalencyclicals.net/Pius10/p10lamen.htm.

———. Oath against Modernism. http://www.papalencyclicals.net/Pius10/p10moath.htm.

———. *Pascendi Dominici Gregis.* http://www.papalencyclicals.net/Pius10/p10pasce.htm.

Pius XII. *Divino Afflante Spiritu.* http://www.papalencyclicals.net/Pius12/P12DIVIN.HTM.

Chapter Six

Richard Coniff. *The Species Seakers.* New York: W. W. Norton and Company, 2011.

Richard Dawkins. *The Blind Watchmaker: Why the Evidence of Evolution Reveals a Universe without Design,* new ed. New York: W. W. Norton and Company, 1996. First edition published by Norton in 1986.

William B. Gatewood, ed. *Controversy in the Twenties: Fundamentalism, Modernism, and Evolution.* Nashville: Vanderbilt University Press, 1969. (Good collection of primary sources.)

Norman Geisler. *Creation and the Courts.* Wheaton, IL: Crossway, 2007.

Peter Harrison. *The Bible, Protestantism, and the Rise of Natural Science.* New York: Cambridge University Press, 1999.

———. *The Fall of Man and the Foundations of Science.* New York: Cambridge University Press, 2007.

William Hutchison. *The Modernist Impulse in American Protestantism.* New York: Oxford University Press, 1982.

Julia Scott Jones. *Being the Chosen: Exploring a Fundamentalist Worldview.* Farnham, Surrey: Ashgate, 2010.

Jerry Korsmeyer. *Evolution and Eden.* Mahwah, NJ: Paulist Press, 1998.

Edward Larson. *Summer for the Gods.* New York: Basic Books, 1997.

Michael Lienesch. *In the Beginning.* Raleigh: University of North Carolina Press, 2007.

George Marsden. *Fundamentalism and American Culture.* New York: Oxford University Press, 2006.

————. *Understanding Fundamentalism and Evangelicalism*. Grand Rapids, MI: William B. Eerdmans Publishing Co., 1991.

Dorothy Nelkin. *The Creation Controversy: Science or Scripture in the Schools*. San Jose: toExcel Press, 2000.

Ronald Numbers. *The Creationists: From Scientific Creationism to Intelligent Design*. Cambridge, MA: Harvard University Press, 2006.

William Paley. *Natural Theology*. New York: Oxford University Press, 2010.

Ernest Sandeen. *The Roots of Fundamentalism: British and American Millenarianism, 1800–1930*. Chicago: University of Chicago Press, 1970.

Mano Singham. *God vs Darwin*. Lanham, MD: Rowan & Littlefield, 2009.

Ferenc Morton Szasz. *The Divided Mind of Protestant America 1880–1930*. Tuscaloosa: University of Alabama Press, 1982.

R. A. Torrey et al., eds. *The Fundamentals*. 2 vols. Los Angeles: Bible Institute of Los Angeles, 1917. Reprinted by Baker Books, Grand Rapids, MI: 2003.

Christopher Toumey. *God's Own Scientists: Creationists in a Secular World*. New Brunswick: Rutgers University Press, 1994.

Index